Bureaucracy and Formal Organizations

From Chapter 7 of *Sociology: A Down-to-Earth Approach*, 9/e. James M. Henslin. Copyright © 2008 by Pearson Education.

Bureaucracy and Formal Organizations

David Tillinghast, *Human Pyramid of Businesspeople*, 1998

THE INTERSECTIONS COLLECTION
PEARSON CUSTOM SOCIOLOGY

Formerly published as Intersections, Crossroads & Inequalities

EDITORS

KATHLEEN A. TIEMANN

University of North Dakota
Introduction to Sociology, Social Problems & Issues, Inequalities & Diversity

RALPH B. MCNEAL, JR.

University of Connecticut
Introduction to Sociology

BETSY LUCAL

Indiana University South Bend
Inequalities & Diversity

MORTEN G. ENDER

United States Military Academy, West Point
Inequalities & Diversity

COMPILED BY:

Professor Joseph Donnermeyer
Rural Sociology 105
Autumn 2009

Pearson Custom Publishing

New York   Boston   San Francisco
London   Toronto   Sydney   Tokyo   Singapore   Madrid
Mexico City   Munich   Paris   Cape Town   Hong Kong   Montreal

Senior Vice President, Editorial and Marketing: Patrick F. Boles
Senior Sponsoring Editor: Robin J. Lazrus
Development Editor: Abbey Lee Briggs
Associate Editor: Ana Díaz-Caneja
Marketing Manager: Jack Cooney
Operations Manager: Eric M. Kenney
Database Product Manager: Jennifer Berry
Rights Manager: Katie Huha
Art Director: Renée Sartell
Cover Designer: Renée Sartell

Cover Art: "Figures," courtesy of Eugenie Lewalski Berg; "Abstract Crowd," courtesy of Diana Ong/Superstock; "R&B Figures," courtesy of Diana Ong/Superstock; "Bramante's Staircase," courtesy of Veer/Photodisc Photography; "Hand Prints," courtesy of Veer/Photodisc Photography; "People Running-Falling," courtesy of Veer/Campbell Laird; "Sunbathers on Beach," courtesy of Veer/Scott Barrow.

**Pearson
Custom Publishing**
is a division of

www.pearsonhighered.com

ISBN 10: 0558267254
ISBN 13: 9780558267254

&❧ CONTENTS ❧&

iii

Imagine for a moment that you are a high school senior and you have applied to Cornell University. It's a long shot, you know, since you aren't in the top of your class—but what the heck? It's worth the extra hour it takes to fill out the application—since you have everything together for the other applications you've already sent to your state universities and regional colleges.

Now imagine the unthinkable. Like betting on the 125-to-1 long shot at the racetrack, your horse comes in! You open the letter from Cornell, expecting to see a polite rejection. Instead, with hands shaking and tears of joy welling up within you, you stare at the first words, scarcely grasping what your eyes are seeing: "Greetings from Cornell, your future alma mater!" and, below this, "Cornell is pleased to welcome you to its incoming freshman class."

You don't know whether to laugh, scream, cry, or what. You shout to your parents, who come running in to see what the problem is. They, too, are flabbergasted. While your Dad and Mom are proudly saying that they knew you could do it, you are already rushing to the phone to call your friends.

The next day, you are the talk of your class at school. Hardly anyone can believe it, for you are just an average student. "They must be trying for diversity of ability," jealously mumbles someone (who just took a sociology course), whom you *used* to count as a friend.

"This is just too good to be true," you keep telling yourself, as you imagine yourself on the ivy-covered campus.

And it is.

The call from the solemn Cornell admissions counselor explains that they had sent the wrong letter to 550 students. "We apologize for any confusion and distress this has caused," she says.

Confusion? How about shattered dreams?

—Based on Arenson 2003

"Just too good to be true," you keep telling yourself, as you imagine yourself on the ivy-covered campus.

Matt Rainey/Star Ledger/Corbis

Some colleges admit thousands of students. To make the job manageable, they have broken the admissions process into several separate steps. Each step is an integrated part of the entire procedure. Computer programs have facilitated this process, but, as this event indicates, things don't always go as planned. In this case, a low-level bureaucrat at Cornell had mixed up the codes, releasing the wrong letter.

Despite their flaws, we need bureaucracies, and in this chapter we'll look at how society is organized to "get its job done." As you read this analysis, you may be able to trace the source of some of your frustrations to this social organization—as well as understand how your welfare depends on it.

The Rationalization of Society

Societies have undergone transformations so extensive that whole new types of societies have emerged. We also saw that we are now in the midst of one of those earth-shattering transformations. Underlying our information society (which may be merging into a biotech society) is an emphasis on **rationality,** the idea that efficiency and practical results should dominate human affairs. Let's examine how this approach to life—which today we take for granted—came about.

Why Did Society Make a Deep Shift in Human Relationships?

Until recently, people were immersed in a **traditional orientation** to life—the idea that the past is the best guide for making decisions today. In this view, what exists is good because it has passed the test of time. Customs—and relationships based on them—have served people well, and they should not be abandoned lightly. A central orientation of a traditional society is to protect the status quo. Change is viewed with suspicion and comes about slowly, if at all.

The traditional orientation to life stands in the way of industrialization. As Table 1 shows, the traditional orientation is based on personal relationships. Deep obligation and responsibility, which are often lifelong, permeate society. What counts in production is not who is best at doing something, but the relationships that people have with one another. Based on origins that are lost in history, everyone—even children—has an established role to play. The past is prized, and it rules the present.

To understand the sociological significance of this photo from Portugal, compare what you see here with the list of characteristics of traditional societies in Table 1.

Peter M. Wilson/Alamy

Table 1 — A Model of Production in Traditional and Nontraditional Societies

Traditional Societies (Horticultural, Agricultural)	Nontraditional Societies (Industrial, Postindustrial)
PRODUCTION	
1. Production is done by family members and same-sex groups (men's and women's groups).	1. Production is done by workers hired for the job.
2. Production takes place in the home, or in fields and other areas adjacent to the home.	2. Production takes place in a centralized location. (Some decentralization is occurring in the information society.)
3. Tasks are assigned according to personal relationships (men, women, and children do specific tasks based on custom).	3. Tasks are assigned according to agreements and training.
4. The "how" of production is not evaluated; the attitude is, "We want to keep doing it the way we've always done it."	4. The "how" of production is evaluated; the attitude is, "How can we make this more efficient?"
RELATIONSHIPS	
5. Relationships are based on history ("the way it's always been").	5. Relationships are based on contracts, which change as the situation changes.
6. Relationships are diffuse (vague, covering many areas of life).	6. Relationships are specific; contracts (even if not written) specify conditions.
7. Relationships are long-term, often lifelong.	7. Relationships are short-term, for the length of the contract.
EVALUATIONS	
8. It is assumed that arrangements will continue indefinitely.	8. Arrangements are evaluated periodically, to decide whether to continue or to change them.
9. People are evaluated according to how they fulfill their traditional roles.	9. People are evaluated according to the "bottom line" (the organization's goals).

Note: This model is an ideal type. Rationality is never totally absent from any society, and no society (or organization) is based entirely on rationality. Even the most rational organizations (those that most carefully and even ruthlessly compute the "bottom line") have traditional components. To properly understand this table, consider these nine characteristics as being "more" or "less" present.

Capitalism requires an entirely different way of looking at life. If a society is to industrialize, a deep shift must occur in people's thinking and relationships. Tradition ("This is the way we've always done it") must be replaced with *rationality* ("Let's find the most efficient way to do it"). As Table 1 shows, personal relationships are replaced by impersonal, short-term contracts. The "bottom line" (results) becomes the primary concern, and rule-of-thumb methods give way to explicit ways of measuring results.

This change to *rationality*—judging things according to the bottom line instead of by personal relationships—is a fundamental divergence from all of human history. Yet today we take rationality so much for granted that it is difficult for us to grasp how different it really is. The following illustration may help.

> Let's suppose that family relationships change from personal to rational. This would be like a wife saying to her husband, "Each year, I'm going to evaluate how much you've contributed to the family budget and how much time you've put in on household tasks—and I'll keep or replace you on that basis."

I'm sure you'll agree that this would be a fundamental change in human relationships, that it would mean a new type of marriage and family. Organizations went through this kind of severe change when they moved from tradition to rationality. What brought about this fundamental change, called the **rationalization of society**—the widespread acceptance of rationality and the construction of social organizations built largely around this idea?

Marx: Capitalism Broke Tradition

An early sociologist, Karl Marx (1818–1883), was one of the first to note how tradition was giving way to rationality. As he thought about why this change was taking place, he

[the] rationalization of society a widespread acceptance of rationality and social organizations that are built largely around this idea

concluded that capitalism was breaking the bonds of tradition. As people who had money experimented with capitalism, they saw that it was more efficient. They were impressed that capitalism produced things they wanted in greater abundance and yielded high profits. This encouraged them to invest capital in manufacturing. As capitalism spread, traditional thinking receded. Gradually, the rationality of capitalism replaced the traditional approach to life. Marx's conclusion: The change to capitalism changed the way people thought about life.

Weber: Religion Broke Tradition

To sociologist Max Weber (1864–1920), this problem was as intriguing as an unsolved murder is to a detective. Weber wasn't satisfied with Marx's answer, and he kept searching for another solution. He found a clue when he noted that capitalism thrived only in certain parts of Europe. "There has to be a reason for this," he mused. As Weber pursued the matter, he noted that capitalism flourished in Protestant countries, while Roman Catholic countries held on to tradition and were relatively untouched by capitalism. "Somehow, then, religion holds the key," he thought.

But why did Roman Catholics cling to the past, while Protestants embraced change? Weber's solution to this puzzle has been the source of controversy ever since he first proposed it in his influential book, *The Protestant Ethic and the Spirit of Capitalism* (1904–1905). Weber concluded that Roman Catholic doctrine emphasized the acceptance of present arrangements: "God wants you where you are. You owe allegiance to the Church, to your family, and to your king. Accept your lot in life and remain rooted." Weber argued that Protestant theology, in contrast, opened its followers to change. Weber was intimately familiar with Calvinism, his mother's religion. Calvinists (followers of the teachings of John Calvin, 1509–1564) believed that before birth, people are destined for either heaven or hell—and they do not know their destiny until after they die. Weber said that this teaching filled Calvinists with anxiety. Salvation became their chief concern—they wanted to know *now* where they were going after death.

To resolve their spiritual dilemma, Calvinists arrived at an ingenious solution: God surely did not want those chosen for heaven to be ignorant of their destiny. Therefore, those who were in God's favor would know it—they would receive a sign from God. But what sign? The answer, claimed Calvinists, would be found not in mystical, spiritual experiences, but in things that people could see and measure. The sign of God's approval was success: Those whom God had predestined for heaven would be blessed with visible success in this life.

This idea transformed the lives of Calvinists. It motivated them to work hard, and because Calvinists also believed that thrift is a virtue, their dedication to work led to an accumulation of money. They could not spend this money on themselves, however, for to purchase items beyond the basic necessities was considered sinful. **Capitalism,** the investment of capital in the hope of making profits, became an outlet for their excess money. The success of those investments, in turn, became another sign of God's approval. In this way, Calvinists transformed worldly success into a spiritual virtue. Other branches of Protestantism, although not in agreement with the notion of predestination, also adopted the creed of thrift and hard work. Consequently, said Weber, Protestant countries embraced capitalism.

But what has this to do with rationalization? Simply put, capitalism demands rationalization, that investors carefully calculate results. If profits are your goal, you must keep track of your income and expenses. You must calculate inventories and wages, the cost of producing goods and how much income they bring. You must determine "the bottom line." Rationality, then, not tradition, becomes the drumbeat to which you march. If traditional ways of doing things are inefficient, they are replaced, for what counts are the results. Weber's equation: A changed way of thinking (God will give a sign to the elect) produced capitalism.

The Two Views Today Who is correct? Weber, who concluded that Protestantism produced rationality, which then paved the way for capitalism? Or Marx, who concluded that capitalism produced rationality? No analyst has yet reconciled these two opposing answers to the satisfaction of sociologists: The two views still remain side by side.

capitalism an economic system characterized by the private ownership of the means of production, the pursuit of profit, and market competition

Formal Organizations and Bureaucracies

Regardless of whether Marx or Weber was right about its cause, rationality was a totally different way of approaching life. As this new orientation began to permeate society, it led to new types of organizations. Let's look at these organizations and how they affect our lives.

Formal Organizations

A major consequence of rationality was the development of **formal organizations,** secondary groups designed to achieve explicit objectives. Although they are fairly new to the human scene, formal organizations have become a central feature of our society. Today, most of us are born within them, we are educated in them, we spend our working lives in them, and we are buried by them.

Prior to industrialization, there were few formal organizations. The guilds of western Europe during the twelfth century are a rare example of a formal organization. People who performed the same type of work organized to control their craft in a local area. They set prices and standards of workmanship (Bridgwater 1953; "Guilds" 2005). Much like modern unions, guilds also prevented outsiders (nonmembers of the guild) from working at their particular craft. Another example of an early formal organization is the army, with its hierarchical structure of senior officers, junior officers, and ranks. Armies with commanders and subleaders, of course, existed far back in history.

With industrialization, secondary groups became common. Today we take their existence for granted and, beginning with grade school, all of us spend a good deal of time in them. Formal organizations tend to develop into bureaucracies, and in general, the larger the formal organization, the more likely it is to be bureaucratic. Because they are so important to our lives, let's look at bureaucracies in detail.

The Characteristics of Bureaucracies

What do the Russian army and the U.S. postal service have in common? Or the government of Mexico and your college? The sociological answer is that all are *bureaucracies*. As Weber (1913/1947) pointed out, **bureaucracies** have

1. *Clear levels, with assignments flowing downward and accountability flowing upward.* Each level assigns responsibilities to the level beneath it, while each lower level is accountable to the level above it for fulfilling those assignments. Figure 1 on the next page shows the bureaucratic structure of a typical university.

formal organization a secondary group designed to achieve explicit objectives

bureaucracy a formal organization with a hierarchy of authority, a clear division of labor, an impersonality of positions, and an emphasis on written rules, communications, and records

©AFP Getty Images

Today's armies, no matter what country they are from, are bureaucracies. They have a strict hierarchy of rank, division of labor, impersonality and replaceability (an emphasis on the office, not the person holding it), and they stress written records, rules, and communications—essential characteristics identified by Max Weber. Though its outward appearance may differ from Western standards, this army in India is no exception to this principle.

Figure 1 **The Typical Bureaucratic Structure of a Medium-Sized University**

This is a scaled-down version of a university's bureaucratic structure. The actual lines of a university are likely to be much more complicated than those depicted here. A large university may have a chancellor and several presidents under the chancellor, each president being responsible for a particular campus. Although in this figure extensions of authority are shown only for the Vice President for Administration and the College of Social Sciences, each of the other vice presidents and colleges has similar positions. If the figure were to be extended, departmental secretaries would be shown, and eventually, somewhere, even students.

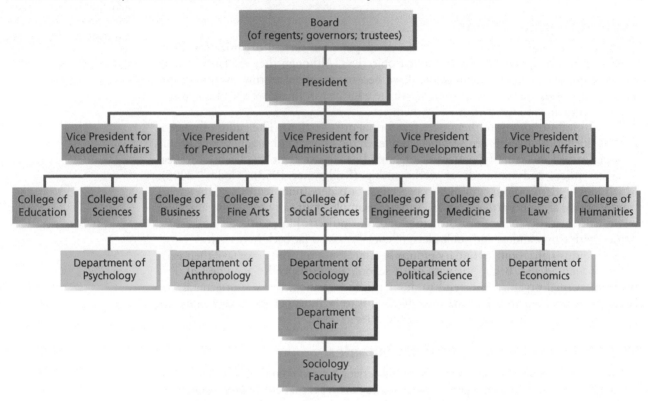

2. *A division of labor.* Each worker has a specific task to fulfill, and all the tasks are coordinated to accomplish the purpose of the organization. In a college, for example, a teacher does not fix the heating system, the president does not teach, and a secretary does not evaluate textbooks. These tasks are distributed among people who have been trained to do them.

3. *Written rules.* In their attempt to become efficient, bureaucracies stress written procedures. In general, the longer a bureaucracy exists and the larger it grows, the more written rules it has. The rules of some bureaucracies cover just about every imaginable situation. In my university, for example, the rules are published in

When society began to be rationalized, production of items was broken into its various components, with individuals assigned only specific tasks. This painting of a pottery shop in England in the late 1800s is by Alfred Morgan (1862–1904).

V&A Images/Alamy

handbooks: separate ones for faculty, students, administrators, civil service workers, and perhaps others that I don't even know about.

4. *Written communications and records.* Records are kept of much of what occurs in a bureaucracy ("Be sure to CC all immediate supervisors."). In some organizations, workers spend a fair amount of time sending memos and e-mail back and forth. Sometimes, workers must detail their activities in written reports. My university, for example, requires that each semester, faculty members compile a summary of the number of hours they spent performing specified activities. They must also submit an annual report listing what they accomplished in teaching, research, and service—all accompanied by copies of publications, evidence of service, and written teaching evaluations from each course. These materials go to committees that evaluate the performance of each faculty member.

5. *Impersonality and replaceability.* It is the office that is important, not the individual who holds the office. You work for the organization, not for the replaceable person who heads some post in the organization. Each worker is a replaceable unit, for many others are available to fulfill each particular function. For example, when a professor retires, someone else is appointed to take his or her place. This makes you a small cog in a large machine.

These five characteristics help bureaucracies reach their goals. They also allow them to grow and endure. One bureaucracy in the United States, the postal service, has become so large that one out of every 175 employed Americans works for it (*Statistical Abstract* 2007:587, 1105). If the head of a bureaucracy resigns, retires, or dies, the organization continues without skipping a beat, for unlike a "mom and pop" operation, its functioning does not depend on the individual who heads it. The expansion (some would say domination) of bureaucracies in contemporary society is illustrated by the Down-to-Earth Sociology box on the next page.

"Ideal" Versus "Real" Bureaucracy

Just as people often act differently from the way the norms say they should, so it is with bureaucracies. The characteristics of bureaucracies that Weber identified are *ideal types*; that is, they are a composite of characteristics based on many specific examples. Think of the judges at a dog show. They have a mental image of how each particular breed of dog should look and behave, and they judge each individual dog according to that mental image. Each dog will rank high on some of these characteristics, and lower on others. In the same way, a particular organization will rank higher or lower on the traits of a bureaucracy, yet still qualify as a bureaucracy. Instead of labeling a particular organization

Bettmann/Corbis

Technology has changed our lives fundamentally. As you can see from this 1904 photo, telephone operators used to make connections by hand. Labor was so intensive and problems so numerous that it required about one supervisor for every four workers. Long distance calls, with their numerous hand-made connections, not only were slower, but also more expensive—perhaps 100 times higher than what they now cost. You can also see that this was "women's" work.

Down-to-Earth Sociology

The McDonaldization of Society

THE MCDONALD'S RESTAURANTS THAT seem to be all over the United States—and, increasingly, the world—have a significance that goes far beyond the convenience of quick hamburgers and milk shakes. As sociologist George Ritzer (1993, 1998, 2001) says, our everyday lives are being "McDonaldized." Let's see what he means by this.

AP Images

McDonald's in Beijing, China

The McDonaldization of society—the standardization of everyday life—does not refer just to the robot-like assembly of food. As Ritzer points out, this process is occurring throughout society—and it is transforming our lives. Want to do some shopping? Shopping malls offer one-stop shopping in controlled environments. Planning a trip? Travel agencies offer "package" tours. They will transport middle-class Americans to ten European capitals in fourteen days. All visitors experience the same hotels, restaurants, and other scheduled sites—and no one need fear meeting a "real" native. Want to keep up with events? *USA Today* spews out McNews—short, bland, unanalytical pieces that can be digested between gulps of the McShake or the McBurger.

Efficiency brings dependability. You can expect your burger and fries to taste the same whether you buy them in Los Angeles or Beijing. Although efficiency also lowers prices, it does come at a cost. Predictability washes away spontaneity, changing the quality of our lives. It produces a sameness, a bland version of what used to be unique experiences. In my own travels, for example, had I taken packaged tours I never would have had the enjoyable, eye-opening experiences that have added so much to my appreciation of human diversity.

For good or bad, our lives are being McDonaldized, and the predictability of packaged settings seems to be our social destiny. When education is rationalized, no longer will our children have to put up with real professors, who insist on discussing ideas endlessly, who never come to decisive answers, and who come saddled with idiosyncrasies. At some point, such an approach to education is going to be a bit of quaint history.

Our programmed education will eliminate the need for discussion of social issues—we will have packaged solutions to social problems, definitive answers that satisfy our need for closure. Computerized courses will teach the same answers to everyone—the approved, "politically correct" ways to think about social issues. Mass testing will ensure that students regurgitate the programmed responses.

Our coming prepackaged society will be efficient, of course. But it also means that we will be trapped in the "iron cage" of bureaucracy—just as Weber warned would happen.

---

as a "bureaucracy" or "not a bureaucracy," it probably makes more sense to think in terms of the *extent* to which it is bureaucratized (Udy 1959; Hall 1963).

As with culture, then, a bureaucracy often differs from its ideal image. The actual lines of authority ("going through channels"), for example, may be different from those portrayed on organizational charts such as the one shown in Figure 1. For example, suppose that before being promoted, the university president taught in the history department. As a result, friends from that department may have direct access to him or her. If they wish to provide "input" (ranging from opinions about how to solve problems to personal grievances or even gossip), these individuals might be able to skip their chairperson or even the dean of their college, and go directly to the president.

Dysfunctions of Bureaucracies

Although in the long run no other form of social organization is more efficient, as Weber recognized, bureaucracies also have a dark side. Let's look at some of their dysfunctions.

Red Tape: A Rule Is a Rule Bureaucracies can be so bound by procedures that their rules impede the purpose of the organization. Some rules ("red tape" in common speech and "correct procedures" in bureaucratic jargon) are enough to try the patience of a saint.

When dealing with the routine, bureaucracies usually function quite efficiently. In emergencies, however, they sometimes fail miserably. This dysfunction was evident during Hurricane Katrina, which hit the U.S. Gulf Coast in 2005. Due to bureaucratic bungling, the pleas of thousands of people in flooded New Orleans went unanswered.

AP Images/David J. Phillip

In the Bronx, Mother Teresa spotted a structurally sound abandoned building and wanted to turn it into a homeless shelter. But she ran head on into a rule: The building must have an elevator for people with disabilities. Not having the funds for the elevator, Mother Teresa struggled to get permission to bypass this rule. Two frustrating years later, she gave up. The abandoned building was left to rot away. (Tobias 1995)

Obviously this rule about elevators was not intended to stop Mother Teresa from ministering to the down and out. But, hey, rules is rules!

Lack of Communication Between Units   Each unit within a bureaucracy performs specialized tasks, which are designed to contribute to the organization's goals. At times, units fail to communicate with one another and end up working at cross purposes. In Granada, Spain, for example, the local government was concerned about the run-down appearance of buildings along one of its main streets. Consequently, one unit of the government fixed the fronts of these buildings, repairing concrete and restoring decorations

This is the way that some people view bureaucracies: stilted, slow-moving, and destructive to the individual. Bureaucracies can be like this, but not all bureaucracies are alike. Some are innovative and unleash creative energy.

of iron and stone. The results were impressive, and the unit was proud of what it had accomplished. The only problem was that another unit of the government had slated these same buildings for demolition (Arías 1993). Because neither unit of this bureaucracy knew what the other was doing, one beautified the buildings while the other planned to turn them into a heap of rubble.

Bureaucratic Alienation   Perceived in terms of roles, rules, and functions rather than as individuals, many workers begin to feel more like objects than people. Marx termed these reactions **alienation,** a result, he said, of workers being cut off from the finished product of their labor. He pointed out that before industrialization, workers used their own tools to produce an entire product, such as a chair or table. Now the capitalists own the tools (machinery, desks, computers), and assign each worker only a single step or two in the entire production process. Relegated to performing repetitive tasks that seem remote from the final product, workers no longer identify with what they produce. They come to feel estranged not only from the results of their labor but also from their work environment.

Resisting Alienation   Because workers need to feel valued and want to have a sense of control over their work, they resist alienation. Forming primary groups at work is a major form of that resistance. Workers band together in informal settings—at lunch, around desks, or for a drink after work. There, they give one another approval for jobs well done and express sympathy for the shared need to put up with cantankerous bosses, meaningless routines, and endless rules. In these contexts, they relate to one another not just as workers, but as people who value one another. They flirt, laugh and tell jokes, and talk about their families and goals. Adding this multidimensionality to their work relationships maintains their sense of being individuals rather than mere cogs in a machine.

As in the photo below, workers often decorate their work areas with personal items. The sociological implication is that of workers who are striving to resist alienation. By staking a claim to individuality, the workers are rejecting an identity as machines that exist simply to perform functions.

The Alienated Bureaucrat   Not all workers succeed in resisting alienation. Some become alienated and leave. Others became alienated but remain in the organization because they see no viable alternative, or they wait it out because they have "only so many years until retirement." They hate every minute of work, and it shows—in their attitudes toward clients, toward fellow workers, and toward authority in the organization.

Workers develop many ways to avoid becoming a depersonalized unit in a bureaucratic-economic machine. In this photo, which I took at a major publisher, you can see how Rebecca, by personalizing her work setting, is claiming an identity that transcends that of worker. What "personalized messages" do you see in this photo?

©James M. Henslin

The alienated bureaucrat does not take initiative, will not do anything for the organization beyond what is absolutely required, and uses company rules to justify doing as little as possible.

Despite poor attitude and performance, alienated workers often retain their jobs. Some keep their jobs because of seniority, while others threaten expensive, time-consuming, and embarrassing legal action if anyone tries to fire them. Some alienated workers are shunted off into small bureaucratic corners, where they spend the day doing trivial tasks and have little chance of coming in contact with the public. This treatment, of course, only alienates them further.

Bureaucratic Incompetence In a tongue-in-cheek analysis of bureaucracies, Laurence Peter proposed what has become known as the **Peter principle:** Each employee of a bureaucracy is promoted to his or her *level of incompetence* (Peter and Hull 1969). People who perform well in a bureaucracy come to the attention of those higher up the chain of command and are promoted. If they continue to perform well, they are promoted again. This process continues *until* they are promoted to a level at which they can no longer handle the responsibilities well—their level of incompetence. There they hide behind the work of others, taking credit for the accomplishments of employees under their direction. In our opening vignette, the employee who sent the wrong mail has already reached his or her level of incompetence.

Although the Peter principle contains a grain of truth, if it were generally true, bureaucracies would be staffed by incompetents, and these organizations would fail. In reality, bureaucracies are remarkably successful. Sociologists Peter Evans and James Rauch (1999) examined the government bureaucracies of 35 developing countries. They found that prosperity comes to the countries that have central bureaucracies that hire workers on the basis of merit and offer them rewarding careers.

Goal Displacement and the Perpetuation of Bureaucracies

Bureaucracies have become a standard feature of our lives because they are a powerful form of social organization. They harness people's energies to reach specific goals. Once in existence, however, bureaucracies tend to take on a life of their own. In a process called **goal displacement,** even after the organization achieves its goal and no longer has a reason to continue, continue it does.

A classic example is the National Foundation for the March of Dimes, organized in the 1930s to fight polio (Sills 1957). At that time, the origin of polio was a mystery. The public was alarmed and fearful, for overnight a healthy child could be stricken with this crippling disease. To raise money to find a cure, the March of Dimes placed posters of children on crutches near cash registers in almost every store in the United States. (See the photo on the next page.) They raised money beyond the organization's wildest dreams. When Dr. Jonas Salk developed a vaccine for polio in the 1950s, the threat was wiped out almost overnight.

The staff that ran the March of Dimes did not quietly fold up their tents and slip away. Instead, they found a way to keep their jobs by targeting a new enemy—birth defects. But then in 2001, researchers finished mapping the human genome system. Perceiving that some day this information could help to eliminate birth defects—and their jobs—officials of the March of Dimes came up with a new slogan, "Breakthroughs for Babies." This latest goal should ensure the organization's existence forever: It is so vague that we are not likely to ever run out of the need for "breakthroughs."

Then there is NATO (North Atlantic Treaty Organization), founded during the Cold War to prevent Russia from invading western Europe. When the Cold War ended, removing the organization's purpose, the Western powers tried to find a reason to continue their organization. I mean, why waste a perfectly good bureaucracy? They appear to have found one: to create "rapid response forces" to combat terrorism and "rogue nations" (Tyler 2002). To keep this bureaucracy going, they even allowed Russia to become a junior partner.

Peter principle a tongue-in-cheek observation that the members of an organization are promoted for their accomplishments until they reach their level of incompetence; there they cease to be promoted, remaining at the level at which they can no longer do good work

goal displacement the adoption of new goals by an organization; also known as *goal replacement*

The March of Dimes was founded by President Franklin Roosevelt in the 1930s to fight polio. When a vaccine for polio was discovered in the 1950s, the organization did not declare victory and disband. Instead, its leaders kept the organization intact by creating new goals, such as combatting premature births. Sociologists use the term *goal displacement* to refer to this process of adopting new goals.

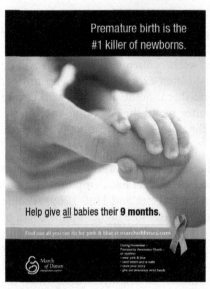

Bettmann/Corbis   March of Dimes Birth Defects Foundation

The Sociological Significance of Bureaucracies

The sociological significance of bureaucracies and the rationalization of society in general go far beyond what is readily visible. Bureaucracies require a fundamental change in the traditional ways that people relate to one another (see Table 1). When work is rooted in personal relationships, much more is at stake than performing tasks efficiently and keeping an eye on the bottom line. Seeing that all relatives and friends have jobs, for example, was once a major factor in making business decisions. Bureaucracies, or the rationalization of society, changed this fundamental aspect of social life, which had been a factor that cemented human relationships.

Voluntary Associations

 Although bureaucracies have become the dominant form of organization for large, task-oriented groups, even more common are voluntary associations. Let's examine their characteristics.

Back in the 1830s, Alexis de Tocqueville, a Frenchman, traveled across the United States, observing the customs of this new nation. His report, *Democracy in America* (1835), was popular both in Europe and in the United States. It is still quoted for its insights into the American character. One of de Tocqueville's observations was that Americans joined a lot of **voluntary associations,** groups made up of volunteers who organize on the basis of some mutual interest.

Over the years, Americans have maintained this pattern and are quite proud of it. A visitor entering one of the thousands of small towns that dot the U.S. landscape is often greeted by a highway sign proclaiming some of the town's volunteer associations: Girl Scouts, Boy Scouts, Kiwanis, Lions, Elks, Eagles, Knights of Columbus, Chamber of Commerce, American Legion, Veterans of Foreign Wars, and perhaps a host of others. One type of voluntary association is so prevalent that a separate sign sometimes indicates which varieties are present in the town: Roman Catholic, Baptist, Lutheran, Methodist, Episcopalian, and so on. Not listed on these signs are many other voluntary associations, such as political parties, unions, health clubs, the National Right to Life, the National Organization for Women, Alcoholics Anonymous, Gamblers Anonymous, Association of Pinto Racers, and Citizens United For or Against This and That.

Americans love voluntary associations, and use them to express a wide variety of interests. Some groups are local, consisting of only a few volunteers; others are national, with a paid professional staff. Some are temporary, organized to accomplish some

voluntary association a group made up of people who voluntarily organize on the basis of some mutual interest; also known as *voluntary memberships* and *voluntary organizations*

specific task, such as arranging for Fourth of July fireworks. Others, such as the Scouts and political parties, are permanent—large, secondary organizations with clear lines of command—and they are also bureaucracies.

Functions of Voluntary Associations

Whatever their form, voluntary associations are numerous because they meet people's needs. People do not *have* to belong to these organizations. They join because they obtain benefits from their participation. Functionalists have identified seven functions of voluntary associations.

1. Voluntary organizations advance particular interests. For example, adults who are concerned about children's welfare volunteer for the Scouts because they think kids are better off joining this group than hanging out on the street. In short, voluntary associations get things done, whether that means organizing a neighborhood crime watch or informing people about the latest legislation on abortion.
2. Voluntary groups offer people an identity. Some even provide a sense of purpose in life. As in-groups, they give their members a feeling of belonging, and, in many cases, a sense of doing something worthwhile. This function is so important for some individuals that their participation in voluntary associations becomes the center of their lives.
3. Voluntary associations help govern the nation and maintain social order. Groups that help "get out the vote" or assist the Red Cross in coping with disasters are obvious examples.

The first two functions apply to all voluntary associations. In a general sense, so does the third. Even though an organization does not focus on politics, it helps to incorporate individuals into society, which helps to maintain social order.

Sociologist David Sills (1968) identified four other functions, which apply only to some voluntary associations.

4. Some voluntary groups mediate between the government and the individual. For example, some groups provide a way for people to join forces to put pressure on lawmakers.
5. By providing training in organizational skills, some groups help individuals climb the occupational ladder.
6. Other groups help bring people into the political mainstream. The National Association for the Advancement of Colored People (NAACP) is an example of such a group.
7. Finally, some voluntary associations pave the way to social change. As they challenge established ways of doing social life, boundaries start to give way. The actions of groups such as Greenpeace, for example, are reshaping taken-for-granted definitions of "normal" when it comes to the environment.

Shared Interests

Voluntary associations, then, represent no single interest or purpose. They can be reactionary, resisting new ways of doing things, or they can be visionary, standing at the vanguard of social change. Despite their diversity, however, a common thread runs through voluntary associations. That thread is mutual interest. Although the particular interest varies from group to group, shared interest in some point of view or activity is the tie that binds group members together.

Motivations for joining these groups differ. Some people join because they hold strong convictions concerning the stated purpose of the organization, others simply because membership helps them politically or professionally—or looks good on a college or job application. Some may even join because they have romantic interests in a group member.

With so many motivations for joining, and because the commitment of some members is fleeting, voluntary associations often have high turnover. Some people move in and out of groups almost as fast as they change clothes. Within each organization, however, is an *inner circle*—individuals who actively promote the group, who stand firmly behind the group's goals, and who are committed to maintaining the organization itself. If this inner circle loses its commitment, the group is likely to fold.

The "Iron Law" of Oligarchy

A significant aspect of voluntary associations is that its key members, its inner circle, often grow distant from the regular members. They become convinced that only they can be trusted to make the group's important decisions. To see this principle at work, let's look at the Veterans of Foreign Wars (VFW).

Sociologists Elaine Fox and George Arquitt (1985) studied three local posts of the VFW, a national organization of former U.S. soldiers who have served in foreign wars. They found that although the leaders conceal their attitudes from the other members, the inner circle views the rank and file as a bunch of ignorant boozers. Because the leaders can't stand the thought that such people might represent them in the community and at national meetings, a curious situation arises. Although the VFW constitution makes rank-and-file members eligible for top leadership positions, they never become leaders. In fact, the inner circle is so effective in controlling these top positions that even before an election they can tell you who is going to win. "You need to meet Jim," the sociologists were told. "He's the next post commander after Sam does his time."

At first, the researchers found this puzzling. The election hadn't been held yet. As they investigated further, they found that leadership is actually determined behind the scenes. The elected leaders appoint their favored people to chair the key committees, which highlights the names and accomplishments of these individuals. This publicity then propels the members to elect these favored ones as their leaders. By appointing its own members to highly visible positions, then, the inner circle maintains control over the entire organization.

Like the VFW, most organizations are run by only a few of their members. Building on the term *oligarchy*, a system in which many are ruled by a few, sociologist Robert Michels (1876–1936) coined the term **the iron law of oligarchy** to refer to how organizations come to be dominated by a small, self-perpetuating elite (Michels 1911). Most members are passive, and an elite inner circle keeps itself in power by passing the leadership positions to one another.

What many find disturbing about the iron law of oligarchy is that people are excluded from leadership because they don't represent the inner circle's values—or, in some instances, their background. This is true even of organizations that are committed to democratic principles. For example, U.S. political parties—supposedly the backbone

In a process called *the iron law of oligarchy*, a small, self-perpetuating elite tends to take control of formal organizations. Veterans' organizations are no exception to this principle, as sociological studies have shown.

Peter Hvizdak/The Image Works

of the nation's representative government are run by an inner circle that passes leadership positions from one elite member to another. This principle also applies to the U.S. Senate. With their statewide control of political machinery and access to free mailing, about 90 percent of U.S. senators who choose to run are reelected (*Statistical Abstract* 2006:Table 394).

The iron law of oligarchy is not without its limitations, of course. Members of the inner circle must remain attuned to the opinions of the other members, regardless of their personal feelings. If the oligarchy gets too far out of line, it runs the risk of a grassroots rebellion that would throw the elite out of office. This threat often softens the iron law of oligarchy by making the leadership responsive to the membership. In addition, because not all organizations become captive to an elite, this is a tendency, not an inevitability.

Working for the Corporation

Since you are likely to end up working in a bureaucracy, let's look at how its characteristics may affect your career.

Self-Fulfilling Stereotypes in the "Hidden" Corporate Culture

Stereotypes can be self-fulfilling. That is, stereotypes can produce the very characteristics that they are built around. Stereotypes also operate in corporate life—and are so powerful that they can affect *your* career. Here's how they work.

Self-Fulfilling Stereotypes and Promotions Corporate and department heads have ideas of "what it takes" to get ahead. Not surprisingly, since they themselves got ahead, they look for people who have characteristics similar to their own. They feed better information to workers with these characteristics, bring them into stronger networks, and put them on "fast track" positions. With such advantages, these workers perform better and become more committed to the company. This, of course, confirms the boss's initial expectation or stereotype. But for workers who don't look or act like the corporate leaders, the opposite happens. Thinking of them as less capable, the bosses give them fewer opportunities and challenges. When these workers see others get ahead, and realize that they are working beneath their own abilities, they lose morale, become less committed to the company, and don't perform as well. This, of course, confirms the stereotypes the bosses had of them.

In her studies of U.S. corporations, sociologist Rosabeth Moss Kanter (1977, 1983) found such self-fulfilling stereotypes to be part of a "hidden" corporate culture. That is, these stereotypes and their powerful effects on workers remain hidden to everyone, even the bosses. What bosses and workers see is the surface: Workers who have superior performance and greater commitment to the company get promoted. To everyone, this seems to be just the way it should be. Hidden below this surface, however, as Kanter found, are these higher and lower expectations and the open and closed opportunities that produce the attitudes and accomplishments—or the lack of them.

Stereotypes and the Iron Law of Oligarchy You can see how the self-fulfilling prophecy contributes to the *iron law of oligarchy* we just reviewed. Often without intending to do so, the inner circle reproduces itself by favoring people who "look" like its own members, generally white and male. Women and minorities, who don't match the stereotype, are often "showcased"—placed in highly visible but powerless positions in order to avoid charges of discrimination or to demonstrate how progressive the company is. The accomplishments of those in these "slow-track" positions seldom come to the attention of top management.

IN SUM | Significant aspects of organizations often lie below the surface. The "hidden" corporate culture, though difficult to perceive, is so significant that it can have a profound effect on your own career. Because workers tend to see only what is readily visible, they usually ascribe differences in people's behaviors and attitudes to their personalities. When sociologists probe beneath the surface, however, they examine how corporate culture shapes people's attitudes, and, by extension, the quality of their work.

As corporations grapple with growing diversity, the stereotypes in the hidden corporate culture are likely to give way, although slowly and grudgingly. In the following Thinking Critically section, we'll consider other aspects of diversity in the workplace.

Thinking Critically

Managing Diversity in the Workplace

Times have changed. The San Jose, California, electronic phone book lists *ten* times more *Nguyens* than *Joneses* (Albanese 2007). More than half of U.S. workers are minorities, immigrants, and women. Diversity in the workplace is much more than skin color. Diversity includes ethnicity, gender, age, religion, social class, and sexual orientation.

In our growing global context of life, diversity is increasing. In the past, the idea was for people to join the "melting pot," to give up their distinctive traits and become like the dominant group. Today, with the successes of the civil rights and women's movements, people are more likely to prize their distinctive traits. Realizing that assimilation (being absorbed into the dominant culture) is probably not the wave of the future, most large companies have "diversity training" (Johnson 2004). They hold lectures and workshops so that employees can learn to work with colleagues of diverse cultures and racial-ethnic backgrounds.

Coors Brewery is a prime example of this change. Coors went into a financial tailspin after one of the Coors brothers gave a racially charged speech in the 1980s. Today, Coors offers diversity workshops, has sponsored a gay dance, and has paid for a corporate-wide mammography program. In 2004, Coors opposed an amendment to the Colorado constitution that would ban the marriage of homosexuals. The company has even had rabbis certify its suds as kosher. Its proud new slogan: "Coors cares" (Cloud 1998). Now, that's quite a change.

What Coors cares about, of course, is the bottom line. It's the same with other corporations. Blatant racism and sexism once made no difference to profitability. Today, they do. To promote profitability, companies must promote diversity—or at least pretend to. The sincerity of corporate leaders is not what's important; diversity in the workplace is.

The cultural and racial-ethnic diversity of today's work force has led to the need for diversity training, the topic of this Thinking Critically section.

Diversity training has the potential to build bridges, but it can backfire. Managers who are chosen to participate can resent it, thinking that it is punishment for some unmentioned insensitivity on their part (Sanchez and Medkik 2004). Some directors of these programs are so incompetent that they create antagonisms and reinforce stereotypes. For example, the leaders of a diversity training session at the U.S. Department of Transportation had women grope men as the men ran by. They encouraged blacks and whites to insult one another and to call each other names (Reibstein 1996). The intention may have been good (understanding the other through role reversal and getting hostilities "out in the open"), but the approach was moronic. Instead of healing, such behaviors wound and leave scars.

Pepsi provides a positive example of diversity training. Managers at Pepsi are given the assignment of sponsoring a group of employees who are unlike themselves. Men sponsor women, African Americans sponsor whites, and so on. The executives are expected to try to understand work from the perspective of the people they sponsor, to identify key talent, and to personally mentor at least three people in their group. Accountability is built in—the sponsors have to give updates to executives even higher up (Terhune 2005).

for your Consideration

Do you think that corporations and government agencies should offer diversity training? If so, how can we develop diversity training that fosters mutual respect? Can you suggest practical ways to develop workplaces that are not divided by gender and race-ethnicity?

Humanizing the Corporate Culture

Bureaucracies have transformed society by harnessing people's energies to reach goals and monitoring their progress to achieve those goals. Weber (1946) predicted that because bureaucracies were so efficient and had the capacity to replace themselves, they would come to dominate social life. More than any prediction in sociology, this one has withstood the test of time (Rothschild and Whitt 1986; Perrow 1991).

Attempts to Humanize the Work Setting

Bureaucracies appear likely to remain our dominant form of social organization, and like it or not, most of us are destined to spend our working lives in bureaucracies. Many people have become concerned about the negative side of bureaucracies, and would like to make them more humane. **Humanizing a work setting** means to organize work in such a way that it develops rather than impedes human potential. Humanized work settings have more flexible rules, are more open in decision making, distribute power more equally, and offer more uniform access to opportunities.

Can bureaucracies adapt to such a model? Contrary to some images, not all bureaucracies are unyielding, unwieldy monoliths. There is nothing in the nature of bureaucracies that makes them *inherently* insensitive to people's needs or that prevents them from fostering a corporate culture that maximizes human potential.

But what about the cost of such changes? The United States faces formidable economic competitors—Japan, Europe, South America, and now China and India. Humanizing corporate culture, however, does not require huge expense. Kanter (1983) compared forty-seven companies that were rigidly bureaucratic with competitors of the same size that were more flexible. Kanter found that the more flexible companies were more profitable—probably because their greater flexibility encouraged greater creativity, productivity, and company loyalty.

In light of such findings, many corporations have experimented with humanizing their work settings. As we look at them, keep in mind that they are not motivated by some altruistic urge to make life better for workers, but by the same motivation as always—the bottom line. It is in management's self-interest to make their company more competitive.

humanizing a work setting organizing a workplace in such a way that it develops rather than impedes human potential

Humanizing the work setting means to make the work site a more pleasant place in order to better meet the needs of workers. In this photo, workers are being instructed in yoga. In some instances, as sociologist Arlie Hochschild discovered, work places have become so rewarding that workers prefer work to the tensions of family life.

Work Teams Work teams are small groups of workers who analyze their work situation to develop creative ideas and solutions to problems. These self-managed teams instill a high sense of loyalty to the company. Employees who belong to work teams work harder, are absent less, and are more productive. Workers in these groups also react more quickly to threats posed by technological change and competitors' advances. Corporations around the world are finding that people work more effectively in small groups than in a centralized command structure (Drucker 1992).

In small work groups, people form primary relationships, and their identities become intertwined with their group. This reduces alienation, for rather than being lost in a bureaucratic maze, their individuality is appreciated and their contributions are more readily recognized. The group's successes become the individual's successes—as do its failures. As a consequence of their accountability within a system of personal ties, workers make more of an effort. The results have been so good that, in what is known as *worker empowerment*, some self-managed teams have even replaced bosses as the ones who control everything from schedules to hiring and firing (Lublin 1991; Vanderburg 2004).

Corporate Child Care Some companies help to humanize the work setting by offering on-site child care facilities. This eases the strain on parents. While they are at work, they can keep in touch with a baby or toddler, and observe the care their child is receiving. They are able to spend time with their children during breaks and lunch hours. Mothers can even nurse their children at the child care center or express milk in the "lactation room" (Kantor 2006).

Most U.S. companies, however, offer no child care at all. In the face of global competition, especially cheap labor in the Least Industrialized Nations, can U.S. firms afford child care? Surprisingly, providing child care can reduce labor costs. When the Union Bank of Monterey, California, decided to measure the cost of its day care center, they found that the annual turnover of employees who used the center was just one-fourth that of employees who did not use it. Users of the center were also absent from work less, and they took shorter maternity leaves. The net cost? After subtracting the center's costs from these savings, the bank saved more than $200,000 (Solomon 1988).

Providing back-up child care falls somewhere in between offering on-site child care and no child care at all. With this approach, parents use their own babysitter, but if the sitter can't make it, parents can use the center's back-up services; this allows them to be at work—and to do their job without worry.

As the number of women in management increases, it is likely that more U.S. firms will offer child care services as part of a benefits package designed to attract and hold capable workers.

Employee Stock Ownership Plans If workers are shareholders, it is thought that their loyalty and productivity will increase. Consequently, many companies let their employees buy the firm's stock either at a discount or as part of their salary. About 10 million U.S. workers own part of 11,000 companies. What are the results? Some studies show that these companies are more profitable than other firms (White 1991; Logue and Yates 2000). Other studies, in contrast, report that their profits are about the same, although their productivity may be higher (Blassi and Conte 1996). We need more definitive research on this matter.

If the employees own *all* or most of the company stock, it should eliminate problems between workers and management. This should be obvious—after all, the workers and owners are the same people. But this is not the case. United Airline pilots, for example, who own the largest stake in their airline, staged a work slowdown during their 2001 contract negotiations, forcing the cancellation of thousands of flights. The machinists, who are also owners, followed suit. The machinists' union even threatened to strike. As passengers fled the airline, United racked up huge losses, and its stock plummeted (Zuckerman 2001). The irony is that the company's losses were the worker-owners' losses.

Profitability, not ownership, appears to be the key to reducing worker-management conflict. Unprofitable firms put more pressure on their employee-owners, while profitable companies are quicker to resolve problems.

The Conflict Perspective

Conflict theorists point out that the term humanizing the work setting is camouflage for what is really going on. The basic relationship between workers and owners is always confrontational. Workers and owners walk different paths in life, with owners exploiting workers to extract greater profits and workers trying to resist that exploitation. Because their basic interests are fundamentally opposed, what employers call humanizing the work setting (or managing diversity) is an attempt to manipulate workers into cooperating in their own exploitation. The term humanizing is intended to conceal the capitalists' goal of exploiting workers.

Fads in Corporate Culture

Business practices go through fads, and something that is hot one day may be cold the next. Twenty years ago, the rage was *quality circles,* workers and a manager or two who met regularly to try to improve the quality of both working conditions and the company's products. Because quality circles were used in Japan, U.S. managers embraced them, thinking they had discovered the secret of Japanese success. At its height of popularity in 1983, tens of thousands of U.S. firms were using quality circles, and 60 consultants specialized in teaching them (Strang and Macy 2001). Plummeting in popularity, quality circle has become a term relegated to dictionaries.

As corporations continue to seek ways to get their employees to solve problems as a team, they hop from one fad to another. "Cook offs" are one of the latest. Going cleaver to cleaver, corporate teams slice, chop, and sauté against the clock (Hafner 2007). Professional chefs lend an aura of credibility by overseeing the cook offs and judging the teams' culinary efforts. It seems safe to predict that, like rope-climbing, these team-building exercises will soon pass—and be replaced by still another fad.

Technology and the Control of Workers

The microchip has brought us higher quality manufactured goods and has reduced drudgery. Records are much easier to keep, and we can type just one letter and let the computer print it out and address it to ten individuals—or to ten thousand. Working on my computer, I can modify this sentence, this paragraph, or any section of this book with ease. The other side of the computer is its potential for abuse. Computers make it easier for governments to operate a police state by monitoring our every move. The Big Brother in Orwell's classic novel, *1984,* may turn out to be a computer.

DILBERT: © Scott Adams/Dist. by United Feature Syndicate, Inc.

Despite the rationality that is essential to them, bureaucracies are also marked by nonrational elements. Fads that sweep businesses and universities are an example.

Perhaps, as Orwell suggests, our destiny is to become servants to a master computer. We'll know shortly. In the meantime, we can see that the computer has allowed managers to increase surveillance without face-to-face supervision. For example, sitting in their office, managers know the exact number of keystrokes workers make each minute. They know precisely how long each worker takes for each telephone call. Workers who fall below the average are singled out for discipline. It doesn't matter that the slower workers may be more polite or more helpful, only that the computer reports slower performance.

Then there are the surveillance cameras mounted in the workplace. These cameras, called "little brothers" (as compared with Orwell's "Big Brother"), let bosses in remote locations peer over the shoulders of workers. As sociologist Gary Marx (1995) says, we may be moving to a *maximum-security workplace.* Computers are able to measure motion, air currents, vibrations, odors, pressure changes, and voice stress. To prevent employees from punching in someone else's time card, some companies are using a device to scan their workers' eyes. It compares retinal images with computerized data on file. Because these scans are so precise, I anticipate that soon we will all have to undergo them to even get a driver's license—and, eventually, to use a credit or debit card.

The maximum-security workplace seems an apt term, but with computers and surveillance cameras, the workplace may be just one aspect of a coming "maximum-security society" (Marx 1995). The Sociology and the New Technology box on the next page discusses how computers are being used to monitor workers who think that their actions have gone unnoticed.

U.S. and Japanese Corporations

How were the Japanese able to recover from the defeat of World War II—including the nuclear devastation of two of their major cities—to become a giant in today's global economy? Some analysts trace part of the answer to the way their corporations are organized. Let's compare Japanese and U.S. corporations.

How the Corporations Differ

One analyst, William Ouchi (1981), pinpointed five ways in which Japanese corporations differ from those of the United States. But are these differences myth or reality?

Hiring and Promoting Teams In *Japan,* teamwork is central. College graduates who join a corporation are all paid about the same starting salary. They also get raises as a team. To learn about the company, they are rotated as a team through the various levels of the organization. They develop intense loyalty to one another and to their company, for the welfare of one represents the welfare of all. Only in later years are individuals singled out for recognition. When there is an opening in the firm, outsiders are not even considered.

In the *United States,* personal achievement is central. A worker is hired on the basis of what the firm thinks that individual can contribute. Employees try to outperform each other, and they strive for raises and promotions as signs of personal success. The individual's loyalty is to himself or herself, not to the company. Outsiders are considered for openings in the firm.

Lifetime Security In *Japan,* lifetime security is taken for granted. Employees can expect to work for the same firm for the rest of their lives. In return for not being laid off or fired, the firm expects employees to be loyal to the company, to stick with it through good and bad times. Workers do not go job shopping, for their careers—and many aspects of their lives—are wrapped up in this one firm.

In the *United States,* lifetime security is unusual. It is limited primarily to teachers and some judges, who receive what is called *tenure.* Companies lay off workers in slow times. To remain competitive, they even reorganize and eliminate entire divisions. Workers, too, "look out for number one." They seek better pay and opportunities elsewhere. Job shopping and job hopping are common.

Almost Total Involvement   In *Japan,* work is like a marriage: The worker and the company are committed to each other. The employee supports the company with loyalty and long hours at work, while the company supports its workers with lifetime security, health services, recreation, sports and social events, even a home mortgage. Involvement with the company does not stop when the workers leave the building. They join company study and exercise groups, and are likely to spend evenings with co-workers in bars and restaurants.

Cyberloafers and Cybersleuths: Surfing at Work

FEW PEOPLE WORK CONSTANTLY at their jobs. Most of us take breaks and, at least once in a while, goof off. We meet fellow workers at the coffee machine, and we talk in the hallway. Much of this interaction is good for the company, for it bonds us to fellow workers and ties us to our jobs.

Our personal lives may even cross over into our workday. Some of us make personal calls from the office. Bosses know that we need to check in with our child's preschool or make arrangements for a babysitter. They expect such calls. Some even wink as we make a date or nod as we arrange to have our car worked on. And most bosses make personal calls of their own from time to time. It's the abuse that bothers bosses, and it's not surprising that they fire anyone who talks on the phone all day for personal reasons.

Using computers at work for personal purposes is called *cyberslacking.* Many workers fritter away some of their workday online. They trade stocks, download music, gamble, and play games. They read books, shop, exchange jokes, send personal e-mail, post messages in chat rooms, and visit online red-light districts. Some cyberslackers even operate their own businesses online—when they're not battling virtual enemies during "work."

To take a day off without the boss knowing it, some use remote devices to make their computer switch screens and their printer spew out documents (Spencer 2003). It looks as though they just stepped away from their desk. Some equip their cell phones with audio recordings: Although they may be sitting on the beach when they call the office, their boss hears background sounds of a dentist's drill or of honking horns (Richtel 2004).

Some workers defend their cyberloafing. They argue, reasonably enough, that since their work invades their homes—forcing them to work evenings and weekends—employers should accommodate their personal lives. Some Web sites protect cyberloafers: They feature a panic button in case the boss pokes her head in your office. Click the button and a phony spreadsheet pops onto your screen while typing sounds emerge from your speakers.

Cyberslacking has given birth to the *cybersleuth.* With specialized software, cybersleuths can recover every note employees have written and every Web site they have visited (Nusbaum 2003). They can bring up every file that employees have deleted, even every word they've erased. What some workers don't know (and what some of us forget) is that "delete" does not mean erase. Hitting the delete button simply pushes the text into the background of our hard drive. With a few clicks, the cybersleuth, like magic ink, exposes our "deleted" information, opening our hidden diary for anyone to read.

for your Consideration

Do you think that cybersleuthing is an abuse of power? An invasion of privacy? Or do employers have a right to check on what their employees are doing with company computers on company time? Can you think of a less invasive solution to cyberloafing?

In the *United States,* work is a specific, often temporary contract. Workers are hired to do a certain job. When they have done that job, they have fulfilled their obligation to the company. Their after-work hours are their own. They go home to their private lives, which usually are separate from the firm.

Broad Training In *Japan,* workers move from one job to another within the company. Not only are they not stuck doing the same thing for years on end but also they gain a bigger picture of the corporation and how the specific jobs they are assigned fit into that bigger picture.

In the *United States,* workers are expected to perform one job, do it well, and then be promoted upward to a job with more responsibility. Their understanding of the company is largely tied to the particular corner they occupy, often making it difficult for them to see how their job fits into the overall picture.

Decision Making by Consensus In *Japan,* decision making is a lengthy process. Each person who will be affected by a decision is consulted. After extensive deliberations, a consensus emerges, and everyone agrees on which suggestion is superior. This makes workers feel that they are an essential part of the organization, not simply cogs in a giant machine.

In the *United States,* the person in charge of the unit to be affected does as much consulting with others as he or she thinks is necessary and then makes the decision.

The Myth Versus Reality

If we peer beneath the surface, we see that a distorting myth clouds the reality of the Japanese corporation. Most Japanese workers never find lifetime job security, for example—only 20 to 30 percent do (Tokoro 2005). Management by consensus is also a myth. This was not how decisions were made at Sony, one of Japan's most successful companies (Nathan 1999). Akio Morita, Sony's founder, was a take-charge entrepreneur, who relied on his gut feeling about products. Before investing company resources in a risky new product called the Walkman, he didn't send memos throughout the company to get consensus–he simply ordered Sony to manufacture it. One day over lunch, without checking with anyone, Morita decided to spend $2 billion to buy CBS Records.

In the Cultural Diversity box with which we close this chapter, we look at the major changes that are transforming Japanese corporations.

For a time, Americans stood in awe of the Japanese corporate model. The passage of time, however, has revealed serious flaws. Lifetime job security, for example, is a myth. These homeless men are living in the Shinjuko train station in Tokyo. Note how they have followed the Japanese custom of placing their shoes outside before entering their "home."

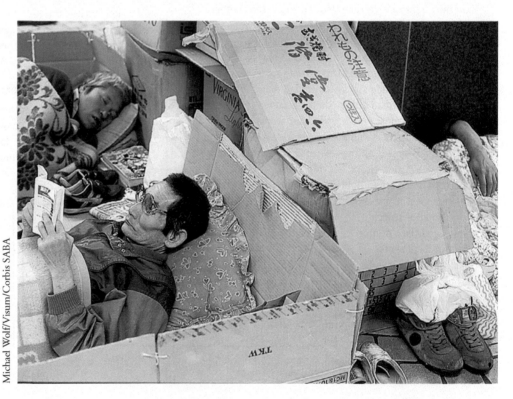

Michael Wolf/Visum/Corbis SABA

DO YOU KNOW WHICH OF THESE statements is false?

The Japanese are more productive than Americans.
The living standard of Americans has fallen behind that of the Japanese.
Japanese workers enjoy lifetime job security.
The Japanese are paid less than Americans.

From what you just read, you know that the third one is false. So are the other three.

A while back, Japanese corporations seemed invincible. There was even talk that the United States had won World War II, but had lost the economic war. Impressed with Japan's success, Western corporations, including those from the United States, sent executives to Japan to study their companies. U.S. corporations then copied parts of that model.

Cracks in the facade soon appeared. Small at first, they grew, destroying some of Japan's major corporations. These companies had been built on personal relationships, on mutual obligations that transcend contracts. This had been a key to creating fierce loyalty, a corporate strength that turned out to be an Achilles heel. When Japan's economy went into a nose dive, companies did not lay off workers; layoffs were not part of their corporate culture. Costs mounted while profits disappeared and debts piled up, sinking companies in a sea of red ink.

In a surprising move, Japan turned to U.S. corporations to see why they were more efficient. Flying in the face of their traditions, Japanese corporations have begun to lay off workers and to use merit pay. Although this is standard U.S. practice, it had been unthinkable in Japan (Tokoro 2005).

Japanese and U.S. Corporations in an Age of Greed

One of the biggest surprises was Ford's takeover of Mazda. With Mazda teetering on the edge of bankruptcy, its creditors decided that Ford knew more about building and marketing cars than Mazda and invited Ford to manage the company. In true U.S. fashion, Ford laid off workers and renegotiated contracts with suppliers. With its work force slashed from 46,000 to 36,000, Mazda again became profitable. Similarly, when Sony's profits plummeted, an American who couldn't even speak Japanese was made its CEO (Kane and Dvorak 2007).

A much leaner, meaner Japanese production machine is emerging.

for your Consideration

The real bottom line is that we live in a global marketplace—of ideas as well as products. Companies from different countries learn from one another. Do you think that it will become common for Japanese corporations—with their cultural background of relationships and cooperation–to lay off workers in order to compete more effectively in global competition?

In another twist, Ford, which had led the successful turnaround of Mazda in Japan, found itself unable to compete successfully with Toyota. Like General Motors, Ford lost market share and billions of dollars, putting itself on the brink of financial disaster. Do you think Toyota will become the poster child of the corporate car world, and, perhaps, in a double twist, be brought back to Japan to apply its U.S. lessons?

Summary *and* Review

The Rationalization of Society

How did the rationalization of society come about?

The term **rationalization of society** refers to a transformation in people's thinking and behaviors—one that shifts the focus from following time-honored ways to being efficient in producing results. Max Weber, who developed this term, traced this change to Protestant theology, which he said brought about capitalism. Karl Marx attributed rationalization to capitalism itself.

Formal Organizations and Bureaucracies

What are formal organizations?

Formal organizations are secondary groups designed to achieve specific objectives. Their dominant form is the **bureaucracy,** which Weber said consists of a hierarchy, a division of labor, written rules and communications, and impersonality and replaceability of positions—characteristics that make bureaucracies efficient and enduring.

What dysfunctions are associated with bureaucracies?

The dysfunctions of bureaucracies include alienation, red tape, lack of communication between units, **goal displacement,** and incompetence (as seen in the **Peter principle**). In Weber's view, the impersonality of bureaucracies tends to produce **alienation** among workers—the feeling that no one cares about them and that they do not really fit in. Marx's view of alienation is somewhat different—workers do not identify with the product of their labor because they participate in only a small part of the production process.

Voluntary Associations

What are the functions of voluntary associations?

Voluntary **associations** are groups made up of volunteers who organize on the basis of common interests. These associations promote mutual interests, provide a sense of identity and purpose, help to govern and maintain order, mediate between the government and the individual, give training in organizational skills, help provide access to political power, and pave the way for social change.

What is "the iron law of oligarchy"?

Sociologist Robert Michels noted that formal organizations have a tendency to become controlled by an inner circle that limits leadership to its own members. The dominance of a formal organization by an elite that keeps itself in power is called **the iron law of oligarchy.**

Working for the Corporation

How does the corporate culture affect workers?

The term **corporate culture** refers to an organization's traditions, values, and unwritten norms. Much of corporate culture, such as its hidden values and stereotypes, is not readily visible. Often, a **self-fulfilling prophecy** is at work: People who match a corporation's hidden values tend to be put on career tracks that enhance their chance of success, while those who do not match those values are set on a course that minimizes their performance.

Humanizing the Corporate Culture

What does it mean to humanize the work setting?

Humanizing a work setting means to organize it in a way that develops rather than impedes human potential. Among the attempts to make bureaucracies more humane are work teams and corporate day care. Employee stock ownership plans give workers a greater stake in the outcomes of their work organizations, but they do not prevent worker-management conflict. Conflict theorists see attempts to humanize work as a way of manipulating workers.

Technology and the Control of Workers

What is the maximum security workplace?

It is the use of computers and surveillance devices to monitor almost all the actions of workers.

U.S. and Japanese Corporations

How do Japanese and U.S. corporations differ?

The Japanese corporate model contrasts sharply with the U.S. model in terms of hiring and promotion, lifetime security, interaction of workers after work, broad training of workers, and collective decision making. Much of this model is a myth, an idealization of reality, and does not reflect Japanese corporate life today.

Thinking Critically

1. You are likely to work for a bureaucracy. How do you think that it will affect your orientations to life? How can you make the "hidden culture" work to your advantage?

2. Do you think the Peter principle is right? Why or why not?

3. Do you think U.S. corporations should have diversity training? Why or why not? If so, how should they go about it?

Additional Resources

What can you use MySocLab for? mysoclab www.mysoclab.com

- **Study and Review:** Pre- and Post-Tests, Practice Tests, Flash Cards, Individualized Study Plans.

- **Current Events:** *Sociology in the News*, the daily *New York Times*, and more.

- **Research and Writing:** *Research Navigator*, *Writing About Sociology*, and more.

Where Can I Read More on This Topic?

Ackoff, Russell L., and Sheldon Rovin. *Beating the System: Using Creativity to Outsmart Bureaucracies.* San Francisco: Berrett-Koehler, Publishers, 2005. This analysis can be applied to everyday situations, such as avoiding getting lost in a maze as you try to solve a problem with the phone company or some other bureaucracy.

Bakan, Joel. *The Corporation: The Pathological Pursuit of Profit and Power.* New York: The Free Press, 2004. The author's thesis is that the corporation's lust for power undermines democracy, social justice, equality, and compassion.

Cyr, Donald. *The Art of Global Thinking: Integrating Organizational Philosophies of East and West.* West Lafayette, Ind.: Ichor Business Books, 2002. The author compares Western and Eastern organizations and their underlying philosophies and suggests ways of extracting and applying the best of both worlds.

Eberly, Don, and Ryan Streeter. *The Soul of Civil Society: Voluntary Associations and the Public Value of Moral Habits.* Lanham, Md.: Lexington Books, 2002. The authors' thesis is that citizens' involvement in voluntary organizations strengthens society.

Fineman, Stephen, Gabriel Yiannis, and David P. Sims. *Organizing and Organizations,* 3rd ed. Thousand Oaks, Calif.: Sage Publications, 2006. The authors draw on many first-hand accounts to help enliven the study of formal organizations.

Freidson, Eliot. *Professionalism: The 3rd Logic.* Chicago: University of Chicago Press, 2001. The author distinguishes between professions, technical occupations, and crafts, analyzing how they differ by knowledge base, educational requirements, career paths, organization, and ideology.

Hall, Richard H., and Pamela S. Tolbert. *Organizations: Structures, Processes, and Outcomes,* 9th ed. Upper Saddle River, N. J.: Prentice Hall, 2005. The focus of this review of the literature on social organizations is on the impacts that organizations have upon individuals and society.

Parkinson, C. Northcote. *Parkinson's Law.* Boston: Buccaneer Books, 1997. Although this exposé of the inner workings of bureaucracies is delightfully satirical, if what Parkinson analyzes were generally true, bureaucracies would always fail.

Ritzer, George. *The McDonaldization of Society: An Investigation into the Changing Character of Contemporary Life,* 4th ed. Thousand Oaks, Calif.: Pine Forge Press, 2004. The author examines how Durkheim's predictions about the rationalization of society are coming true in everyday life.

Want, Jerome. *Corporate Culture: Illuminating the Black Hole.* New York: St. Martin's Press, 2007. The author uses real-life examples to show how culture determines the success of an organization.

Social Class in the United States

From Chapter 10 of *Sociology: A Down-to-Earth Approach*, 9/e. James M. Henslin. Copyright © 2008 by Pearson Education. All rights reserved.

Social Class in the United States

Frank Freed, *Have and Have Not*, 1970

Ah, New Orleans, that fabled city on the Mississippi Delta. Images from its rich past floated through my head—pirates, treasure, intrigue. Memories from a pleasant vacation stirred my thoughts—the exotic French Quarter with its enticing aroma of Creole food and sounds of earthy jazz drifting through the air.

The shelter for the homeless, however, forced me back to an unwelcome reality. The shelter was the same as those I had visited in the North, West, and East—only dirtier. The dirt, in fact, was the worst that I had encountered during my research, and this shelter was the only one to insist on payment in exchange for sleeping in one of its filthy beds.

The men looked the same—disheveled and haggard, wearing that unmistakable expression of despair—just like the homeless anywhere in the country. Except for the accent, you wouldn't know what region you were in. Poverty wears the same tired face wherever you are, I realized. The accent may differ, but the look remains the same.

I had grown used to the sights and smells of abject poverty. Those no longer surprised me. But after my fitful sleep with the homeless, I saw something that did.

> **I was startled by a sight so out of step with the misery and despair that I stopped in midtrack.**

Hou Jun/Xinhua News Agency/WpN

Just a block or so from the shelter, I was startled by a sight so out of step with the misery and despair I had just experienced that I stopped in midtrack.

Indignation swelled within me. Confronting me were life-size, full-color photos mounted on the transparent plexiglass shelter of a bus stop. Staring back at me were images of finely dressed men and women proudly strutting about as they modeled elegant suits, dresses, diamonds, and furs.

A wave of disgust swept over me. "Something is cockeyed in this society," I thought, my mind refusing to stop juxtaposing these images of extravagance with the suffering I had just witnessed. Occasionally, the reality of social class hits home with brute force. This was one of those moments.

The disjunction that I felt in New Orleans was triggered by the ads, but it was not the first time that I had experienced this sensation. Whenever my research abruptly transported me from the world of the homeless to one of another social class, I experienced a sense of disjointed unreality. Each social class has its own way of being, and because these fundamental orientations to the world contrast so sharply, the classes do not mix well.

What Is Social Class?

If you ask most Americans about their country's social class system, you are likely to get a blank look. If you press the matter, you are likely to get an answer like this: "There are the poor and the rich—and then there are you and I, neither poor nor rich." This is just about as far as most Americans' consciousness of social class goes. Let's try to flesh out this idea.

Our task is made somewhat difficult because sociologists have no clear-cut, agreed-on definition of social class. Conflict sociologists (of the Marxist orientation) see only two social classes: those who own the means of production and those who do not. The problem with this view, say most sociologists, is that it lumps too many people together. Teenage "order takers" at McDonald's who work for $15,000 a year are lumped together with that company's executives who make $500,000 a year—because they both are workers at McDonald's, not owners.

Most sociologists agree with Weber that there is more to social class than just a person's relationship to the means of production. Consequently, most sociologists use the components Weber identified and define **social class** as a large group of people who rank closely to one another in property, prestige, and power. These three elements separate people into different lifestyles, give them different chances in life, and provide them with distinct ways of looking at the self and the world.

Let's look at how sociologists measure these three components of social class.

Property

Property comes in many forms, such as buildings, land, animals, machinery, cars, stocks, bonds, businesses, furniture, and bank accounts. When you add up the value of someone's property and subtract that person's debts, you have what sociologists call **wealth.** This term can be misleading, as some of us have little wealth—especially most college students. Nevertheless, if your net total comes to $10, then that is your wealth. (Obviously, wealth as a sociological term does not equal wealthy.)

Distinguishing Between Wealth and Income   Wealth and income are sometimes confused, but they are not the same. Where *wealth* is a person's net worth, **income** is a flow of money. Income can come from a number of sources: usually a business or wages, but also from rent, interest, or royalties, even from alimony, an allowance, or gambling. Some people have much wealth and little income. For example, a farmer may own much land (a form of wealth), but bad weather, combined with the high cost of fertilizers and machinery, can cause the income to dry up. Others have much income and little wealth. An executive with a $250,000 annual income may be debt-ridden. Below the surface prosperity—the exotic vacations, country club membership, private schools for the children, sports cars, and an elegant home—the credit cards may be maxed out, the sports cars in danger of being repossessed, and the mortgage payments "past due." Typically, however, wealth and income go together.

Distribution of Property   Who owns the property in the United States? One answer, of course, is "everyone." Although this statement has some merit, it overlooks how the nation's property is divided among "everyone."

Overall, Americans are worth a hefty sum, about $38 trillion (*Statistical Abstract* 2007:Table 704). This includes all real estate, stocks, bonds, and business assets in the entire country. Figure 1 shows how highly concentrated this wealth is. Most wealth, 70 percent, is owned by only *10 percent* of the nation's families. As you can also see from this figure, 1 percent of Americans own one third of all the U.S. assets.

Distribution of Income   How is income distributed in the United States? Economist Paul Samuelson (Samuelson and Nordhaus 2005) put it this way: "If we made an income pyramid out of a child's blocks, with each layer portraying $500 of income, the peak would be far higher than Mount Everest, but most people would be within a few feet of the ground."

Actually, if each block were 1-½ inches tall, the typical American would be just 9 *feet off the ground,* for the average per capita income in the United States is about $35,000 per year. (This average income includes every American, even children.) The typical family climbs a little higher, for most families have more than one worker, and together they average about $54,000 a year. Compared with the few families who are on the mountain's peak, the average U.S. family would find itself only 14 feet off the ground (*Statistical Abstract* 2007:Tables 660, 677). Figure 2 portrays these differences.

Figure 1 Distribution of the Property of Americans

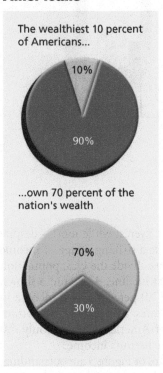

The wealthiest 10 percent of Americans...

10%

90%

...own 70 percent of the nation's wealth

70%

30%

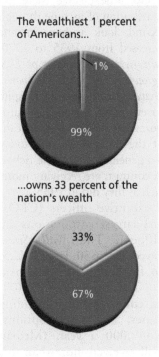

The wealthiest 1 percent of Americans...

1%

99%

...owns 33 percent of the nation's wealth

33%

67%

Source: By the author. Based on Beeghley 2008.

Figure 2 Distribution of the Income of Americans

Some U.S. families have incomes that exceed the height of Mt. Everest, 29,028 feet

Average U.S. family income
$54,000
or 14 feet

Average U.S. individual income
$35,000
or 9 feet

If a 1 1/2 inch child's block equals $500 of income, the average individual's annual income of $35,000 would represent a height of 9 feet, and the average family's annual income of $54,000 would represent a height of 14 feet. The income of some families, in contrast, would represent a height greater than that of Mt. Everest.

Source: By the author.

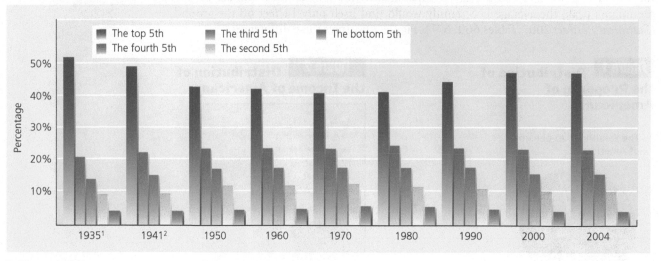

¹Earliest year available.
²No data for 1940.

Source: By the author. Based on *Statistical Abstract* 1960:Table 417; 1970:Table 489; 2007:Table 678.

The fact that some Americans enjoy the peaks of Mount Everest while most—despite their efforts—make it only 9 to 14 feet up the slope presents a striking image of income inequality in the United States. Another picture emerges if we divide the U.S. population into five equal groups and rank them from highest to lowest income. As Figure 3 shows, the top 20 percent of the population receive *almost half* (47.9 percent) of all income in the United States. In contrast, the bottom 20 percent of Americans receive only 4.0 percent of the nation's income.

Two features of Figure 3 are outstanding. First, notice how little change there has been in the distribution of income through the years. Second, look at how income inequality decreased from 1935 to 1970. *Since 1970, the richest 20 percent of U.S. families have grown richer, while the poorest 20 percent have grown poorer.* Despite numerous government antipoverty programs, the poorest 20 percent of Americans receive *less* of the nation's income today than they did a generation ago. The richest 20 percent, in contrast, are receiving more, but not as much as they did in 1935.

The chief executive officers (CEOs) of the nation's largest corporations are especially affluent. The *Wall Street Journal* surveyed the 350 largest U.S. companies to find out what they paid their CEOs ("The Boss's Pay" 2007). Their median compensation (including salaries, bonuses, and stock options) came to $6,549,000 a year. (Median means that half received more than this amount, and half less.)

CBS/Landov LLC

A mere one-half of 1 percent of Americans owns over a quarter of the entire nation's wealth. Very few minorities are numbered among this 0.5 percent. An exception is Oprah Winfrey, who has had an ultra-successful career in entertainment and investing. Worth $1.3 billion, she is the 215th richest person in the United States. Winfrey, who has given millions of dollars to help minority children, is shown here as she is interviewed by David Letterman.

The CEOs' income—which does *not* include their income from interest, dividends, or rents, or the value of company-paid limousines and chauffeurs, airplanes and pilots, and private boxes at the symphony and sporting events—is *166 times* higher than the average pay of U.S. workers (*Statistical Abstract* 2007:Table 629). To really see the disparity consider this: The average U.S. worker would have to work *1,475 years* to earn the amount received by the highest-paid executive listed in Table 1.

Imagine how you could live with an income like this. And this is precisely the point. Beyond cold numbers lies a dynamic reality that profoundly affects people's lives. The difference in wealth between those at the top and those at the bottom of the U.S. class structure means that these individuals experience vastly different lifestyles. For example, a colleague of mine who was teaching at an exclusive Eastern university piqued his students' curiosity when he lectured on poverty in Latin America. That weekend, one of the students borrowed his parents' corporate jet and pilot, and in class on Monday, he and his friends related their personal observations on poverty in Latin America. Americans who are at the low end of the income ladder, in contrast, lack the funds to travel even to a neighboring town for the weekend. For young parents, choices may revolve around whether to spend the little they have at the laundromat or on milk for the baby. The elderly might have to choose between purchasing the medicines they need or buying food. In short, divisions of wealth represent not "mere" numbers, but choices that make vital differences in people's lives, a topic that we explore in the Down-to-Earth Sociology box on the next page.

Table 1	The 5 Highest-Paid CEOs	
Executive	Company	Compensation
1. Lloyd Blankfein	Goldman Sachs Group	$55 million
2. Stanley O'Neal	Merrill Lynch	$50 million
3. Ray Irani	Occidental Petroleum	$48 million
4. John Mack	Morgan Stanley	$40 million
5. Lawrence Ellison	Oracle	$39 million

Note: Compensation includes salary, bonuses, and stock options.
Source: "The Boss's Pay" 2007.

Power

Like many people, you may have said to yourself, "Sure, I can vote, but somehow the big decisions are always made despite what I might think. Certainly *I* don't make the decision to send soldiers to Afghanistan or Iraq. *I* don't launch missiles against Kosovo or Baghdad. *I* don't decide to raise taxes or lower interest rates. It isn't *I* who decides to change Social Security or Medicare benefits."

And then another part of you may say, "But I do participate in these decisions through my representatives in Congress, and by voting for president." True enough—as far as it goes. The trouble is, it just doesn't go far enough. Such views of being a participant in the nation's "big" decisions are a playback of the ideology we learn at an early age—an ideology that Marx said is promoted by the elites to both legitimate and perpetuate their power. Sociologists Daniel Hellinger and Dennis Judd (1991) call this the "democratic facade" that conceals the real source of power in the United States.

Back in the 1950s, sociologist C. Wright Mills (1956) was criticized for insisting that **power**—the ability to carry out your will despite resistance—was concentrated in the hands of a few, for his analysis contradicted the dominant ideology of equality. Mills coined the term **power elite** to refer to those who make the big decisions in U.S. society.

Mills and others have stressed how wealth and power coalesce in a group of like-minded individuals who share ideologies and values. These individuals belong to the same private clubs, vacation at the same exclusive resorts, and even hire the same bands for their daughters' debutante balls. Their shared backgrounds and vested interests reinforce their view of both the world and their special place in it (Domhoff 1999a, 2006). This elite wields extraordinary power in U.S. society, so much so that *most* U.S. presidents have come from this group—millionaire white men from families with "old money" (Baltzell and Schneiderman 1988).

Continuing in the tradition of Mills, sociologist William Domhoff (1990, 2006) argues that this group is so powerful that no major decision of the U.S. government is

power the ability to carry out your will, even over the resistance of others

power elite C. Wright Mills' term for the top people in U.S. corporations, military, and politics who make the nation's major decisions

made without its approval. He analyzed how this group works behind the scenes with elected officials to determine both the nation's foreign and domestic policy—from setting Social Security taxes to imposing trade tariffs. Although Domhoff's conclusions are controversial—and alarming—they certainly follow logically from the principle that wealth brings power, and extreme wealth brings extreme power.

Prestige

Occupations and Prestige What are you thinking about doing after college? Chances are, you don't have the option of lolling under palm trees at the beach. Almost all of us have to choose an occupation and go to work. Look at Table 2 to see how the career you are considering stacks up in terms of **prestige** (respect or regard). Because we are moving toward a global society, this table also shows how the rankings given by Americans compare with those of the residents of sixty other countries.

Down-to-Earth Sociology

How the Super-Rich Live

IT'S GOOD TO SEE how other people live. It gives us a different perspective on life. Let's take a glimpse at the life of John Castle (his real name). After earning a degree in physics at MIT and an MBA at Harvard, John went into banking and securities, where he made more than $100 million (Lublin 1999).

Wanting to be connected to someone famous, John bought President John F. Kennedy's "Winter White House," an ocean-front estate in Palm Beach, Florida. John spent $11 million to remodel the 13,000-square-foot house so that it would be more to his liking. Among those changes: adding bathrooms numbers 14 and 15. He likes to show off John F. Kennedy's bed and also the dresser that has the drawer labeled "black underwear," carefully hand-lettered by Rose Kennedy.

At his beachfront estate, John gives what he calls "refined feasts" to the glitterati ("On History . . . " 1999). If he gets tired of such activities—or weary of swimming in the Olympic-size pool where JFK swam the weekend before his assassination—he entertains himself by riding one of his thoroughbred horses at his nearby 10-acre ranch. If this fails to ease his boredom, he can relax aboard his custom-built 42-foot Hinckley yacht.

The yacht is a real source of diversion. John once boarded it for an around-the-world trip. He didn't stay on board, though—just joined the cruise from time to time. A captain

©Brian Smith/Corbis OUTLINE

How do the super-rich live? This photo helps give you an idea of how different their lifestyles are from most of us. Shown here is Wayne Huizenga, who is featured in this box, with one of his vintage automobiles.

and crew kept the vessel on course, and whenever John felt like it he would fly in and stay a few days. Then he would fly back to the States to direct his business. He did this about a dozen times, flying perhaps 150,000 miles. An interesting way to go around the world.

How much does a custom-built Hinckley yacht cost? John can't tell you. As he says, "I don't want to know what anything costs. When you've got enough money, price doesn't make a difference. That's part of the freedom of being rich."

Right. And for John, being rich also means paying $1,000,000 to charter a private jet to fly Spot, his Appaloosa horse, back and forth to the vet. John didn't want Spot to have to endure a long trailer ride. Oh, and of course, there was the cost of Spot's medical treatment, another $500,000.

Other wealthy people put John to shame. Wayne Huizenga, the founder of Blockbuster, wanted more elbow room for his estate at Nantucket, so he added the house next door for $2.5 million (Fabrikant 2005). He also bought a 2,000-acre country club, complete with an 18-hole golf course, a 55,000-square-foot-clubhouse, and 68 slips for visiting vessels. The club is so exclusive that its only members are Wayne and his wife.

Why do people give more prestige to some jobs than to others? If you look at Table 2, you will notice that the jobs at the top share four features:

1. They pay more.
2. They require more education.
3. They entail more abstract thought.
4. They offer greater autonomy (independence, or self-direction).

If you look at the bottom of the list, you can see that people give less prestige to jobs with the opposite characteristics: These jobs are low-paying, require less preparation or education, involve more physical labor, and are closely supervised. In short, the professions and the white-collar jobs are at the top of the list, the blue-collar jobs at the bottom.

One of the more interesting aspects of these rankings is how consistent they are across countries and over time. For example, people in every country rank college professors higher than nurses, nurses higher than social workers, and social workers higher than janitors. Similarly, the occupations that were ranked high 25 years ago still rank high today—and likely will rank high in the years to come.

Displaying Prestige People want others to acknowledge their prestige. In times past, in some countries only the emperor and his family could wear purple—for it was the royal color. In France, only the nobility could wear lace. In England, no one could sit while the king was on his throne. Some kings and queens required that subjects walk backward as they left the room—so no one would "turn their back" on the "royal presence."

Concern with displaying prestige has not let up. For some, it is almost an obsession. Military manuals specify precisely who must salute whom. The U.S. president enters a room only after everyone else attending the function is present (to show that *he* isn't the one waiting for *them*). They also must be standing when he enters. In the courtroom, bailiffs, sometimes armed, make certain that everyone stands when the judge enters.

The display of prestige permeates society. In parts of Los Angeles, some people list their address as the prestigious Beverly Hills and then add their own correct ZIP code. When East Detroit changed its name to East Pointe to play off its proximity to swank Grosse Pointe, property values shot up (Fletcher 1997). Many pay more for clothing that bears a "designer" label. Prestige is often a primary factor in deciding which college to attend. Everyone knows how the prestige of a generic sheepskin from Regional State College compares with a degree from Harvard, Princeton, Yale, or Stanford.

Status symbols vary with social class. Clearly, only the wealthy can afford certain items, such as

Table 2 — Occupational Prestige: How the United States Compares with 60 Countries

Occupation	United States	Average of 60 Countries
Physician	86	78
Supreme court judge	85	82
College president	81	86
Astronaut	80	80
Lawyer	75	73
College professor	74	78
Airline pilot	73	66
Architect	73	72
Biologist	73	69
Dentist	72	70
Civil engineer	69	70
Clergy	69	60
Psychologist	69	66
Pharmacist	68	64
High school teacher	66	64
Registered nurse	66	54
Professional athlete	65	48
Electrical engineer	64	65
Author	63	62
Banker	63	67
Veterinarian	62	61
Police officer	61	40
Sociologist	61	67
Journalist	60	55
Classical musician	59	56
Actor or actress	58	52
Chiropractor	57	62
Athletic coach	53	50
Social worker	52	56
Electrician	51	44
Undertaker	49	34
Jazz musician	48	38
Real estate agent	48	49
Mail carrier	47	33
Secretary	46	53
Plumber	45	34
Carpenter	43	37
Farmer	40	47
Barber	36	30
Store sales clerk	36	34
Truck driver	30	33
Cab driver	28	28
Garbage collector	28	13
Waiter or waitress	28	23
Bartender	25	23
Lives on public aid	25	16
Bill collector	24	27
Factory worker	24	29
Janitor	22	21
Shoe shiner	17	12
Street sweeper	11	13

Note: For five occupations not located in the 1994 source, the 1991 ratings were used: Supreme Court judge, astronaut, athletic coach, lives on public aid, and street sweeper.

Sources: Treiman 1977, Appendices A and D; Nakao and Treas 1991; 1994: Appendix D.

Display of prestige and social position varies over time and from one culture to another. Shown here is Elizabeth I, Queen of England and Ireland. Elizabeth became queen in 1558 at the age of 25 and ruled for 45 years, until 1603. This painting hangs in the National Portrait Gallery.

yachts and huge estates. But beyond affordability lies a class-based preference in status symbols. For example, people who are striving to be upwardly mobile are quick to flaunt labels, Hummers, Land Rovers, and other material symbols to show that they have "arrived," while the rich, more secure in their status, often downplay such images. The wealthy regard the designer labels of the "common" classes as cheap and showy. They, of course, flaunt their own status symbols, such as $50,000 Rolex watches. Like the other classes, they, too, try to outdo one another; they boast about who has the longest yacht or that they have a helicopter fly them to their meetings or their golf games (Fabrikant 2005).

Status Inconsistency

Ordinarily, a person has a similar rank on all three dimensions of social class—property, power, and prestige. The homeless men in the opening vignette are an example. Such people are **status consistent.** Sometimes that match is not there, however, and someone has a mixture of high and low ranks, a condition called **status inconsistency.** This leads to some interesting situations.

Sociologist Gerhard Lenski (1954, 1966) analyzed how people try to maximize their **status,** their position in a social group. Individuals who rank high on one dimension of social class but lower on others want people to judge them on the basis of their highest status. Others, however, who are trying to maximize their own position, may respond to status inconsistent individuals according to their lowest ranking.

A classic study of status inconsistency was done by sociologist Ray Gold (1952). He found that after apartment-house janitors unionized, they made more money than some of the tenants whose garbage they carried out. Tenants became upset when they saw their janitors driving more expensive cars than they did. Some attempted to "put the janitor in his place" by making "snotty" remarks to him. For their part, the janitors took delight in knowing "dirty" secrets about the tenants, gleaned from their garbage.

Individuals with status inconsistency, then, are likely to confront one frustrating situation after another (Heames et al. 2006). They claim the higher status, but are handed the lower one. The significance of this condition, said Lenski (1954), is that such people tend to be more politically radical. An example is college professors. Their prestige is very high, as we saw in Table 2, but their incomes are relatively low. Hardly anyone in U.S. society is more educated, and yet college professors don't even come close to the top of the income pyramid. In line with Lenski's prediction, the politics of most college professors are left of center. This hypothesis may also hold true among academic departments; that is, the higher a department's average pay, the less radical are the members' politics. Teachers in departments of business and medicine, for example, are among the most highly paid in the university—and they also are the most politically conservative.

Instant wealth, the topic of the Down-to-Earth Sociology box on the next page, provides an interesting case of status inconsistency.

status consistency ranking high or low on all three dimensions of social class

status inconsistency ranking high on some dimensions of social class and low on others, also called *status discrepancy*

status the position that someone occupies in society or a social group

anomie Durkheim's term for a condition in which people become detached from the norms that usually guide their behavior

Sociological Models of Social Class

The question of how many social classes there are is a matter of debate. Sociologists have proposed several models, but no single model has gained universal support. There are two main models: one that builds on Marx, the other on Weber.

Updating Marx

Marx argued that there are just two classes—capitalists and workers—with membership based solely on a person's relationship to the means of production (see Figure 4). Sociologists have criticized this view, saying that these categories are too broad. For example, because executives, managers, and supervisors don't own the means

Down-to-Earth Sociology

The Big Win: Life After the Lottery

"IF I JUST WIN THE LOTTERY, life will be good. These problems I've got, they'll be gone. I can just see myself now."

So goes the dream. And many Americans shell out megabucks every week, with the glimmering hope that "Maybe this week, I'll hit it big."

Most are lucky to get $20, or maybe just win another scratch-off ticket.

But there are the big hits. What happens to these winners? Are their lives all wine, roses, and chocolate afterward?

Unfortunately, we don't yet have any systematic studies of the big winners, so I can't tell you what life is like for the average winner. But several themes are apparent from reporters' interviews.

The most common consequence of hitting it big is that life becomes topsy-turvy (Ross 2004). All of us are rooted somewhere. We have connections with others that provide the basis for our orientations to life and how we feel about the world. Sudden wealth can rip these moorings apart, and the resulting *status inconsistency* can lead to a condition sociologists call **anomie.**

First comes the shock. As Mary Sanderson, a telephone operator in Dover, New Hampshire, who won $66 million, said, "I was afraid to believe it was real, and afraid to believe it wasn't." Mary says that she never slept worse than her first night as a multimillionaire. "I spent the whole time crying—and throwing up" (Tresniowski 1999).

Reporters and TV camera operators appear on your doorstep. "What are you going to do with all that money?" they demand. You haven't the slightest idea, but in a daze you mumble something.

Then come the calls. Some are welcome. Your Mom and Dad call to congratulate you. But long-forgotten friends and distant relatives suddenly remember how close they really are to you—and strangely enough, they all have emergencies that your money can solve. You even get calls from strangers who have ailing mothers, terminally ill kids, sick dogs . . .

You have to unplug the phone and get an unlisted number.

Some lottery winners are flooded with marriage proposals. These individuals certainly didn't become more attractive or sexy overnight—or did they? Maybe money makes people sexy.

You can no longer trust people. You don't know what their real motives are. Before, no one could be after your money because you didn't have any. You may even fear kidnappers. Before, this wasn't a problem—unless some kidnapper wanted the ransom of a seven-year-old car.

The normal becomes abnormal. Even picking out a wedding gift is a problem. If you give the usual toaster, everyone will think you're stingy. But should you write a check for $25,000? If you do, you'll be invited to every wedding in town—and everyone will expect the same.

©Doral Chenoweth III/Columbus Dispatch/Corbis Sygma

Status inconsistency is common for lottery winners, whose new wealth is vastly greater than their education and occupational status. Shown here are John and Sandy Jarrell of Chicago, after they learned that they were one of 13 families to share a $295 million jackpot. How do you think their $22 million will affect their lives?

Here is what happened to some lottery winners:

As a tip, a customer gave a lottery ticket to Tonda Dickerson, a waitress at the Waffle House in Grand Bay, Alabama. She won $10 million. (Yes, just like the Nicholas Cage movie, *It Could Happen to You.*) Her coworkers sued her, saying that they had always agreed to split such winnings ("House Divided" 1999).

Then there is Michael Klinebiel of Rahway, New Jersey. When he won $2 million, his mother, Phyllis, said that they had pooled $20 a month for years to play the lottery. He said that was true, but his winning ticket wasn't from their pool. He had bought this one on his own. Phyllis sued her son ("Sticky Ticket" 1998).

Frank Capaci, a retired electrician in Streamwood, Illinois, who won $195 million, is no longer welcome at his old neighborhood bar. Two bartenders had collected $5 from customers and driven an hour to Wisconsin to buy tickets. When Frank won, he gave $10,000 to each of them. They said that he promised them more. Also, his former friends say that Capaci started to act "like a big shot," buying rounds of drinks but saying, "Except him," while pointing to someone he didn't like (Annin 1999).

Mack Metcalf of Corbin, Kentucky, wasn't as fortunate as Frank Capaci. After Mark hit the jackpot for $34 million, he built a beautiful home—but his former wife sued him, his current wife divorced him, his new girlfriend got $500,000 while he was drunk, and within three years of his good fortune he had drunk himself to death (Dao 2005).

Winners who avoid *anomie* seem to be people who don't make sudden changes in their lifestyle or their behavior. They hold onto their old friends, routines, and other anchors in life that give them identity and a sense of belonging. Some even keep their old jobs—not for the money, of course, but because working anchors them to an identity with which they are familiar and comfortable.

Sudden wealth, in other words, poses a threat that has to be guarded against.

And I can just hear you say, "I'll take the risk!"

Figure 4 Marx's Model of the Social Classes

Figure 4 Marx's Model of the Social Classes

Capitalists
(*Bourgeoisie*, those who own the means of production)

Workers
(*Proletariat*, those who work for the capitalists)

Inconsequential Others
(beggars, etc.)

Table 3 Wright's Modification of Marx's Model of the Social Classes

1. Capitalists
2. Petty bourgeoisie
3. Managers
4. Workers

of production, they would be classified as workers. But what do these people have in common with assembly-line workers? The category of "capitalist" is also too broad. Some people, for example, employ a thousand workers, and their decisions directly affect a thousand families. Compare these people with a man I know in Godfrey, Illinois, who used to fix cars in his backyard. As Frank gained a following, he quit his regular job, and in a few years he put up a building with five bays and an office. Frank is now a capitalist, for he employs five or six mechanics and owns the tools and the building (the "means of production"). But what does he have in common with a factory owner who controls the lives of one thousand workers? Not only is Frank's work different but so are his lifestyle and the way he looks at the world.

To resolve this problem, sociologist Erik Wright (1985) suggests that some people are members of more than one class at the same time. They occupy what he calls **contradictory class locations.** By this, Wright means that a person's position in the class structure can generate contradictory interests. For example, the automobile mechanic-turned-business owner may want his mechanics to have higher wages because he, too, has experienced their working conditions. At the same time, his current interests—making profits and remaining competitive with other repair shops—lead him to resist pressures to raise their wages.

Because of such contradictory class locations, Wright modified Marx's model. As summarized in Table 3, Wright identifies four classes: (1) *capitalists,* business owners who employ many workers; (2) *petty bourgeoisie,* small business owners; (3) *managers,* who sell their own labor but also exercise authority over other employees; and (4) *workers,* who simply sell their labor to others. As you can see, this model allows finer divisions than the one Marx proposed, yet it maintains the primary distinction between employer and employee.

Problems persist, however. For example, in which category would we place college professors? And as you know, there are huge differences in the power of managers. An executive at Toyota, for example, may manage a thousand workers, while a shift manager at McDonald's may be responsible for only a handful. They, too, have little in common.

Updating Weber

Sociologists Joseph Kahl and Dennis Gilbert (Gilbert and Kahl 1998; Gilbert 2003) developed a six-tier model to portray the class structure of the United States and other capitalist countries. Think of this model, illustrated in Figure 5 on the next page, as a ladder. Our discussion starts with the highest rung and moves downward. In line with Weber, on each lower rung you find less property (wealth), less power, and less prestige. Note that in this model education is also a primary measure of class.

The Capitalist Class   Sitting on the top rung of the class ladder is a powerful elite that consists of just 1 percent of the U.S. population. As you saw in Figure 1, this capitalist class is so wealthy that it owns one-third of all U.S. assets. *This tiny 1 percent is worth more than the entire bottom 90 percent of the country* (Beeghley 2008).

Power and influence cling to this small elite. They have direct access to top politicians, and their decisions open or close job opportunities for millions of people. They even help to shape the consciousness of the nation: They own our major media and entertainment outlets—newspapers, magazines, radio and television stations, and sports franchises. They also control the boards of directors of our most influential colleges and universities. The super-rich perpetuate themselves in privilege by passing on their assets and social networks to their children.

The capitalist class can be divided into "old" and "new" money. The longer that wealth has been in a family, the more it adds to the family's prestige. The children of "old" money seldom mingle with "common" folk. Instead, they attend exclusive private schools where they learn views of life that support their privileged position. They don't work for wages; instead, many study business or enter the field of law so that they can manage the family fortune. These old-money capitalists (also called "blue-bloods") wield vast power as they use their extensive political connections to protect their economic empires (Sklair 2001; Domhoff 1990, 1999b, 2006).

contradictory class locations Erik Wright's term for a position in the class structure that generates contradictory interests

Figure 5   **The U.S. Social Class Ladder**

Social Class	Education	Occupation	Income	Percentage of Population
Capitalist	Prestigious university	Investors and heirs, a few top executives	$1,000,000+	1%
Upper Middle	College or university, often with postgraduate study	Professionals and upper managers	$125,000+	15%
Lower Middle	High school or college; often apprenticeship	Semiprofessionals and lower managers, craftspeople, foremen	About $60,000	34%
Working	High school	Factory workers, clerical workers, low-paid retail sales, and craftspeople	About $35,000	30%
Working Poor	Some high school	Laborers, service workers, low-paid salespeople	About $17,000	16%
Underclass	Some high school	Unemployed and part-time, on welfare	Under $10,000	4%

Source: Based on Gilbert and Kahl 1998 and Gilbert 2003; income estimates are modified from Duff 1995.

At the lower end of the capitalist class are the *nouveau riche,* those who have "new money." Although they have made fortunes in business, the stock market, inventions, entertainment, or sports, they are outsiders to the upper class. They have not attended the "right" schools, and they don't share the social networks that come with old money. Not blue-bloods, they aren't trusted to have the right orientations to life (Burris 2000). Even their "taste" in clothing and status symbols is suspect (Fabricant 2005). Donald Trump, whose money is "new," is not listed in the *Social Register,* the "White Pages" of the blue-bloods that lists the most prestigious and wealthy one-tenth of 1 percent of the U.S. population. Trump says he "doesn't care," but he reveals his true feelings by adding that his heirs will be in it

With a fortune of $48 billion, Bill Gates, a cofounder of Microsoft Corporation, is the second wealthiest person in the world. His 40,000-square-foot home (sometimes called a "technopalace") in Seattle, Washington, was appraised at $110 million.

Gates has given more money to the poor and minorities than any individual in history. His foundation is now focusing on fighting infectious diseases, developing vaccines, and improving schools.

©Scott Gries/Getty Images

(Kaufman 1996). He is probably right, for the children of the new-moneyed can ascend into the top part of the capitalist class—if they go to the right schools *and* marry old money.

Many in the capitalist class are philanthropic. They establish foundations and give huge sums to "causes." Their motivations vary. Some feel guilty because they have so much while others have so little. Others seek prestige, acclaim, or fame. Still others feel a responsibility—even a sense of fate or purpose—to use their money for doing good. Bill Gates, who has given more money to the poor and to medical research than anyone else has, seems to fall into this latter category.

The Upper Middle Class Of all the classes, the upper middle class is the one most shaped by education. Almost all members of this class have at least a bachelor's degree, and many have postgraduate degrees in business, management, law, or medicine. These people manage the corporations owned by the capitalist class or else operate their own business or profession. As Gilbert and Kahl (1998) say, these positions

> may not grant prestige equivalent to a title of nobility in the Germany of Max Weber, but they certainly represent the sign of having "made it" in contemporary America. . . . Their income is sufficient to purchase houses and cars and travel that become public symbols for all to see and for advertisers to portray with words and pictures that connote success, glamour, and high style.

Consequently, parents and teachers push children to prepare for upper-middle-class jobs. About 15 percent of the population belong to this class.

Sociologists use income, education, and occupational prestige to measure social class. For most people, this classification works well, but not for everyone. Entertainers sometimes are difficult to fit in. To what social class do Depp, Cruz, Oh, and James belong? Johnny Depp makes $10 million a year, Penelope Cruz $1 to 2 million, and Sandra Oh around $300,000. When Lebron James got out of high school, he signed more than $100 million in endorsement contracts, as well as a $4 million contract to play basketball for the Cleveland Cavaliers.

Johnny Depp

LeBron James

Penelope Cruz

Sandra Oh

The Lower Middle Class   About 34 percent of the population belong to the lower middle class. Members of this class have jobs that call for them to follow orders given by those who have upper-middle-class credentials. With their technical and lower-level management positions, they can afford a mainstream lifestyle, and many anticipate being able to move up the social class ladder. Feelings of insecurity are common, however, with the threat of inflation, recession, and job insecurity bringing a nagging sense that they might fall down the class ladder (Kefalas 2007).

The distinctions between the lower middle class and the working class on the next rung below are more blurred than those between other classes. In general, however, members of the lower middle class work at jobs that have slightly more prestige, and their incomes are generally higher.

The Working Class   About 30 percent of the U.S. population belong to this class of relatively unskilled blue-collar and white-collar workers. Compared with the lower middle class, they have less education and lower incomes. Their jobs are also less secure, more routine, and more closely supervised. One of their greatest fears is that of being laid off during a recession. With only a high school diploma, the average member of the working class has little hope of climbing up the class ladder. Job changes usually bring "more of the same," so most concentrate on getting ahead by achieving seniority on the job rather than by changing their type of work. They tend to think of themselves as having "real jobs," and regard the "suits" above them as paper pushers who have no practical experience (Morris and Grimes 2005).

The Working Poor   Members of this class, about 16 percent of the population, work at unskilled, low-paying, temporary and seasonal jobs, such as sharecropping, migrant farm work, housecleaning, and day labor. Most are high school dropouts. Many are functionally illiterate, finding it difficult to read even the want ads. They are not likely to vote (Gilbert and Kahl 1998; Beeghley 2008), for they believe that no matter what party is elected to office, their situation won't change.

Although they work full time, millions of the working poor depend on help such as food stamps and donations from local food pantries to survive on their meager incomes (O'Hare 1996b). It is easy to see how you can work full time and still be poor. Suppose that you are married and have a baby 3 months old and another child 3 years old. Your spouse stays home to care for them, so earning the income is up to you. But as a high-school dropout, all you can get is a minimum wage job. At $7.25 an hour, you earn $290 for 40 hours. In a year, this comes to $15,080—before deductions. Your nagging fear—and daily nightmare—is of ending up "on the streets."

The Underclass   On the lowest rung, and with next to no chance of climbing anywhere, is the **underclass.** Concentrated in the inner city, this group has little or no connection with the job market. Those who are employed—and some are—do menial, low-paying, temporary work. Welfare, if it is available, along with food stamps and food pantries, is their main support. Most members of other classes consider these people the "ne'er-do-wells" of society. Life is the toughest in this class, and it is filled with despair. About 4 percent of the population fall into this class.

The homeless men described in the opening vignette of this chapter, and the women and children like them, are part of the underclass. These are the people whom most Americans wish would just go away. Their presence on our city streets bothers passersby from the more privileged social classes—which includes just about everyone. "What are those obnoxious, dirty, foul-smelling people doing here, cluttering up my city?" appears to be a common response. Some people react with sympathy and a desire to do something. But what? Almost all of us just shrug our shoulders and look the other way, despairing of a solution and somewhat intimidated by their presence.

"There are plenty of jobs around. People just don't want to work."

A primary sociological principle is that people's views are shaped by their social location. Many people from the middle and upper classes cannot understand how anyone can work and still be poor.

underclass a group of people for whom poverty persists year after year and across generations

The homeless are the "fallout" of our postindustrial economy. In another era, they would have had plenty of work. They would have tended horses, worked on farms, dug ditches, shoveled coal, and run the factory looms. Some would have explored and settled the West. Others would have been lured to California, Alaska, and Australia by the prospect of gold. Today, however, with no frontiers to settle, factory jobs scarce, and farms that are becoming technological marvels, we have little need for unskilled labor.

Social Class in the Automobile Industry

Let's use the automobile industry to illustrate the social class ladder. The Fords, for example, own and control a manufacturing and financial empire whose net worth is truly staggering. Their power matches their wealth, for through their multinational corporation, their decisions affect production and employment in many countries. The family's vast fortune and its accrued power are now several generations old. Consequently, Ford children go to the "right" schools, know how to spend money in the "right" way, and can be trusted to make family and class interests paramount in life. They are without question at the top level of the *capitalist* class.

Next in line come top Ford executives. Although they may have an income of several hundred thousand dollars a year (and some, with stock options and bonuses, earn several million dollars annually), most are new to wealth and power. Consequently, they would be classified at the lower end of the capitalist class.

A husband and wife who own a Ford agency are members of the *upper middle class*. Their income clearly sets them apart from the majority of Americans, and their reputation in the community is enviable. More than likely, they also exert greater-than-average influence in their community, but their capacity to wield power is limited.

A Ford salesperson, as well as people who work in the dealership office, belongs to the *lower middle class*. Although there are some exceptional salespeople–even a few who make handsome incomes selling prestigious, expensive cars to the capitalist class—those at a run-of-the-mill Ford agency are lower middle class. Compared with the owners of the agency, their income is less, their education is likely to be less, and their work is less prestigious.

Mechanics who repair customers' cars are members of the *working class*. A mechanic who is promoted to supervise the repair shop joins the lower middle class. Those who "detail" used cars (making them appear newer by washing and polishing the car, painting the tires, spraying "new car scent" into the interior, and so on) belong to the *working poor*. Their income and education are low, and the prestige accorded to their work minimal. They are laid off when selling slows down.

Ordinarily, the *underclass* is not represented in the automobile industry. It is conceivable, however, that the agency might hire a member of the underclass to do a specific job such as mowing the grass or cleaning up the used car lot. In general, however, personnel at the agency do not trust members of the underclass and do not want to associate with them—even for a few hours. They prefer to hire someone from the working poor for such jobs.

Consequences of Social Class

Each social class can be thought of as a broad subculture with distinct approaches to life. Social class affects people's health, family life, and education. It also influences their religion and politics, and even their experiences with crime and the criminal justice system. Let's look at these consequences of social class, as well as how the new technology is related to social class.

Physical Health

If you want to get a sense of how social class affects health, take a ride on Washington's Metro system. Start in the blighted Southeast section of downtown D.C. For every mile you travel to where the wealthy live in Montgomery County in Maryland, life expectancy rises about a year and a half. By the time you get off, you will find a twenty-year gap between the poor blacks where you started your trip and the rich whites where you ended it. (Cohen 2004). (The foldout at the front of the book illustrates these effects of social class.)

The effects of social class on physical health are startling. The principle is simple: The lower a person's social class, the more likely that individual is to die before the expected age. This principle holds true at all ages. Infants born to the poor are more likely than other infants to die before their first birthday. In old age—whether 75 or 95—a larger proportion of the poor die each year than do the wealthy.

How can social class have such dramatic effects? While there is some controversy over the reasons, there seem to be three basic explanations. First, social class opens and closes doors to medical care. Consider this example:

> Terry Takewell (his real name), a 21-year-old diabetic, lived in a trailer park in Somerville, Tennessee. When Zettie Mae Hill, Takewell's neighbor, found the unemployed carpenter drenched with sweat from a fever, she called an ambulance. Takewell was rushed to nearby Methodist Hospital, where, it turned out, he had an outstanding bill of $9,400. A notice posted in the emergency room told staff members to alert supervisors if Takewell ever returned.
>
> When the hospital administrator was informed of the admission, Takewell was already in a hospital bed. The administrator went to Takewell's room, helped him to his feet, and escorted him to the parking lot. There, neighbors found him under a tree and took him home.
>
> Takewell died about twelve hours later.
>
> Zettie Mae Hill wonders whether Takewell would be alive today if she had directed his ambulance to a different hospital. She said, "I didn't think a hospital would just let a person die like that for lack of money." (Based on Ansberry 1988)

Why was Terry Takewell denied medical treatment and his life cut short? The fundamental reason is that health care in the United States is not a citizens' right but a commodity for sale. This gives us a two-tier system of medical care: superior care for those who can afford the cost and inferior care for those who cannot (Budrys 2003). Unlike the middle and upper classes, few poor people have a personal physician, and they often spend hours waiting in crowded public health clinics. After waiting most of a day, some don't even get to see a doctor. Instead, they are told to come back the next day. And when the poor are hospitalized, they are likely to find themselves in understaffed and underfunded public hospitals, treated by rotating interns who do not know them and cannot follow up on their progress.

A second reason is lifestyles, which are shaped by social class. People in the lower social classes are more likely to smoke, eat a lot of fats, be overweight, abuse drugs and alcohol, get little or no exercise, and practice unsafe sex (Chin et al. 2000; Navarro 2002; Liu 2007). This, to understate the matter, does not improve people's health.

There is a third reason, too. Life is hard on the poor. The persistent stresses they face cause their bodies to wear out faster (Spector 2007). The rich find life better. They have fewer problems and more resources to deal with the ones they have. This gives them a sense of control over their lives, a source of both physical and mental health.

Mental Health

From the 1930s until now, sociologists have found that the mental health of the lower classes is worse than that of the higher classes (Faris and Dunham 1939; Srole et al. 1978; Pratt et al. 2007). Greater mental problems are part of the higher stress that accompanies poverty. Compared with middle- and upper-class Americans, the poor have less job security and lower wages. They are more likely to divorce, to be the victims of crime, and to have more physical illnesses. Couple these conditions with bill collectors and the threat of eviction, and you can see how they can deal severe blows to people's emotional well-being.

People higher up the social class ladder experience stress in daily life, of course, but their stress is generally less, and their coping resources are greater. Not only can they afford vacations, psychiatrists, and counselors but also *their class position gives them greater control over their lives, a key to good mental health.*

Family Life

Social class also plays a significant role in family life. It even affects our choice of spouse, our chances of getting divorced, and how we rear our children.

Choice of Husband or Wife   Members of the capitalist class place strong emphasis on family tradition. They stress the family's ancestors, history, and even a sense of purpose or destiny in life (Baltzell 1979; Aldrich 1989). Children of this class learn that their choice of husband or wife affects not just themselves but also the entire family, that their spouse will have an impact on the "family line." Because of these background expectations, the field of "eligible" marriage partners is much narrower than it is for the children of any other social class. As a result, parents in this class play a strong role in their children's mate selection.

Divorce   The more difficult life of the lower social classes, especially the many tensions that come from insecure jobs and inadequate incomes, leads to higher marital friction and a greater likelihood of divorce. Consequently, children of the poor are more likely to grow up in broken homes.

Child Rearing   Sociologists have found significant class differences in child rearing. Lower-class parents focus on getting their children to follow rules and obey authority, while middle-class parents focus on developing their children's creative and leadership skills. The reason for this difference appears to be the parents' occupation (Kohn 1977). Lower-class parents are closely supervised at work, and they anticipate that their children will have similar jobs. Consequently, they try to teach their children to defer to authority. Middle-class parents, in contrast, enjoy greater independence at work.

©Dale Berman/Corbis Outline

©Alison Wright/Corbis

How much difference does social class make in our lives? Shown here are actress Jillian Barberie in the walk-in closet of her home in Los Angeles, California, and Paulina Rodriguez in the living room of her home in Rio Grande Valley, Texas. Can you see why these women are likely to see the world in highly distinctive ways, and why even their politics and aspirations in life are likely to differ?

Anticipating similar jobs for their children, they encourage them to be more creative. Out of these contrasting orientations arise different ways of disciplining children; lower-class parents are more likely to use physical punishment, while the middle classes rely more on verbal persuasion.

Working-class and middle-class parents also have different ideas about child development and children's play (Lareau 2002). Working-class parents think that children develop naturally, a sort of unfolding from within. If parents provide comfort, food, shelter, and other basic support, the child's development will take care of itself. Consequently, they set limits and let their children play as they wish. Middle-class parents, however, think that children need a lot of guidance to develop correctly, and they encourage play and extracurricular activities that they think will help develop their children's mental and social skills.

Education

As we saw in Figure 5, education increases as one goes up the social class ladder. It is not just the amount of education that changes, but also the type of education. Children of the capitalist class bypass public schools. They attend exclusive private schools where they are trained to take a commanding role in society. Prep schools such as Phillips Exeter Academy, Groton School, and Woodberry Forest School teach upper-class values and prepare their students for prestigious universities (Cookson and Persell 2005; Beeghley 2008).

Keenly aware that private schools can be a key to social mobility, some upper middle class parents do their best to get their children into the prestigious preschools that feed into these exclusive prep schools. Although some preschools cost $23,000 a year, they have a waiting list (Rohwedder 2007). Parents even elicit letters of recommendation for their 2- and 3-year-olds. Such parental expectations and resources are major reasons why children from the more privileged classes are more likely to go to college—and to graduate.

Religion

One area of social life that we might think would not be affected by social class is religion. ("People are just religious, or they are not. What does social class have to do with it?") The classes tend to cluster in different denominations. Episcopalians, for example, are more likely to attract the middle and upper classes, while Baptists draw heavily from the lower classes. Patterns of worship also follow class lines: The lower classes are attracted to more expressive worship services and louder music, while the middle and upper classes prefer more "subdued" worship.

Politics

As has been stressed throughout this text, symbolic interactionists emphasize that people perceive events from their own corner in life. Political views are no exception to this principle, and the rich and the poor walk different political paths. The higher that people are on the social class ladder, the more likely they are to vote for Republicans (Burris 2005). In contrast, most members of the working class believe that the government should intervene in the economy to provide jobs and to make citizens financially secure. They are more likely to vote for Democrats. Although the working class is more liberal on *economic* issues (policies that increase government spending), it is more conservative on *social* issues (such as opposing abortion and the Equal Rights Amendment) (Lipset 1959; Houtman 1995). People toward the bottom of the class structure are also less likely to be politically active—to campaign for candidates or even to vote (Soss 1999; Gilbert 2003; Beeghley 2008).

Crime and Criminal Justice

If justice is supposed to be blind, it certainly is not when it comes to one's chances of being arrested (Henslin 2008). Upper and lower social classes have different styles of crime. The white-collar crimes of the more privileged classes are more likely to be dealt with outside the criminal justice system, while the police and courts deal with the street crimes of the lower classes. One consequence of this class standard is that members of the lower classes are more likely to be in prison, on probation, or on parole. In addition, since people tend to commit crimes in or near their own neighborhoods, the lower classes are more likely to be robbed, burglarized, or murdered.

The Changing Economy

Two major forces in today's world are the globalization of capitalism and rapidly changing technology. If the United States does not remain competitive by producing low-cost, high-quality, state-of-the-art goods, its economic position will decline. The result will be dwindling opportunities—fewer jobs, shrinking paychecks, and vast downward social mobility.

The upheaval in the economy does not affect all social classes in the same way. For the *capitalist class,* globalization is a dream come true: Although the competition is keen, by minimizing the obstacles of national borders, capitalists are able to move factories to countries that provide cheaper labor. They produce components in one country, assemble them in another, and market the product throughout the world. Members of the *upper middle class* are well prepared for this change. Their higher education enables them to take a leading role in managing this global system for the capitalist class, or for using the new technology to advance in their professions.

Below these two most privileged classes, however, changes in capitalism and technology add to the insecurities to life. As job markets shift, the skills of many in the *lower middle class* become outdated. Those who work at specialized crafts are especially at risk, for changing markets and technology can reduce or even eliminate the need for their skills. People in lower management are more secure, for they can transfer their skills from one job to another.

From this middle point on the ladder down, these changes in capitalism and technology hit people the hardest. The threat of plant closings haunts the *working class,* for they have few alternatives. The *working poor* are even more vulnerable, for they have even less to offer in the new job market. As unskilled jobs dry up, many workers are tossed into the industrial garbage bin.

The *underclass* has been bypassed altogether. This point was driven home to me when I saw the homeless sitting dejected in the shelters. There were our high school dropouts, our technological know-nothings. Of what value are they to this new technological society competing on a global level? They simply have no productive place in it. Their base of social belonging and self-esteem—tied into work and paychecks—has been pulled out from under them.

Social Mobility

▌▐ ▄ ▟ ▙ ▟ No aspect of life, then—from marriage to politics—goes untouched by social class. Because life is so much more satisfying in the more privileged classes, people strive to climb the social class ladder. What affects their chances?

Three Types of Social Mobility

There are three basic types of social mobility: intergenerational, structural, and exchange. **Intergenerational mobility** refers to a change that occurs between generations—when grown-up children end up on a different rung of the social class ladder from the one occupied by their parents. If the child of someone who sells used cars graduates from college and buys a Saturn dealership, that person experiences **upward social mobility.** Conversely, if a child of the dealership's owner parties too much, drops out of college, and ends up selling cars, he or she experiences **downward social mobility.**

We like to think that individual efforts are the reason people move up the class ladder—and their faults the reason they move down. In these examples, we can identify hard work,

intergenerational mobility the change that family members make in social class from one generation to the next

upward social mobility movement up the social class ladder

downward social mobility movement down the social class ladder

sacrifice, and ambition on the one hand, versus indolence and substance abuse on the other. Although individual factors such as these do underlie social mobility, sociologists consider **structural mobility** to be the crucial factor. This second basic type of mobility refers to changes in society that cause large numbers of people to move up or down the class ladder.

To better understand structural mobility, think of how opportunities opened when computers were invented. New types of jobs appeared overnight. Huge numbers of people attended workshops and took crash courses, switching from blue-collar to white-collar work. Although individual effort certainly was involved—for some seized the opportunity while others did not—the underlying cause was a change in the *structure* of work. Consider the opposite—how opportunities disappear during a depression, which forces millions of people downward on the class ladder. In this instance, too, their changed status is due less to individual behavior than to *structural* changes in society.

The term *structural mobility* refers to changes in society that push large numbers of people either up or down the social class ladder. A remarkable example was the stock market crash of 1929, when tens of thousands of people suddenly lost immense amounts of wealth. People who once "had it made" found themselves standing on street corners selling apples or, as depicted here, selling their possessions at fire-sale prices.

The third type of social mobility, **exchange mobility,** occurs when large numbers of people move up and down the social class ladder, but, on balance, the proportions of the social classes remain about the same. Suppose that a million or so working-class people are trained in some new technology, and they move up the class ladder. Suppose also that because of a surge in imports, about a million skilled workers have to take lower-status jobs. Although millions of people change their social class, there is, in effect, an *exchange* among them. The net result more or less balances out, and the class system remains basically untouched.

Women in Studies of Social Mobility

In classic studies, sociologists concluded that about half of sons passed their fathers on the social class ladder; about one-third stayed at the same level, and about one-sixth moved down (Blau and Duncan 1967; Featherman and Hauser 1978; Featherman 1979).

Feminists objected that it wasn't good science to focus on sons and ignore daughters (Davis and Robinson 1988). They also pointed out that it was wrong to assume that women had no social class position of their own, that wives should not simply be assigned the class of their husbands. The defense made by male sociologists of the time was that too few women were in the labor force to make a difference.

With huge numbers of women now working for pay, more recent studies include women (Gofen 2007; Beeghley 2008). Sociologists Elizabeth Higginbotham and Lynn Weber (1992), for example, studied 200 women from working-class backgrounds who became professionals, managers, and administrators in Memphis. They found that almost without exception, the women's parents had encouraged them while they were still little girls to postpone marriage and get an education. This study confirms how important the family is in the socialization process. It also supports the observation that the primary entry to the upper middle class is a college education. At the same time, if there had not been a *structural* change in society, the millions of new positions that women occupy would not exist.

Interpreting Statistics on Social Mobility

The United States is famous worldwide for its intergenerational mobility. That children can pass up their parents on the social class ladder is one of the attractions of this country. How much mobility is there? It turns out that most apples don't fall far from the tree. Of children who are born to the poorest 10 percent of Americans, about a third are

structural mobility movement up or down the social class ladder because of changes in the structure of society, not to individual efforts

exchange mobility about the same numbers of people moving up and down the social class ladder, such that, on balance, the social class system shows little change

still there when they are grown up—half end up in the poorest 20 percent. Similarly, of children who are born to the richest 10 percent of families, about a third stay there—two of five end up among the richest 20 percent (Krueger 2002). In short, the benefits that high-income parents enjoy tend to keep their children afloat, while the obstacles that low-income parents confront tend to weigh their children down.

But is the glass half empty or half full? We could also stress the other end of these findings: Two-thirds of the very poorest kids move upward, and two-thirds of the very richest kids drop down. Remember that statistics don't lie, but liars use statistics. In this case, you can stress either part of these findings, depending on what you are trying to prove.

The Pain of Social Mobility

You know that to be knocked down the social class ladder is painful, but were you aware that climbing it also brings pain? Sociologist Steph Lawler (1999) interviewed British women who had moved from the working class to the middle class. The women were caught between two worlds—their working-class background and their current middle-class life. As the women's mothers criticized their new middle-class ways—their tastes in furniture and food, their speech, and even the way they reared their children—the relationship between daughters and mothers grew strained. Sociologists Richard Sennett and Jonathan Cobb (1972/1988), who studied working-class parents in Boston, found something similar. The parents had made deep sacrifices so their children could go to college, and they expected their children to appreciate their sacrifice. Because the children's educated world was so distant from that of their parents, however, the children grew aloof, and the family members had difficulty talking to one another. Not surprisingly, the parents felt betrayed and bitter.

In short, social class separates people into worlds so distinct that communication and mutual understanding become difficult. Sociologists also have studied fellow sociologists: Those who make the jump from the working class to college and university positions also feel a tearing away of their roots. Some never become comfortable with their new social class (Morris and Grimes 2005). The Cultural Diversity box on the next page discusses other costs that come with the climb up the social class ladder.

Poverty

Many Americans find that the "limitless possibilities" on which the American dream is based are really quite elusive. As is illustrated in Figure 5, the working poor and underclass together form about one-fifth of the U.S. population. This translates into a huge number, about 60 million people. Who are these people?

Drawing the Poverty Line

To determine who is poor, the U.S. government draws a **poverty line.** This measure was set in the 1960s, when poor people were thought to spend about one-third of their incomes on food. On the basis of this assumption, each year the government computes a low-cost food budget and multiplies it by 3. Families whose incomes are less than this amount are classified as poor; those whose incomes are higher—even by a dollar—are determined to be "not poor."

This official measure of poverty is grossly inadequate. Poor people actually spend only about 20 percent of their incomes on food, so to determine a poverty line, we ought to multiply their food budget by 5 instead of 3 (Uchitelle 2001). No political party in power wants to do this, as redrawing the line in this way would make it appear that poverty increased under their watch. Another problem with the poverty line is that some mothers work outside the home and have to pay for child care, but they are treated the same as mothers who don't have this expense. The poverty line is also the same for everyone across the nation, even though the cost of living is much higher in New York than in Alabama. In addition, the government does not count food stamps as income.

poverty line the official measure of poverty; calculated to include incomes that are less than three times a low-cost food budget

Cultural Diversity *in the* United States

Social Class and the Upward Social Mobility of African Americans

THE OVERVIEW OF SOCIAL CLASS presented in this chapter doesn't apply equally to all the groups that make up U.S. society. Consider geography: What constitutes the upper class of a town of 5,000 people will be quite different from that of a city of a million. The extremes of wealth and the diversity and prestige of occupations will be less in the small town, where family background is likely to play a more significant role.

So, too, there are differences within racial-ethnic groups. While all racial-ethnic groups are marked by divisions of social class, what constitutes a particular social class can differ from one group to another—as well as from one historical period to another. Consider social class among African Americans (Cole and Omari 2003).

The earliest class divisions can be traced to slavery—to slaves who worked in the fields and those who worked in the "big house." Those who worked in the plantation home were exposed to more "genteel" manners and forms of speech. Their more privileged position—which brought with it better food, clothing, and lighter work—was often based on skin color. Mulattos, lighter-skinned slaves, were often chosen for this more desirable work. One result was the development of a "mulatto elite," a segment of the slave population that, proud of its distinctiveness, distanced itself from the other slaves. At this time, there also were free blacks. Not only were they able to own property but some of them even owned black slaves.

After the War Between the States (as the Civil War is known in the South), these two groups, the mulatto elite and the free blacks, became the basis of an upper class. Proud of their earlier status, they distanced themselves from other blacks. From these groups came most of the black professionals.

After World War II, just as with whites, the expansion of the black middle class opened access to a wider range of occupations and residential neighborhoods. Beginning about 1960, the numbers of African Americans who were middle class surged. Today, more than half of all African American adults work at white-collar jobs, with twenty-two percent working at the professional or managerial level (Beeghley 2008). As with members of other racial-ethnic groups, African Americans who move up the social class ladder experience a hidden cost: They feel an uncomfortable distancing from their roots, a separation from significant others—parents, siblings, and childhood friends (hooks 2000). The upwardly mobile individual has entered a world unknown to those left behind.

The cost of upward mobility that comes with trying to straddle two worlds is common to individuals from all groups. What appears to be different for African Americans, however, is a sense of leaving one's racial-ethnic group,

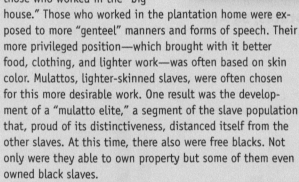

David Deas/DK Stock/Getty Images

of the necessity—if one is to succeed in the new world—of conforming to a dominant culture. This includes appearance and speech, but also something much deeper—values, aspirations, and ways of evaluating the self. In addition, the increased contact with whites that comes with social mobility often brings a greater sense of deprivation. Whites become a primary reference group, yet racism, mostly subtle and beneath the surface, continues. Awareness that they are not fully accepted in their new world engenders frustration, dissatisfaction, and cynicism.

for your Consideration

If you review the box on upward social mobility, you will find that Latinos face a similar situation. Why do you think this is? What connections do you see among upward mobility, frustration, and strong racial-ethnic identity? How do you think that the upward mobility of whites is different? Why?

That a change in the poverty line would instantly make millions of people poor—or take away their poverty—would be a laughable matter, if it weren't so serious. (The absurdity has not been lost on Parker and Hart, as you can see from their sarcastic cartoon two pages ahead.) Although this line is arbitrary, it is the official measure of poverty, and the government uses it to decide who will receive help and who will not. On the basis of this line, let's see who in the United States is poor. Before we do this, though, compare your ideas of the poor with the myths explored in the Down-to-Earth Sociology box on the next page.

Down-to-Earth Sociology

Exploring Myths About the Poor

Myth 1 Most poor people are lazy. They are poor because they do not want to work. Half of the poor are either too old or too young to work: About 40 percent are under age 18, and another 10 percent are age 65 or older. About 30 percent of the working-age poor work at least half the year.

Myth 2 Poor people are trapped in a cycle of poverty that few escape. Long-term poverty is rare. Most poverty lasts less than a year (Lichter and Crowley 2002). Only 12 percent remain in poverty for five or more consecutive years (O'Hare 1996a). Most children who are born in poverty are *not* poor as adults (Ruggles 1989; Corcoron 2001).

Myth 3 Most of the poor are African Americans and Latinos. As shown in Figure 6, the poverty rates of African Americans and Latinos are much higher than that of whites. Because there are so many more whites in the U.S. population, however, *most of the poor are white*. Of the 37 million U.S. poor, about 57 percent are white, 20 percent African American, 20 percent Latino, and 3 percent Asian American (*Statistical Abstract* 2007:Table 694).

Myth 4 Most of the poor are single mothers and their children. Although about 38 percent of the poor match this stereotype, 34 percent of the poor live in married-couple families, 22 percent live alone or with nonrelatives, and 6 percent live in other settings.

Myth 5 Most of the poor live in the inner city. This one is close to fact, as about 42 percent do live in the inner city. But 36 percent live in the suburbs, and 22 percent live in small towns and rural areas.

Myth 6 The poor live on welfare. This stereotype is far from reality. Only about 25 percent of the income of poor adults comes from welfare. About half comes from wages and pensions, and about 22 percent from Social Security.

Sources: Primarily O'Hare 1996a, 1996b, with other sources as indicated.

Figure 6 **Poverty in the United States, by Age and Race-Ethnicity**

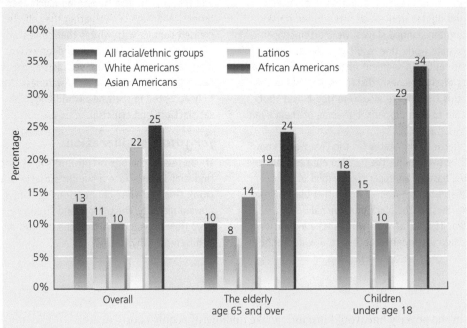

Note: Only these groups are listed in the source. The poverty line on which this figure is based is $19,307 for a family of four.

Source: By the author. Based on *Statistical Abstract* 2007:Table 694.

WIZARD OF ID

By permission of Johnny Hart and
Creators Syndicate

Who Are the Poor?

Geography   As you can see from the Social Map below, the poor are not evenly distributed among the states. This map shows a clustering of poverty in the South, a pattern that has prevailed for more than 150 years.

A second aspect of geography is also significant. About 59 million Americans live in rural areas. Of these, 9 million are poor. At 16 percent, the rate of poverty of rural Americans is higher than the national average of 13 percent. The rural poor are less likely to be single parents, and more likely to be married and to have jobs. Compared with urban Americans, the rural poor are less educated, and the jobs available to them pay less than similar jobs in urban areas (Lichter and Crowley 2002; Arseneault 2006).

Geography, however, is not the main factor in poverty. The greatest predictors of poverty are race-ethnicity, education, and the sex of the person who heads the family. Let's look at these factors.

Race-Ethnicity   One of the strongest factors in poverty is race-ethnicity. As Figure 6 on the previous page shows, only 10 percent of Asian Americans and 11 percent of whites are poor, but 22 percent of Latinos and 25 percent of African Americans live in

Figure 7   Patterns of Poverty

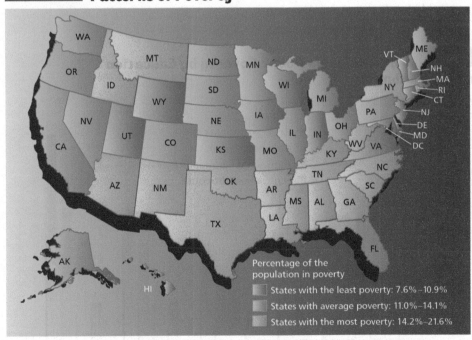

Note: Poverty varies tremendously from one state to another. In the extreme, poverty is about three times greater in Mississippi (21.6%) than in Connecticut and New Hampshire (7.6% each).

Source: By the author. Based on *Statistical Abstract of the United States* 2007:Table 690.

Beyond the awareness of most Americans are the rural poor, such as this family in Kentucky. This family is typical of the rural poor: white and headed by a woman. What do you think the future holds for these children?

(the) feminization of poverty a trend in U.S. poverty whereby most poor families are headed by women

poverty. The stereotype that most poor people are African Americans and Latinos is untrue. Because there are so many more whites in U.S. society, their much lower rate of poverty translates into larger numbers. As a result, most poor people are white.

Education You are aware that education is a vital factor in poverty, but you may not know just how powerful it is. Figure 8 below shows that 3 of 100 people who finish college end up in poverty, but one of every four people who drop out of high school is poor. As you can see, the chances that someone will be poor become less with each higher level of education. Although this principle applies regardless of race-ethnicity, this figure shows that at every level of education race-ethnicity makes an impact.

The Feminization of Poverty One of the best indicators of whether or not a family is poor is family structure. Those least likely to be poor are families that are headed by both the mother and the father. Families headed by only a father or a mother are more likely to be poor, with poverty the most common among mother-headed families. The reason for this can be summed up in this one statistic: On average, women who head families earn only 70 percent of the income of men who head families (*Statistical Abstract* 2007:Table 679). With our high rate of divorce combined with our high number of births to single women, mother-headed families have become more common. This association of poverty with women has come to be known by sociologists as the **feminization of poverty.**

Old Age As Figure 6 shows, the elderly are *less* likely than the general population to be poor. This is quite a change. It used to be that growing old increased people's chances of being poor, but government policies to redistribute income—Social Security and subsidized housing, food, and medical care—slashed the rate of poverty among the elderly. This figure also shows how the prevailing racial-ethnic patterns carry over into old age. You can see how much more likely an elderly African American or Latino is to be poor than an elderly white or Asian American.

Figure 8 **Who Ends Up Poor? Poverty by Education and Race-Ethnicity**

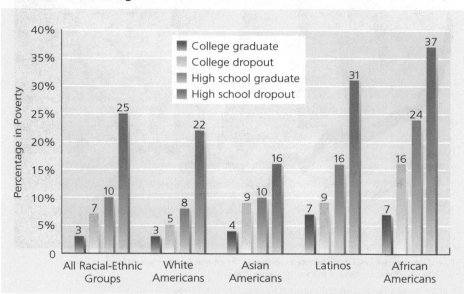

Source: By the author. Based on *Statistical Abstract of the United States* 2007:Table 697.

Children of Poverty

Children are more likely to live in poverty than are adults or the elderly. This holds true regardless of race-ethnicity, but from Figure 6, you can see how much greater poverty is among Latino and African American children. That millions of U.S. children are reared in poverty is shocking when one considers the wealth of this country and the supposed concern for the well-being of children. This tragic aspect of poverty is the topic of the following Thinking Critically section.

Thinking Critically

The Nation's Shame: Children in Poverty

One of the most startling statistics in sociology is shown in Figure 6. Look at the rate of child-hood poverty: For Asian Americans, one of ten children is poor; for whites, one of seven; for Latinos, one of three or four; and for African Americans, an astounding one of three. These percentages translate into incredible numbers—approximately *16 million* children live in poverty: 8 million white children, 4 million Latino children, 4 million African American children, and 300,000 Asian American children.

Why do so many U.S. children live in poverty? The main reason, said sociologist and former U.S. Senator Daniel Moynihan (1991), is an increase in births outside marriage. In 1960, one of twenty U.S. children was born to a single woman. Today that total is about *seven times higher,* and single women now account for one of three (36 percent) of all U.S. births (*Statistical Abstract* 2007:Table 84). Sociologists Lee Rainwater and Timothy Smeeding (2003), who note that *the poverty rate of U.S. children is the highest in the industrialized world,* point to another cause: the lack of government support to children.

Births to single women follow patterns that are significant for their children's welfare. The less education a woman has, the more likely she is to bear children when she is not married. As you can see from Figure 9, births to single women drop with each gain in education. Because people with lower education earn less, this means that the single women who can least afford children are those most likely to give birth. Their children are likely to live in poverty and to face the suffering and obstacles to a satisfying life that poverty entails. They are more likely to die in infancy, to go hungry, to be malnourished, to develop more slowly, and to have more health problems. They also are more likely to drop out of school, to become

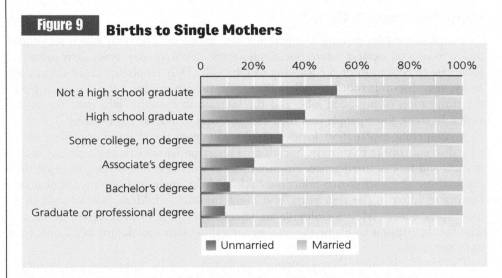

Figure 9 **Births to Single Mothers**

Note: Based on a national U.S. sample of all births in the preceding 12 months.

Source: Dye 2005.

involved in criminal activities, and to have children while still in their teens—thus perpetuating the cycle of poverty.

for your Consideration

With education so important to obtain jobs that pay better, in light of Figure 9, what programs would you suggest for helping women attain more education? Be specific and practical.

The Dynamics of Poverty

Some have suggested that the poor tend to get trapped in a **culture of poverty** (Harrington 1962; Lewis 1966a). They assume that the values and behaviors of the poor "make them fundamentally different from other Americans, and that these factors are largely responsible for their continued long-term poverty" (Ruggles 1989:7).

Lurking behind this concept is the idea that the poor are lazy people who bring poverty on themselves. Certainly, some individuals and families match this stereotype—many of us have known them. But is a self-perpetuating culture—one that is transmitted across generations and that locks people in poverty—the basic reason for U.S. poverty?

Researchers who began following 5,000 U.S. families in 1968 uncovered some surprising findings. Contrary to common stereotypes, most poverty is short-lived, lasting only a year or less. The researchers found that most poverty comes about because of a dramatic life change such as divorce, the loss of a job, or even the birth of a child (O'Hare 1996a). As Figure 10 shows, only 12 percent of poverty lasts five years or longer. Contrary to the stereotype of lazy people content to live off the government, few poor people enjoy poverty—and they do what they can to avoid being poor.

Yet from one year to the next, the number of poor people remains about the same. This means that the people who move out of poverty are replaced by people who move *into* poverty. Most of these newly poor will also move out of poverty within a year. Some people even bounce back and forth, never quite making it securely out of poverty. Poverty, then, is dynamic, touching a lot more people than the official totals indicate. Although 12 percent of Americans may be poor at any one time, twice that number—about one-fourth of the U.S. population—is or has been poor for at least a year.

Figure 10 **How Long Does Poverty Last?**

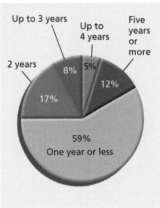

Up to 3 years	Up to 4 years	Five years or more
2 years	8%	5%	12%
17%		
59% One year or less		

Source: Gottschalk et al. 1994:89.

Why Are People Poor?

Two explanations for poverty compete for our attention. The first, which sociologists prefer, focuses on *social structure.* Sociologists stress that *features of society* deny some people access to education or the learning of job skills. They emphasize racial-ethnic, age, and gender discrimination, as well as changes in the job market—the closing of plants, the elimination of unskilled jobs, and the increase in marginal jobs that pay poverty wages. In short, some people find their escape routes to a better life blocked.

A competing explanation focuses on the *characteristics of individuals* that are assumed to contribute to poverty. Sociologists reject individualistic explanations such as laziness and lack of intelligence, viewing these as worthless stereotypes. Individualistic explanations that sociologists reluctantly acknowledge include dropping out of school, bearing children in the teen years, and averaging more children than women in the other social classes. Most sociologists are reluctant to speak of such factors in this context, for they appear to blame the victim, something that sociologists bend over backward not to do.

The tension between these competing explanations is of more than just theoretical interest. Each explanation affects our perception and has practical consequences, as is illustrated in the following Thinking Critically section.

culture of poverty the assumption that the values and behaviors of the poor make them fundamentally different from other people, that these factors are largely responsible for their poverty, and that parents perpetuate poverty across generations by passing these characteristics to their children

Thinking Critically

The Welfare Debate: The Deserving and the Undeserving Poor

Throughout U.S. history, Americans have divided the poor into two types: the deserving and the undeserving. The deserving poor are people who, in the public mind, are poor through no fault of their own. Most of the working poor, such as the Lewises, are considered deserving:

> Nancy and Ted Lewis are in their early 30s and have two children. Ted works three part-time jobs, earning $13,000 a year; Nancy takes care of the children and house and is not employed. To make ends meet, the Lewises rely on food stamps, Medicaid, and housing subsidies.

The undeserving poor, in contrast, are viewed as people who brought on their own poverty. They are freeloaders who waste their lives in laziness, alcohol and drug abuse, and promiscuous sex. They don't deserve help, and, if given anything, will waste it on their dissolute lifestyles. Some would see Joan as an example:

> Joan, her mother, and her three brothers and two sisters lived on welfare. Joan started having sex at 13, bore her first child at 15, and, now, at 23, is expecting her fourth child. Her first two children have the same father, the third a different father, and Joan isn't sure who fathered her coming child. Joan parties most nights, using both alcohol and whatever drugs are available. Her house is filthy, the refrigerator usually empty, and social workers have threatened to take away her children.

This division of the poor into deserving and undeserving underlies the heated debate about welfare. "Why should we use *our* hard-earned money to help *them*? They are just going to waste it. Of course, there are others who want to get back on their feet, and helping them is okay."

for your Consideration

Why do people make a distinction between deserving and undeserving poor? Should we let some people starve because they "brought poverty upon themselves"? Should we let children go hungry because their parents are drug abusers? Does "unworthy" mean that we should not offer assistance to people who "squander" the help they are given?

In contrast to thinking of poor people as deserving or undeserving, use the sociological perspective to explain poverty without blaming the victim. What *social* conditions (conditions of society) create poverty? Are there *social* conditions that produce the lifestyles that the middle class so despises?

Welfare Reform

After decades of criticism, the U.S. welfare system was restructured in 1996. A federal law—the Personal Responsibility and Work Opportunity Reconciliation Act—requires states to place a lifetime cap on welfare assistance and compels welfare recipients to look for work and to take available jobs. The maximum length of time that someone can collect welfare is five years. In some states, it is less. Unmarried teen parents must attend school and live at home or in some other adult-supervised setting.

This law set off a storm of criticism. Some called it an attack on the poor. Defenders replied that the new rules would rescue people from poverty. They would transform welfare recipients into self-supporting and hard-working citizens—and reduce welfare costs. National welfare rolls plummeted, dropping by about 60 percent (Urban Institute 2006). Two out of five who left welfare also moved out of poverty (Hofferth 2002).

This is only the rosy part of the picture, however. Three of five are still in poverty or are back on welfare. A third of those who were forced off welfare have no jobs (Hage 2004; Urban Institute 2006). Some can't work because they have health problems. Others lack transportation. Some are addicted to drugs and alcohol. Still others are trapped in economically depressed communities where there are no jobs. Then there are those who have jobs, but earn so little that they remain in poverty. Consider one of the "success stories":

> JoAnne Sims, 37, lives in Erie, New York, with her 7-year-old daughter Jamine. JoAnne left welfare, and now earns $6.75 an hour as a cook for Head Start. Her 37-hour week brings $239.75 before deductions. With the help of medical benefits and a mother who provides child care, JoAnne "gets by." She says, "From what I hear, a lot of us who went off welfare are still poor . . . let me tell you, it's not easy." (Peterson 2000)

Conflict theorists have an interesting interpretation of welfare. They say that welfare's purpose is not to help people, but, rather, to maintain a *reserve labor force.* It is designed to keep the unemployed alive during economic downturns until they are needed during the next economic boom. Reducing the welfare rolls through the 1996 law fits this model, as it occurred during the longest economic boom in U.S. history. Recessions are inevitable, however, and just as inevitable is surging unemployment. In line with conflict theory, we can predict that during the coming recession, welfare rules will be softened—in order to keep the reserve labor force ready for the next time they are needed.

Deferred Gratification

One consequence of a life of deprivation punctuated by emergencies—*and of viewing the future as promising more of the same*—is a lack of **deferred gratification,** giving up things in the present for the sake of greater gains in the future. It is difficult to practice this middle-class virtue if one does not have a middle-class surplus—or middle-class hope.

Back in 1967, sociologist Elliot Liebow noted that black streetcorner men did not defer gratification. Their jobs were low-paying and insecure, their lives pitted with emergencies. With the future looking exactly like the present, and any savings they did manage gobbled up by emergencies, it seemed pointless to save for the future. The only thing that made sense from their perspective was to enjoy what they could at that moment. Immediate gratification, then, was not the cause of their poverty, but, rather, its consequence. Cause and consequence loop together, however, for their immediate gratification helped perpetuate their poverty. For another look at this "looping," see the Down-to-Earth Sociology box on the next page, in which I share my personal experiences with poverty.

If both causes are at work, why do sociologists emphasize the structural explanation? Reverse the situation for a moment. Suppose that members of the middle class drove old cars that broke down, faced threats from the utility company to shut off the electricity and heat, and had to make a choice between paying the rent or buying medicine and food and diapers. How long would they practice deferred gratification? Their orientations to life would likely make a sharp U-turn.

Sociologists, then, do not view the behaviors of the poor as the cause of their poverty, but, rather, as the result of their poverty. Poor people would welcome the middle-class opportunities that would allow them the chance to practice the middle-class virtue of deferred gratification. Without those opportunities, though, they just can't afford it.

Where Is Horatio Alger? The Social Functions of a Myth

In the late 1800s, Horatio Alger was one of the country's most talked-about authors. The rags-to-riches exploits of his fictional boy heroes and their amazing successes in overcoming severe odds motivated thousands of boys of that period. Although Alger's characters have disappeared from U.S. literature, they remain alive and well in the psyche of Americans. From real-life examples of people of humble origin who climbed the social class ladder, Americans know that anyone can get ahead if they really try. In fact, they believe that most Americans, including minorities and the working poor, have an average or better-than-average chance of getting ahead—obviously a statistical impossibility (Kluegel and Smith 1986).

A society's dominant ideologies are reinforced throughout the society, including its literature. Horatio Alger provided inspirational heroes for thousands of boys. The central theme of these many novels, immensely popular in their time, was rags to riches. Through rugged determination and self-sacrifice, a boy could overcome seemingly insurmountable obstacles to reach the pinnacle of success. (Girls did not strive for financial success, but were dependent on fathers and husbands.)

Down-to-Earth Sociology

Poverty: A Personal Journey

I WAS BORN IN POVERTY. MY PARENTS, who could not afford to rent a house or apartment, rented the tiny office in their minister's house. That is where I was born.

My father began to slowly climb the social class ladder. His fitful odyssey took him from laborer to truck driver to the owner of a series of small businesses (tire repair shop, bar, hotel), then to vacuum cleaner salesman, and back to bar owner. He converted a garage into a house. Although it had no indoor plumbing or insulation (in northern Minnesota!), it was a start. Later, he bought a house, and then he built a new home. After that we moved into a trailer, and then back to a house. My father's seventh grade education was always an obstacle. Although he never became wealthy, poverty eventually become a distant memory for him.

My social class took a leap—from working class to upper middle class—when, after attending college and graduate school, I became a university professor. I entered a world that was unknown to my parents, one that was much more pampered and privileged. I had opportunities to do research, to publish, and to travel to exotic places. My reading centered on sociological research, and I read books in Spanish as well as in English. My father, in contrast, never read a book in his life, and my mother read only detective stories and romance paperbacks. One set of experiences isn't "better" than the other, just significantly different in determining what windows of perception it opens onto the world.

My interest in poverty, which was rooted in my own childhood experiences, stayed with me. I traveled to a dozen or so skid rows across the United States and Canada, talking to homeless people and staying in their shelters. In my own town, I spent considerable time with people on welfare, observing how they lived. I constantly marveled at the connections between *structural* causes of poverty (low education and skills, undependable transportation, the lack of unskilled jobs) and *personal* causes (the *culture of poverty*—alcohol and drug abuse, multiple out-of-wedlock births, frivolous spending, all-night partying, and a seeming incapacity to keep appointments—except to pick up the welfare check).

Sociologists haven't unraveled this connection, and as much as we might *like* for only structural causes to apply, clearly *both* are at work (Duneier 1999:122). The situation can be illustrated by looking at the perennial health problems I observed among the poor—the constant colds, runny noses, backaches, and injuries. The health problems stem from the *social structure* (less access to medical care, less trained or less capable physicians, drafty houses, lack of education regarding nutrition, and more dangerous jobs). At the same time, *personal* characteristics— hygiene, eating habits, and overdrinking—cause health problems. Which is the cause and which the effect? Both, of course, for one feeds into the other. The medical problems (which are based on both personal and structural causes) feed into the poverty these people experience, making them less able to perform their jobs successfully— or even to show up at work regularly. What an intricate puzzle for sociologists!

The accuracy of the **Horatio Alger myth** is less important than the belief that limitless possibilities exist for everyone. Functionalists would stress that this belief is functional for society. On the one hand, it encourages people to compete for higher positions, or, as the song says, "to reach for the highest star." On the other hand, it places blame for failure squarely on the individual. If you don't make it—in the face of ample opportunities to get ahead—the fault must be your own. The Horatio Alger myth helps to stabilize society: Since the fault is viewed as the individual's, not society's, current social arrangements can be regarded as satisfactory. This reduces pressures to change the system.

As Marx and Weber pointed out, social class penetrates our consciousness, shaping our ideas of life and our "proper" place in society. When the rich look at the world around them, they sense superiority and anticipate control over their own destiny. When the poor look around them, they are more likely to sense defeat, and to anticipate that unpredictable forces will batter their lives. Both rich and poor know the dominant ideology, that their particular niche in life is due to their own efforts, that the reasons for success—or failure—lie solely with the self. Like fish that don't notice the water, people tend not to perceive the effects of social class on their own lives.

Horatio Alger myth the belief that due to limitless possibilities anyone can get ahead if he or she tries hard enough

Summary *and* Review

What Is Social Class?

What is meant by the term social class?

Most sociologists have adopted Weber's definition of **social class:** a large group of people who rank closely to one another in terms of property (wealth), power, and prestige. **Wealth**—consisting of the value of property and income—is concentrated in the upper classes. From the 1930s to the 1970s, the trend in the distribution of wealth in the United States was toward greater equality. Since that time, it has been toward greater inequality.

Power is the ability to get one's way even though others resist. C. Wright Mills coined the term **power elite** to refer to the small group that holds the reins of power in business, government, and the military. **Prestige** is linked to occupational status. People's rankings of occupational prestige have changed little over the decades and are similar from country to country. Globally, the occupations that bring greater prestige are those that pay more, require more education and abstract thought, and offer greater independence.

What is meant by the term status inconsistency?

Status is social position. Most people are **status consistent;** that is, they rank high or low on all three dimensions of social class. People who rank higher on some dimensions than on others are status inconsistent. The frustrations of **status inconsistency** tend to produce political radicalism.

Sociological Models of Social Class

What models are used to portray the social classes?

Erik Wright developed a four-class model based on Marx: (1) capitalists (owners of large businesses), (2) petty bourgeoisie (small business owners), (3) managers, and (4) workers. Kahl and Gilbert developed a six-class model based on Weber. At the top is the capitalist class. In descending order are the upper middle class, the lower middle class, the working class, the working poor, and the **underclass.**

Consequences of Social Class

How does social class affect people's lives?

Social class leaves no aspect of life untouched. It affects our chances of benefiting from the new technology, dying early, becoming ill, receiving good health care, and getting divorced. Social class membership also affects child rearing, educational attainment, religious affiliation, political participation, the crimes people commit, and contact with the criminal justice system.

Social Mobility

What are three types of social mobility?

The term **intergenerational mobility** refers to changes in social class from one generation to the next. **Structural mobility** refers to changes in society that lead large numbers of people to change their social class. **Exchange mobility** is the movement of large numbers of people from one class to another, with the net result that the relative proportions of the population in the classes remain about the same.

Poverty

Who are the poor?

Poverty is unequally distributed in the United States. Racial–ethnic minorities (except Asian Americans), children, women-headed households, and rural Americans are more likely than others to be poor. The poverty rate of the elderly is less than that of the general population.

Why are people poor?

Some social analysts believe that characteristics of *individuals* cause poverty. Sociologists, in contrast, examine *structural* features of society, such as employment opportunities, to find the causes of poverty. Sociologists generally conclude that life orientations are a consequence, not the cause, of people's position in the social class structure.

How is the Horatio Alger myth functional for society?

The **Horatio Alger myth**—the belief that anyone can get ahead if only he or she tries hard enough—encourages people to strive to get ahead. It also deflects blame for failure from society to the individual.

Thinking Critically

1. The belief that the United States is the land of opportunity draws millions of legal and illegal immigrants to the United States each year. How do the materials in this chapter support or undermine this belief?

2. How does social class affect people's lives?

3. What social mobility has your own family experienced? In what ways has this affected your life?

Additional Resources

What can you use MySocLab for?      www.mysoclab.com

- **Study and Review:** Pre- and Post-Tests, Practice Tests, Flash Cards, Individualized Study Plans.
- **Current Events:** *Sociology in the News,* the daily *New York Times,* and more.

- **Research and Writing:** *Research Navigator, Writing About Sociology,* and more.

Where Can I Read More on This Topic?

Beeghley, Leonard. *The Structure of Social Stratification in the United States,* 5th ed. Boston: Pearson, 2008. The author presents a concise overview of the U.S. social classes.

Bowles, Samuel, Herbert Gintis, and Melissa Osborne Groves, eds. *Unequal Chances: Family Background and Economic Success.* Princeton, N.J.: Princeton University Press., 2005. The authors of these articles focus on how our economic origins affect our social destination as adults.

Florida, Richard. *The Rise of the Creative Class: And How It's Transforming Work, Leisure, Community and Everyday Life.* New York: Basic Books, 2004. The author's thesis is that a new social class has evolved, consisting of scientists, engineers, architects, educators, writers, artists, and entertainers, and that this class needs to become cohesive and work for the common good.

Gatewood, Willard B. *Aristocrats of Color: The Black Elite, 1880–1920.* Fayetteville: University of Arkansas Press, 2000. Analyzing the rise and decline of the African American upper class that developed after the Civil War, the author focuses on marriage, occupations, education, religion, clubs, and relationships with whites and with African Americans of lower classes.

Hartmann, Heidi I., ed. *Women, Work, and Poverty: Women Centered Research for Policy Change.* Binghamton, N.Y.: Haworth Press, 2006. The authors present research on women living at or below the poverty line. Major themes are work, marriage, motherhood, and welfare reform.

Iceland, John. *Poverty in America, A Handbook,* 2nd ed. Berkeley, Calif.: University of California Press, 2006. This picture of poverty in the United States shows how both poverty and its related public policies have changed over time.

Neckerman, Kathryn. *Social Inequality.* New York: Russell Sage, 2004. The author examines implications of the increasing economic inequality analyzed in this chapter for the quality of family and neighborhood life, access to education and health care, job satisfaction, and political participation.

Perucci, Robert, and Earl Wyson. *The New Class Society,* 3rd ed. Lanham, Md.: Rowman and Littlefield, 2007. An overview of the U.S. social class structure, with the suggestion that no longer is there a middle class.

Sherman, Rachel. *Class Acts: Service and Inequality in Luxury Hotels.* Berkeley, Calif.: University of California Press, 2007. Based on participant observation, the author explores the relationship between workers and guests at a luxury hotel.

Wilson, William Julius, and Richard P. Taub. *There Goes the Neighborhood: Racial, Ethnic, and Class Tensions in Four Chicago Neighborhoods and Their Meaning for America.* New York: Alfred A. Knopf, 2007. This study of four working- and lower-middle class neighborhoods in Chicago is enlivened with personal narratives that provide insight into how race, class, and ethnicity influence our lives.

Journals

Journal of Children and Poverty and *Journal of Poverty* analyze issues that affect the quality of life of people who live in poverty.

Race, Gender, and Class publishes interdisciplinary articles on the topics listed in its title.

Marriage and Family

From Chapter 16 of *Sociology: A Down-to-Earth Approach*, 9/e. James M. Henslin. Copyright © 2008 by Pearson Education.

Marriage and Family

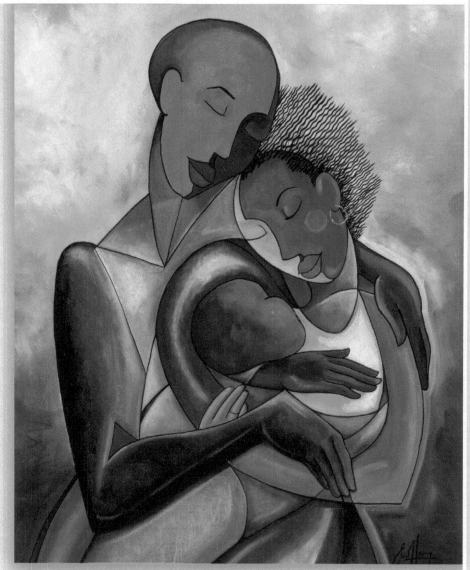

Michael Escoffery, *Circle of Love*, 1996

"**H**old still. We're going to be late," said Sharon as she tried to put shoes on 2-year-old Michael, who kept squirming away.

Finally succeeding with the shoes, Sharon turned to 4-year-old Brittany, who was trying to pull a brush through her hair. "It's stuck, Mom," Brittany said.

"Well, no wonder. Just how did you get gum in your hair? I don't have time for this, Brittany. We've got to leave."

Getting to the van fifteen minutes behind schedule, Sharon strapped the kids in, and then herself. Just as she was about to pull away, she remembered that she had not checked the fridge for messages.

"Just a minute, kids. I'll be right back."

Running into the house, she frantically searched for a note from Tom. She vaguely remembered him mumbling something about being held over at work. She grabbed the Post-It and ran back to the van.

"He's picking on me," complained Brittany when her mother climbed back in.

"Oh, shut up, Brittany. He's only 2. He can't pick on you."

"Yes, he did," Brittany said, crossing her arms defiantly as she stretched out her foot to kick her brother's seat.

"Oh, no! How did Mikey get that smudge on his face? Did you do that, Brit?"

Brittany crossed her arms again, pushing out her lips in her classic pouting pose.

"Yes, he did," Brittany said, crossing her arms defiantly as she kicked her brother's seat.

©DP Clark/The Image Bank/Getty Images

As Sharon drove to the day care center, she tried to calm herself. "Only two more days of work this week, and then the weekend. Then I can catch up on housework and have a little relaxed time with the kids. And Tom can finally cut the grass and buy the groceries," she thought. "And maybe we'll even have time to make love. Boy, that's been a long time."

At a traffic light, Sharon found time to read Tom's note. "Oh, no. That's what he meant. He has to work Saturday. Well, there go those plans."

What Sharon didn't know was that her boss had also made plans for Sharon's Saturday. And that their emergency Saturday babysitter wouldn't be available. And that Michael was coming down with the flu. And that Brittany would follow next. And that . . .

polygyny a form of marriage in which men have more than one wife

polyandry a form of marriage in which women have more than one husband

family two or more people who consider themselves related by blood, marriage, or adoption

household people who occupy the same housing unit

nuclear family a family consisting of a husband, wife, and child(ren)

extended family a nuclear family plus other relatives, such as grandparents, uncles, and aunts

family of orientation the family in which a person grows up

family of procreation the family formed when a couple's first child is born

"There just isn't enough time to get everything done!" Most of us have this complaint, but it is especially true for working parents of young children. Unlke the past, today's young partents find themselves without the support systems that parents used to take for granted: stay-at-home moms who provided stability to the neighborhood, husbands whose sole income was enough to support a wife and several children, a safe neighborhood where even small children could play outside, and grandmas who could pitch in during emergencies.

Those days are gone, most likely forever. Today, more and more families are like Sharon and Tom's. They are harried, working more but staying in debt, and seeming to have less time for one another. In this chapter, we shall try to understand what is happening to the U.S. family, and to families worldwide.

Marriage and Family in Global Perspective

To better understand U.S. patterns of marriage and family, let's first look at how customs differ around the world. This will give us a context for interpreting our own experience in this vital social institution.

What Is a Family?

"What is a family, anyway?" asked William Sayres at the beginning of an article on this topic. In posing this question, Sayres (1992) meant that although the family is so significant to humanity that it is universal—every human group in the world organizes its members in families—the world's cultures display so much variety that the term *family* is difficult to define. For example, although the Western world regards a family as a husband, wife, and children, other groups have family forms in which men have more than one wife (**polygyny**) or women more than one husband (**polyandry**). How about the obvious? Can we define the family as the approved group into which children are born? Then we would be overlooking the Banaro of New Guinea. In this group, a young woman must give birth *before* she can marry—and she *cannot* marry the father of her child (Murdock 1949).

What if we were to define the family as the unit in which parents are responsible for disciplining children and providing for their material needs? This, too, is not universal. Among the Trobriand Islanders, it is not the parents but the wife's eldest brother who is responsible for providing the children's discipline and their food (Malinowski 1927).

Such remarkable variety means that we have to settle for a broad definition. A **family** consists of people who consider themselves related by blood, marriage, or adoption. A **household,** in contrast, consists of people who occupy the same housing unit—a house, apartment, or other living quarters.

We can classify families as **nuclear** (husband, wife, and children) and **extended** (including people such as grandparents, aunts, uncles, and cousins in addition to the nuclear unit). Sociologists also refer to the **family of orientation** (the family in which an individual grows up) and the **family of procreation** (the family that is formed when a couple have their first child).

What Is Marriage?

We have the same problem here. For just about every element you might regard as essential to marriage, some group has a different custom.

Consider the sex of the bride and groom. Until recently, this was a taken-for-granted assumption. Then in the 1980s and 1990s, several European countries legalized same-sex marriages. In 2003, so did Canada, followed by the state of Massachusetts in 2004.

Courtesy of the National Parenting Association (NPA), N.Y. copyright 1994 by the NPA

Often one of the strongest family bonds is that of mother–daughter. The young artist, an eleventh grader, wrote: "This painting expresses the way I feel about my future with my child. I want my child to be happy and I want her to love me the same way I love her. In that way we will have a good relationship so that nobody will be able to take us apart. I wanted this picture to be alive; that is why I used a lot of bright colors."

These, however, were not the first groups to approve marriage between people of the same sex. When Columbus landed in the Americas, some Native American tribes were already practicing same-sex marriage. A man or woman who wanted to be a member of the opposite sex went through a ceremony (*berdache*) that officially *declared* that their sex was changed. The "new" man or woman then wore the clothing of the opposite sex, performed the tasks associated with his or her new sex, and was allowed to marry.

Even sexual relationships don't universally characterize marriage. The Nayar of Malabar never allow a bride and groom to have sex. After a three-day celebration of the marriage, they send the groom packing—and never allow him to see his bride again (La Barre 1954). (In case you're wondering, the groom comes from another tribe. Nayar women are allowed to have sex, but only with approved lovers—who can never be the husband. This system keeps family property intact—along matrilineal lines.)

At least we can be certain that a man and a woman have to be alive to get married. Or so it would seem. Even here, however, we find an exception. On the Loess Plateau in China, if a man dies without a wife, his parents look for a dead woman to be his bride. After finding one—and there are families who sell their dead unmarried daughters—the dead man and woman are married and then buried together. The parents, who feel that having a bride gives their son comfort and support in the afterlife, celebrate the marriage by inviting friends to a reception (Fremson 2006).

With such cultural variety, we can conclude that, regardless of its form, **marriage** is a group's approved mating arrangements—usually marked by a ritual of some sort (the wedding) to indicate the couple's new public status.

Common Cultural Themes

Despite this diversity, several common themes run through marriage and family. As Table 1 illustrates, all societies use marriage and family to establish patterns of mate selection, descent, inheritance, and authority. Let's look at these patterns.

Mate Selection   Each human group establishes norms to govern who marries whom. If a group has norms of **endogamy,** it specifies that its members must marry *within* their group. For example, some groups prohibit interracial marriage. In some societies, these

marriage a group's approved mating arrangements, usually marked by a ritual of some sort

endogamy the practice of marrying within one's own group

Table 1 **Common Cultural Themes: Marriage in Traditional and Industrialized Societies**		
Characteristic	Traditional Societies	Industrial (and Postindustrial) Societies
What is the structure of marriage?	*Extended* (marriage embeds spouses in a large kinship network of explicit obligations)	*Nuclear* (marriage brings fewer obligations toward the spouse's relatives)
What are the functions of marriage?	Encompassing (see the six functions listed on the next two pages)	More limited (many functions are fulfilled by other social institutions)
Who holds authority?	*Patriarchal* (authority is held by males)	Although some patriarchal features remain, authority is divided more equally
How many spouses at one time?	Most have one spouse (*monogamy*), while some have several (*polygamy*)	One spouse
Who selects the spouse?	Parents, usually the father, select the spouse	Individuals choose their own spouse
Where does the couple live?	Couples usually reside with the groom's family (*patrilocal residence*), less commonly with the bride's family (*matrilocal residence*)	Couples establish a new home (*neolocal residence*)
How is descent figured?	Usually figured from male ancestors (*patrilineal kinship*), less commonly from female ancestors (*matrilineal kinship*)	Figured from male and female ancestors equally (*bilateral kinship*)
How is inheritance figured?	Rigid system of rules; usually patrilineal, but can be matrilineal	Highly individualistic; usually bilateral

norms are written into law, but in most cases they are informal. In the United States most whites marry whites and most African Americans marry African Americans—not because of any laws but because of informal norms. In contrast, norms of **exogamy** specify that people must marry *outside* their group. The best example of exogamy is the **incest taboo,** which prohibits sex and marriage among designated relatives.

As you can see from Table 1, how people find mates varies around the world, from the father selecting them, with no choice by the individuals, to the highly individualistic, personal choices of members of Western cultures. Changes in mate selection are the focus of the Sociology and the New Technology box on the next page.

Descent   How are you related to your father's father or to your mother's mother? The answer to this question is not the same all over the world. Each society has a **system of descent,** the way people trace kinship over generations. We use a **bilineal system,** for we think of ourselves as related to *both* our mother's and our father's sides of the family. "Doesn't everyone?" you might ask. Ours, however, is only one logical way to reckon descent. Some groups use a **patrilineal system,** tracing descent only on the father's side; they don't think of children as being related to their mother's relatives. Others follow a **matrilineal system,** tracing descent only on the mother's side, and not considering children to be related to their father's relatives. The Naxi of China, for example, don't even have a word for father (Hong 1999).

Inheritance   Marriage and family—in whatever form is customary in a society—are also used to compute rights of inheritance. In a bilineal system, property is passed to both males and females, in a patrilineal system only to males, and in a matrilineal system (the rarest form), only to females. No system is natural. Rather, each matches a group's ideas of justice and logic.

Authority   Historically, some form of **patriarchy,** a social system in which men dominate women, has formed a thread that runs through all societies. Contrary to what some think, there are no historical records of a true **matriarchy,** a social system in which women as a group dominate men as a group. Our marriage and family customs, then, developed within a framework of patriarchy. Although U.S. family patterns are becoming more **egalitarian,** or equal, some of today's customs still reflect their patriarchal origin. One of the most obvious examples is U.S. naming patterns. Despite some changes, the typical bride still takes the groom's last name, and children usually receive the father's last name.

Marriage and Family in Theoretical Perspective

As we have seen, human groups around the world have chosen numerous forms of mate selection, ways to trace descent, and ways they view the parent's responsibility. Although these patterns are arbitrary, each group perceives its own forms of marriage and family as natural. Now let's see what picture emerges when we view marriage and family theoretically.

The Functionalist Perspective: Functions and Dysfunctions

Functionalists stress that to survive, a society must fulfill basic functions (that is, meet its basic needs). When functionalists look at marriage and family, they examine how they are related to other parts of society, especially the ways they contribute to the well-being of society.

Why the Family Is Universal   Although the form of marriage and family varies from one group to another, the family is universal. The reason for this, say functionalists, is that the family fulfills six needs that are basic to the survival of every society. These needs, or functions, are (1) economic production, (2) socialization of children,

exogamy   the practice of marrying outside one's group

incest taboo   the rule that prohibits sex and marriage among designated relatives

system of descent   how kinship is traced over the generations

bilineal (system of descent) a system of reckoning descent that counts both the mother's and the father's side

patrilineal (system of descent) a system of reckoning descent that counts only the father's side

matrilineal (system of descent) a system of reckoning descent that counts only the mother's side

patriarchy   a society or group in which men dominate women; authority is vested in males

matriarchy   a society in which women as a group dominate men as a group

egalitarian   authority more or less equally divided between people or groups, in this instance between husband and wife

Finding a Mate: Not the Same as It Used to Be

THINGS HAVEN'T CHANGED ENTIRELY. Boys and girls still get interested in each other at their neighborhood schools, and men and women still meet at college. Friends still serve as matchmakers and introduce friends, hoping they might click. People still meet at churches and bars, at the mall and at work.

But technology is bringing about some fundamental changes.

Among traditional people—Jews, Arabs, and in the villages of China and India—for centuries matchmakers have brought couples together. They carefully match a prospective couple by background—or by the position of the stars, whatever their tradition dictates—arranging marriages to please the families of the bride and groom, and, hopefully, the couple, too.

In China, this process is being changed by technology. Matchmakers use computerized records—age, sex, education, personal interests, and, increasingly significant, education and earnings—to identify compatibility and predict lifelong happiness.

But parents aren't leaving the process up to technology. They want their input, too. In one park in Beijing, hundreds of mothers and fathers gather twice a week to try to find spouses for their adult children. They bring photos of their children and share them with one another, talking up their kids' virtues while evaluating the sales pitch they get from the other parents. Some of the parents even sit on the grass, next to handwritten ads they've written about their children (Ang 2006).

Closer to home, Americans are turning more and more to the Internet. Numerous sites advertise that they offer thousands of potential companions, lovers, or spouses. For a low monthly fee, you, too, can meet the person of your dreams.

The photos are fascinating in their variety. Some seem to be lovely people, attractive and vivacious, and one wonders why they are posting their photos and personal information online. Do they have some secret flaw that they need to do this? Others seem okay, although perhaps, a bit needy. Then there are the pitiful, and one wonders if they will ever find a mate, or even a hookup, for that matter. Some are desperate, begging for someone—anyone—to make contact with them: women who try for sexy poses, exposing too much flesh, suggesting the promise of at least a good time; and men who try their best to look like hulks, their muscular presence promising the same.

The Internet dating sites are not filled with losers, although there are plenty of them. A lot of regular, ordinary people post their profiles, too. And some do so successfully. More and more, Internet postings are losing their stigma, and couples are finding mates via electronic matchmaking.

A frustrating aspect of these sites is that the "thousands of eligible prospects" that they tout are spread over the nation. You might find that a person who piques your interest lives in another part of the country. You can do a search for your area, but there are likely to be few from it.

Not to worry. Technology to the rescue.

The latest is dating on demand. You sit at home, turn on your TV, and search for your partner. Your local cable company has already done all the hard work. They have hosted singles events at bars and malls and helped singles make three-to-five minute tapes talking about themselves and what they are looking for in a mate (Grant 2005).

You can view the videos free—which is often more interesting than watching reruns of old TV shows. But if you get interested, for a small fee—again—you have the opportunity to contact the individuals who have caught your interest.

Now all you need is to get a private detective service—also available by online contact, for another fee—to see if this engaging person is already married, has a dozen kids, has been sued for paternity or child support, or is a child molester or a rapist.

Hmm, maybe the old village matchmaker wasn't such a bad idea, after all.

for your Consideration

What is your opinion of electronic dating sites? Would you consider using an electronic dating site (if you were single and unattached)?

(3) care of the sick and aged, (4) recreation, (5) sexual control, and (6) reproduction. To make certain that these functions are performed, every human group has adopted some form of the family.

Functions of the Incest Taboo   Functionalists note that the incest taboo helps families to avoid *role confusion*. This, in turn, facilitates the socialization of children. For example, if father-daughter incest were allowed, how should a wife treat her daughter—as a daughter, as a subservient second wife, or even as a rival? Should the daughter consider her mother as a mother, as the first wife, or as a rival? Would her father be a father or a lover? And would the wife be the husband's main wife, a secondary wife—or even the "mother of the other wife" (whatever role that might be)? And if the daughter had a child by her father, what relationships would everyone have? Maternal incest would also lead to complications every bit as confusing as these.

The incest taboo also forces people to look outside the family for marriage partners. Anthropologists theorize that *exogamy* was especially functional in tribal societies, for it forged alliances between tribes that otherwise might have killed each other off. Today, exogamy still extends both the bride's and the groom's social networks by adding and building relationships with their spouse's family and friends.

Isolation and Emotional Overload   As you know, functionalists also analyze dysfunctions. One of those dysfunctions comes from the relative isolation of today's nuclear family. Because extended families are enmeshed in large kinship networks, their members can count on many people for material and emotional support. In nuclear families, in contrast, the stresses that come with crises such as the loss of a job—or even the routine pressures of a harried life, as depicted in our opening vignette—are spread among fewer people. This places greater strain on each family member, creating *emotional overload*. In addition, the relative isolation of the nuclear family makes it vulnerable to a "dark side"— incest and various other forms of abuse, matters that we examine later in this chapter.

The Conflict Perspective: Struggles Between Husbands and Wives

Anyone who has been married or who has seen a marriage from the inside knows that— regardless of a couple's best intentions—conflict is a part of marriage. It is inevitable that conflict will arise between two people who live intimately and who share most everything in life—from their goals and checkbooks to their bedroom and children. At some point, their desires and approaches to life clash, sometimes mildly and sometimes quite harshly. Conflict among married people is so common that it is the grist of soap operas, movies, songs, and novels.

Throughout the generations, power has been a major source of conflict between wives and husbands: Husbands have had more power, and wives have resented it. Power differences show up throughout marriage, from disagreements over responsibilities for doing housework and taking care of children to quarrels about spending money and the lack of attention, respect, and sex.

As you know well, divorce is one way that couples try to end marital conflict. Divorce can mark the end of hostilities, or it can merely indicate a changed legal relationship within which the hostilities persist as the couple continues to quarrel about finances and children. We will return to the topic of divorce later in this chapter.

The Symbolic Interactionist Perspective: Gender, Housework, and Child Care

Throughout the generations, housework has been regarded as "women's work," and men have resisted getting involved. Child care, too, has traditionally been considered women's work. As more women began to work for wages, however, men came to feel pressure to do housework and to be more involved in the care of their children. But no man wanted to be labeled a sissy or be accused of being under the control of a woman. That would conflict with his culturally rooted feelings of manhood and the reputation he wanted to maintain in the community, especially around his friends.

As women put in more hours at paid work, men gradually began to do more housework and to take on more responsibility for the daily care of their children. When men first began to change diapers—at least openly—it was big news. Comedians even told jokes about Mr. Mommy, giving expression to common concerns of what the future would be like if men continued to be feminized.

Ever so slowly, cultural ideas changed. Eventually, doing housework and helping care for children came to be regarded in terms of fairness. No longer was it a sissy thing, but it became the right thing to do for husbands whose wives were in the paid labor force. Husband/fathers who refused to participate in these activities were labeled Neanderthals, and their wives pitied.

Now this is quite a change. This fundamental reorientation does not apply across the board, of course. Not all segments of the population have undergone the same change to the same degree, and we have not reached equality in housework and child care, but this is the general direction of our changing orientations.

One of the best indicators of this change is the research sociologists have done on how husbands and wives divide up housework and child care. If you look at Table 2, you can see how husbands have increased the amount of housework they do, and how wives have decreased the amount they do. Look at the changes in child care. Husbands are spending more time taking care of the children, and so are wives. This is fascinating: *Both* husbands and wives are spending more time in child care.

Contrary to popular assumptions, then, children are getting *more* attention from their parents than they used to. This flies in the face of common ideas of the *Leave It to Beaver* and *Ozzie and Harriet* families, part of our mythical past that colors our perception of the present. But if wives are working so many more hours in paid jobs *and* spending more time with their children, just where is the time coming from?

Today's parents have squeezed out more hours for their children by visiting other couples less and by reducing their participation in organizations. But this accounts for only a little bit. Look again at Table 2, but this time focus on women's hours at housework. You can see how women have cut down the amount of time they spend doing housework. Although husbands are doing more housework than they used to, the combined hours that husbands and wives spend doing housework have dropped from 38.9 to 29.1 hours a week. One explanation is that today's parents aren't as fussy as their parents were, leaving today's houses dirtier and messier. Another explanation is that the microwaves, more efficent washing machines and clothes dryers, and wrinkle-free clothing have saved hours of drudgery, leaving home hygiene about the same as before (Bianchi et al. 2006).

With the many changes in how married couples divide up family responsibilities, today's husbands and wives put in about the same number of hours per week at supporting the family. Wives spend more of their time in housework and child care but less in paid work. Husbands, in contrast, spend less of their time in housework and child care but more in paid work. Husbands and wives are following what sociologists call a *gendered division of labor;* that is, husbands remain primarily responsible for earning the income and wives primarily responsible for the house and children. If you follow the changes over time, shown in Figure 1, you can see something more significant than a growing equality in the time that husbands and wives spend in supporting the family: The trend is for wives to take on more of the responsibility

Table 2 Husbands and Wives: Who Does What?

	HOURS PER WEEK				
	1965	1975	1985	1995	2000
Housework					
Husbands	4.4	5.6	10.7	10.9	9.7
Wives	34.5	25.2	22.5	21.6	19.4
Child Care					
Husbands	2.6	2.7	3.0	5.0	6.5
Wives	10.6	8.8	9.3	11.0	12.9
Paid Work					
Husbands	47.8	47.2	42.5	39.8	42.5
Wives	6.0	15.2	19.7	24.9	23.8
Other Services to the Family					
Husbands	5.3	3.7	5.2	5.1	5.3
Wives	7.7	5.8	7.9	7.9	8.8
Total Hours					
Husbands	60.1	59.2	61.4	60.8	64.0
Wives	58.8	55.0	59.4	65.4	64.9

Note: Housework includes cooking, cleaning, and laundry, as well as plant and pet care. Husbands/wives refers to married couples who have children and are living together. Other services includes shopping, paying bills, and running errands.

Source: By the author. Based on Bianchi et al. 2006. Housework hours are from Table 5.1, child care from Table 4.1, and total hours from Table 3.4. Other services is derived by subtracting the hours for housework, child care, and paid work from total hours.

romantic love feelings of erotic attraction accompanied by an idealization of the other

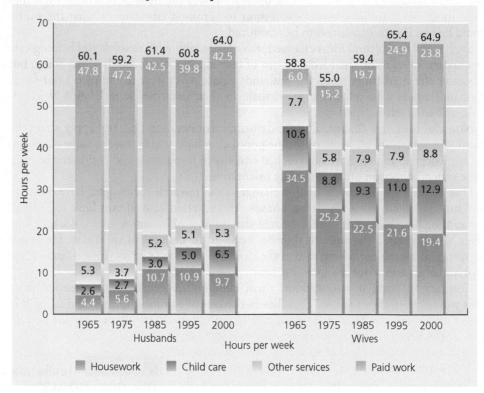

Figure 1 In Two Paycheck Marriages, How Do Husbands and Wives Divide Up the Responsibilities?

Source: By the author. Based on Bianchi et al. 2006. Housework hours are from Table 5.1, child care from Table 4.1, and work hours and total hours from Table 3.4. Other services is derived by subtracting the hours for housework, child care, and paid work from the total hours.

for earning the income and for husbands to take on more of the responsibilty for household and child care. This trend is firmly in place, and we can anticipate more changes like this in the future.

The Family Life Cycle

We have seen how the forms of marriage and family vary widely, and we have examined marriage and family theoretically. Now let's discuss love, courtship, and the family life cycle.

Love and Courtship in Global Perspective

Until recently, social scientists thought that romantic love originated in western Europe during the medieval period (Mount 1992). When anthropologists William Jankowiak and Edward Fischer (1992) surveyed the data available on 166 societies around the world, however, they found that this was not so. **Romantic love**—people being sexually attracted to one another and idealizing each other—showed up in 88 percent (147) of these groups. The role of love, however, differs from one society to another. As the Cultural Diversity box on the next page details, for example, Indians don't expect love to occur until *after* marriage.

In Hindu marriages, the roles of husband and wife are firmly established. Neither this woman, whom I photographed in Chittoor, India, nor her husband question whether she should carry the family wash to the village pump. Women here have done this task for millennia. As India industrializes, as happened in the West, who does the wash will be questioned—and may eventually become a source of strain in marriage.

©James M. Henslin

MARRIAGE AND FAMILY

Cultural Diversity *around the* World

East Is East and West Is West: Love and Arranged Marriage in India

AFTER ARUN BHARAT RAM returned to India with a degree from the University of Michigan, his mother announced that she wanted to find him a wife. Arun would be a good catch anywhere: 27 years old, educated, well mannered, intelligent, handsome—and, not incidentally, heir to a huge fortune.

Arun's mother already had someone in mind. Manju came from a middle-class family and was a college graduate. Arun and Manju met in a coffee shop at a luxury hotel—along with both sets of parents. He found her pretty and quiet. He liked that. She was impressed that he didn't boast about his background.

After four more meetings, including one at which the two young people met by themselves, the parents asked their children whether they were willing to marry. Neither had any major objections.

©James M. Henslin

This billboard in Chennai, India, caught my attention. As the text indicates, even though India is industrializing, most of its people still follow traditional customs. This billboard is a sign of changing times.

The Prime Minister of India and fifteen hundred other guests came to the wedding.

"I didn't love him," Manju says. "But when we talked, we had a lot in common." She then adds, "But now I couldn't live without him. I've never thought of another man since I met him."

Although India has undergone extensive social change, Indian sociologists estimate that parents still arrange 90 to 95 percent of marriages. Today, however, as with Arun and Manju, couples have veto power over their parents' selection. Another innovation is that the prospective bride and groom are allowed to talk to each other before the wedding—unheard of just a generation ago.

Why do Indians have arranged marriages? And why does this practice persist today, even among the educated and upper classes? We can also ask why the United States has such an individualistic approach to marriage.

The answers to these questions take us to two sociological principles. First, *a group's marriage practices match its values.* Individual mate selection matches U.S. values of individuality and independence, while arranged marriages match the Indian

value of children deferring to parental authority. To Indians, allowing unrestricted dating would mean entrusting important matters to inexperienced young people.

Second, *a group's marriage practices match its patterns of social stratification.* Arranged marriages in India affirm caste lines by channeling marriage within the same caste. Unchaperoned dating would encourage premarital sex, which, in turn, would break down family lines. Virginity at marriage, in contrast, assures the upper castes that they know the fatherhood of the children. Consequently, Indians socialize their children to think that parents have superior wisdom in these matters. In the United States, where family lines are less important and caste is an alien concept, the practice of young people choosing their own dating partners mirrors the relative openness of our social class system.

These different backgrounds have produced contrasting ideas of love. Americans idealize love as being mysterious, a passion that suddenly seizes an individual. Indians view love as a peaceful feeling that develops when a man and a woman are united in intimacy and share common interests and goals in life. For Americans, love just "happens," while Indians think of love as something that can be created between two people by arranging the right conditions. Marriage is one of those right conditions.

The end result is this startling difference: *For Americans, love produces marriage—while for Indians, marriage produces love.*

for your Consideration

What advantages do you see to the Indian approach to love and marriage? Do you think that the Indian system could work in the United States? Why or why not? Do you think that love can be created? Or does love suddenly "seize" people? What do you think love is?

Sources: Based on Gupta 1979; Bumiller 1992; Sprecher and Chandak 1992; Dugger 1998; Gautham 2002; Derne 2003; Easley 2003, Berger 2004.

Because love plays such a significant role in Western life—and often is regarded as the *only* proper basis for marriage—social scientists have probed this concept with the tools of the trade: experiments, questionnaires, interviews, and observations. In a fascinating experiment, psychologists Donald Dutton and Arthur Aron discovered that fear can produce romantic love (Rubin 1985). Here's what they did.

> About 230 feet above the Capilano River in North Vancouver, British Columbia, a rickety footbridge sways in the wind. It makes you feel like you might fall into the rocky gorge below. A more solid footbridge crosses only ten feet above the shallow stream.
>
> The experimenters had an attractive woman approach men who were crossing these bridges. She told them she was studying "the effects of exposure to scenic attractions on creative expression." She showed them a picture, and they wrote down their associations. The sexual imagery in their stories showed that the men on the unsteady, frightening bridge were more sexually aroused than were the men on the solid bridge. More of these men also called the young woman afterward—supposedly to get information about the study.

You may have noticed that this research was really about sexual attraction, not love. The point, however, is that romantic love usually begins with sexual attraction. Finding ourselves sexually attracted to someone, we spend time with that person. If we discover mutual interests, we may label our feelings "love." Apparently, then, *romantic love has two components*. The first is emotional, a feeling of sexual attraction. The second is cognitive, a label that we attach to our feelings. If we attach this label, we describe ourselves as being "in love."

Marriage

In the typical case, marriage in the United States is preceded by "love," but, contrary to folklore, whatever love is, it certainly is not blind. That is, love does not hit us willy-nilly, as if Cupid had shot darts blindly into a crowd. If it did, marital patterns would be unpredictable. An examination of who marries whom, however, reveals that love is socially channeled.

The Social Channels of Love and Marriage The most highly predictable social channels are age, education, social class, and race-ethnicity. For example, a Latina with a college degree whose parents are both physicians is likely to fall in love with and marry a Latino slightly older than herself who has graduated from college. Similarly, a girl who drops out of high school and whose parents are on welfare is likely to fall in love with and marry a man who comes from a background similar to hers.

Sociologists use the term **homogamy** to refer to the tendency of people who have similar characteristics to marry one another. Homogamy occurs largely as a result of *propinquity*, or spatial nearness. That is, we tend to "fall in love" with and marry people who live near us or whom we meet at school, church, or work. The people with whom we associate are far from a random sample of the population, for social filters produce neighborhoods, schools, and places of worship that follow racial-ethnic and social class lines.

As with all social patterns, there are exceptions. Although 93 percent of Americans who marry choose someone of their same racial-ethnic background, 7 percent do not. Because there are 60 million married couples in the United States, those 7 percent add up, totaling over 4 million couples (*Statistical Abstract* 2007:Table 58).

One of the more dramatic changes in U.S. marriage patterns is a sharp increase in marriages between African Americans and whites. Today it is difficult to realize how norm shattering such marriages are, but in some states they used to be illegal and carry a jail sentence. In Mississippi, the penalty for interracial marriage was life in prison (Crossen 2004b). The last law of this type (called *antimiscegenation* laws) was not repealed until 2000. It had been a part of the Alabama constitution (Lee and Edmonston 2005).

There always have been a few couples who crossed the "color line," but the social upheaval of the 1960s broke this barrier permanently.

Figure 2 illustrates this increase. Look at the racial-ethnicity of the husbands and wives in these marriages. You can see that here, too, Cupid's arrows strike far from random. If you look closely, you can see an emerging change. Since 2000, marriages between African American women and white men are increasing faster than those between African American men and white women.

Childbirth

Marital Satisfaction   Sociologists have found that after the birth of a child marital satisfaction usually decreases (Rogers and Amato 2000; Twenge et al. 2003). To understand why, a dyad (two persons) provides greater intimacy than a triad (after adding a third person, interaction must be shared). In addition, the birth of a child unbalances the roles that the couple have worked out (Knauth 2000). To move from the abstract to the concrete, think about the implications for marriage of coping with a fragile newborn's 24-hour-a-day needs of being fed, soothed, and diapered—while having less sleep and heavier expenses.

Yet husbands and wives continue to have children, not because they don't know how to avoid conceiving them, but because having their own child brings them so much satisfaction. New parents bubble over with joy, saying things like, "There's no feeling to compare with holding your own child in your arms. Those little hands, those tiny feet, those big eyes, that little nose, that sweet face . . ." and they gush on and on.

This is why there really is no equivalent to parents. It is *their* child, and no one else takes such delight in a baby's first steps, its first word, and so on. Let's turn, then, to child rearing.

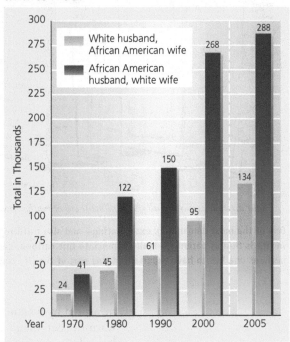

Figure 2   Marriages Between Whites and African Americans: The Race-Ethnicity of the Husbands and Wives

Source: By the author. Based on *Statistical Abstract* 1990:Table 53; 2007:Table 58.

No adequate substitute has been found for the family. Although its form and functions vary around the world, the family remains the primary socializer of children.

"Your attitude is sucking all the fulfillment out of motherhood."

One of the most demanding, exasperating—and also fulfilling—roles in life is that of parent. To really appreciate this cartoon, however, perhaps one has to have experienced this part of the life course.

Child Rearing

As you saw in Table 1 and Figure 2, today's parents—both mothers and fathers—are spending more time with their children than parents did in the 1970s and 1980s. Despite this trend, with mothers and fathers spending so many hours away from home at work, we must ask: Who's minding the kids while the parents are at work?

Married Couples and Single Mothers   Figure 3 on the next page compares the child care arrangements of married couples and single mothers. As you can see, their overall arrangements are similar. A main difference is the role of the child's father while the mother is at work. For married couples, about one of five children is cared for by the father, while for single mothers, care by the father drops to one of ten. As you can see, grandparents help fill the gap left by the absent father. Single mothers also rely more on organized day care.

Day Care   Figure 3 also shows that about one of four or five children is in day care. Apparently only a minority of U.S. day care centers offer high-quality care as measured by whether they provide stimulating learning activities, safety, and emotional warmth (Bergmann 1995; Blau 2000). A primary reason for this dismal situation is the low salaries paid to day care workers, who average only about $15,000 a year (*Statistical Abstract* 2007:Table 561, adjusted for inflation).

It is difficult for parents to judge the quality of day care, since they don't know what takes place when they are not there. If you ever look for day care, however, two factors best predict that children will receive quality care: staff who have taken courses in early childhood development and a low ratio of children per staff member (Blau 2000; Belsky et al. 2007). If you have nagging fears that your children might be neglected or even abused, choose a center that streams live Web cam images on the Internet. While at work, you can "visit" each room of the day care center via cyberspace, and monitor your toddler's activities and care.

Nannies   For upper-middle-class parents, nannies have become a popular alternative to day care centers. Parents love the one-on-one care. They also like the convenience of in-home care, which eliminates the need to transport the child to an unfamiliar environment, reduces the chances of their child catching illnesses, and eliminates the hardship of parents having to take time off from work when their child becomes ill. A recurring problem, however, is tensions between the parents and the nanny: jealousy that the nanny might see the first step, hear the first word, or—worse yet—be called "mommy." There are also tensions over different discipline styles; disdain on the part of the nanny that the mother isn't staying home with her child; and feelings of guilt or envy as the child cries when the nanny leaves but not when the mother goes to work.

Social Class   Social class makes a huge difference in child rearing. If you thought about it, you probably would guess that people's views on how children develop affect their child-rearing practices. Sociologists have found this to be true—and that the working and middle classes hold different views of how children develop (Lareau 2002). Working-class parents think of children as wild flowers that develop naturally, while middle-class parents think of children as garden flowers that need a lot of nurturing if they are to bloom. Consequently, working-class parents are more likely to set limits on their children and then let them choose their own activities. Middle-class parents, in contrast, are more likely to try to involve their children in leisure activities that they think will develop the children's thinking and social skills.

Figure 3 Who Takes Care of Preschooolers While Their Mothers Are at Work?

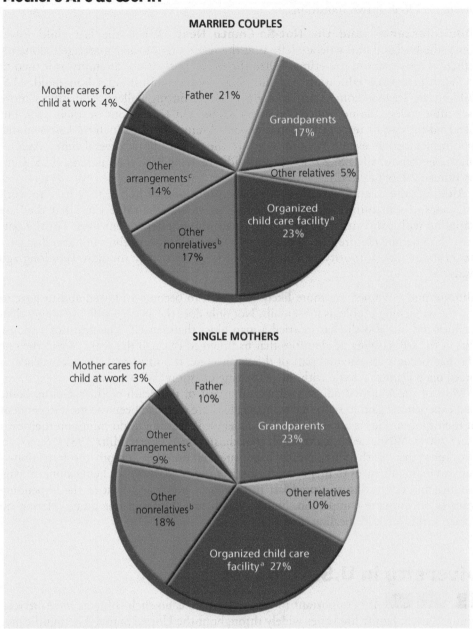

MARRIED COUPLES

Mother cares for child at work 4%

Father 21%

Grandparents 17%

Other arrangements[c] 14%

Other relatives 5%

Organized child care facility[a] 23%

Other nonrelatives[b] 17%

SINGLE MOTHERS

Mother cares for child at work 3%

Father 10%

Grandparents 23%

Other arrangements[c] 9%

Other relatives 10%

Other nonrelatives[b] 18%

Organized child care facility[a] 27%

[a] Includes in-home babysitters and other non-relatives providing care in either the child's or the provider's home.

[b] Includes self-care and no regular arrangements.

[c] Includes daycare center, nursery schools, preschools, and Head Start programs.

*Source: America's Children 2005:*Table POP8.B.

Sociologist Melvin Kohn (1963, 1977; Kohn and Schooler 1969) also found that the type of work that parents do has an impact on how they rear their children. Because members of the working class are closely supervised on their jobs, where they are expected to follow explicit rules, their concern is less with their children's motivation and more with their outward conformity. These parents are more apt to use physical punishment—which brings about outward conformity without regard for internal attitude. Middle-class workers, in contrast, are expected to take more initiative on the job. Consequently, middle-class parents have more concern that their children develop curiosity and self-expression. They are also more likely to withdraw privileges or affection than to use physical punishment.

Family Transitions

The later stages of family life bring their own pleasures to be savored and problems to be solved. Let's look at two transitions.

"Adultolescents" and the Not-So-Empty Nest When the last child leaves home, the husband and wife are left, as at the beginning of their marriage, "alone together." This situation, sometimes called the *empty nest*—is not as empty as it used to be. With prolonged education and the high cost of establishing a household, U.S. children are leaving home later. Many stay home during college, and others move back after college. Some (called "boomerang children") strike out on their own, but then find the cost or responsibility too great and return home. Much to their own disappointment, some even leave and return to the parent's home several times. As a result, 42 percent of all U.S. 25- to 29-year-olds are living with their parents (U.S. Census Bureau 2006:Table A2).

Although these "adultolescents" enjoy the protection of home, they have to work out issues of remaining dependent on their parents at the same time that they are grappling with concerns and fears about establishing independent lives. For the parents, "boomerang children" mean not only a disruption of routines but also disagreements about turf, authority, and responsibilities—items they thought were long ago resolved.

Widowhood Women are more likely than men to become widowed and to have to face the wrenching problems this entails. Not only does the average wife live longer than her husband but also she has married a man older than herself. The death of a spouse tears at the self, clawing at identities that had merged through the years. When the one who had become an essential part of the self is gone, the survivor, as in adolescence, is forced once again to wrestle with the perplexing question "Who am I?"

Most of the widowed adjust well within a year of the death of their spouse. Some even experience a gain in self-esteem, especially those who had been the most dependent on their spouse. This is apparently a consequence of learning to do things on their own (Carr 2004). When death is expected, the adjustment is easier (Hiltz 1989). Survivors who know that death is impending make preparations that smooth the transition—from arranging finances to preparing themselves psychologically for being alone. Saying goodbye and cultivating treasured last memories help people adjust to the impending death of an intimate companion. Sudden death rips the loved one away, offering no chance at this predeath healing process.

Diversity in U.S. Families

It is important to note that there is no such thing as *the* American family. Rather, family life varies widely throughout the United States. The significance of social class, noted earlier, will continue to be evident as we examine diversity in U.S. families.

African American Families

Note that the heading reads African American *families,* not *the* African American family. There is no such thing as *the* African American family any more than there is *the* white family or *the* Latino family. The primary distinction is not between African Americans and other groups, but between social classes (Willie and Reddick 2003). Because African Americans who are members of the upper class follow the class interests preservation of privilege and family fortune, they are especially concerned about the family background of those whom their children marry (Gatewood 1990). To them, marriage is viewed as a merger of family lines. Children of this class marry later than children of other classes.

Middle-class African American families focus on achievement and respectability. Both husband and wife are likely to work outside the home. A central concern is that

©Jeff Greenberg/Alamy

There is no such thing as *the* African American family, any more than there is *the* Native American, Asian American, Latino, or Irish American family. Rather, each racial-ethnic group has different types of families, with the primary determinant being social class.

their children go to college, get good jobs, and marry well—that is, marry people like themselves, respectable and hardworking, who want to get ahead in school and pursue a successful career.

African American families in poverty face all the problems that cluster around poverty (Wilson 1987, 1996; Anderson 1990/2006; Venkatesh 2006). Because the men are likely to have few skills and to be unemployed, it is difficult for them to fulfill the cultural roles of husband and father. Consequently, these families are likely to be headed by a woman and to have a high rate of births to single women. Divorce and desertion are also more common than among other classes. Sharing scarce resources and "stretching kinship" are primary survival mechanisms. People who have helped out in hard times are considered brothers, sisters, or cousins to whom one owes obligations as though they were blood relatives; and men who are not the biological fathers of their children are given fatherhood status (Stack 1974; Fischer et al. 2005). Sociologists use the term *fictive kin* to refer to this stretching of kinship.

From Figure 4 you can see that, compared with other groups, African American families are the least likely to be headed by married couples and the most likely to be headed by women. Because African American women tend to go farther in school than African American men, they are more

Figure 4 Family Structure: The Percentage of U.S. Families Headed by Men, Women, and Married Couples

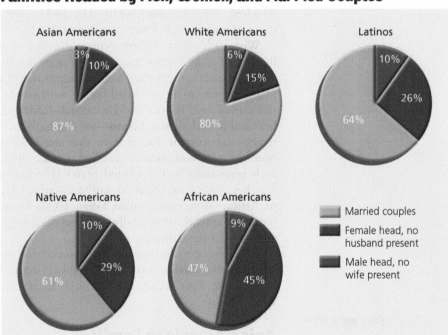

Sources: By the author. For Native Americans, "American Community . . ." 2004. For other groups, *Statistical Abstract* 2007:Tables 41, 44, 62. Data for Asian Americans are for families with children under 18, while the other groups don't have this limitation. Totals may not equal 100 percent due to rounding.

As with other groups, there is no such thing as *the* Latino family. Some Latino families have assimilated into U.S. culture to such an extent that they no longer speak Spanish. Others maintain Mexican customs, such as this family, which is celebrating *quincianera*, the "coming of age" of girls at age 15 (traditionally, an announcement to the community that a girl is eligible for courtship).

Spencer Grant/PhotoEdit, Inc.

likely than women in other racial-ethnic groups to marry men who are less educated than themselves (South 1991; Eshleman 2000).

Latino Families

As Figure 4 shows, the proportion of Latino families headed by married couples and women falls in between that of whites and African Americans. The effects of social class on families, which I just sketched, also apply to Latinos. In addition, families differ by country of origin. Families from Mexico, for example, are more likely to be headed by a married couple than are families from Puerto Rico (*Statistical Abstract* 2007:Table 44). The longer that Latinos have lived in the United States, the more their families resemble those of middle-class Americans (Saenz 2004).

With such a wide variety, experts disagree on what is distinctive about Latino families. Some point to the Spanish language, the Roman Catholic religion, and a strong family orientation coupled with a disapproval of divorce. Others add that Latinos emphasize loyalty to the extended family, with an obligation to support the extended family in times of need (Cauce and Domenech-Rodriguez 2002). Descriptions of Latino families used to include **machismo**—an emphasis on male strength, sexual vigor, and dominance—but current studies show that *machismo* now characterizes only a small proportion of Latino husband-fathers (Torres et al. 2002). *Machismo* apparently decreases with each generation in the United States (Hurtado et al. 1992; Wood 2001). Some researchers have found that the husband-father plays a stronger role than in either white or African American families (Vega 1990; Torres et al. 2002). Apparently, the wife-mother is usually more family-centered than her husband, displaying more warmth and affection for her children.

It is difficult to draw generalizations because, as with other racial–ethnic groups, individual Latino families vary considerably (Contreras et al. 2002). Some Latino families, for example, have acculturated so such an extent that they are Protestants who do not speak Spanish.

Asian American Families

As you can see from Figure 4 on the previous page, Asian American children are more likely than children in any other racial-ethnic group to grow up with both parents. As

machismo an emphasis on male strength and dominance

with the other groups, family life also reflects social class. In addition, because Asian Americans emigrated from many different countries, their family life reflects those many cultures (Xie and Goyette 2004). As with Latino families, the more recent their immigration, the more closely their family life reflects the patterns in their country of origin (Kibria 1993; Glenn 1994).

Despite such differences, sociologist Bob Suzuki (1985), who studied Chinese American and Japanese American families, identified several distinctive characteristics of Asian American families. Although Asian Americans have adopted the nuclear family structure, they have retained Confucian values that provide a framework for family life: humanism, collectivity, self-discipline, hierarchy, respect for the elderly, moderation, and obligation. Obligation means that each member of a family owes respect to other family members and is responsible never to bring shame on the family. Conversely, a child's success brings honor to the family (Zamiska 2004). To control their children, Asian American parents are more likely to use shame and guilt rather than physical punishment.

The ideal does not always translate into the real, however, and so it is here. The children born to Asian immigrants confront a bewildering world of incompatible expectations—those of the new culture and those of their parents. As a result, they experience more family conflict and mental problems than do children of Asian Americans who are not immigrants (Meyers 2006).

Native American Families

Perhaps the single most significant issue that Native American families face is whether to follow traditional values or to assimilate into the dominant culture (Garrett 1999). This primary distinction creates vast differences among families. The traditionals speak native languages and emphasize distinctive Native American values and beliefs. Those who have assimilated into the broader culture do not.

Figure 4 depicts the structure of Native American families. You can see how close it is to that of Latinos. In general, Native American parents are permissive with their children and avoid physical punishment. Elders play a much more active role in their children's families than they do in most U.S. families: Elders, especially grandparents, not only provide child care but also teach and discipline children. Like others, Native American families differ by social class.

To search for *the* Native American family would be fruitless. There are rural, urban, single-parent, extended, nuclear, rich, poor, traditional, and assimilated Native American families, to name just a few. Shown here is a Shoshone family in Fort Hall, Idaho.

©Marilyn Angel Wynn/Nativestock Pictures/Corbis

From this brief review, you can see that race-ethnicity signifies little for understanding family life. Rather, social class and culture hold the keys. The more resources a family has, the more it assumes the characteristics of a middle-class nuclear family. Compared with the poor, middle-class families have fewer children and fewer unmarried mothers. They also place greater emphasis on educational achievement and deferred gratification.

One-Parent Families

Another indication of how extensively U.S. families are changing is the increase in one-parent families. From Figure 5, you can see that the percentage of U.S. children who live with two parents (not necessarily their biological parents) has dropped sharply. The concerns that are often expressed about one-parent families may have more to do with their poverty than with children being reared by one parent. Because women head most one-parent families, these families tend to be poor. Most divorced women earn less than their former husbands, yet about 85 percent of children of divorce live with their mothers ("Child Support" 1995; Aulette 2002).

To understand the typical one-parent family, then, we need to view it through the lens of poverty, for that is its primary source of strain. The results are serious, not just for these parents and their children but also for society as a whole. Children from one-parent families are more likely to drop out of school, to get arrested, to have emotional problems, and to get divorced (McLanahan and Sandefur 1994; Menaghan et al. 1997; McLanahan and Schwartz 2002; Amato and Cheadle 2005). If female, they are more likely to become sexually active at a younger age and to bear children while still unmarried teenagers.

Families Without Children

While most married women give birth, about one of five (19 percent) do not (DeOilos and Kapinus 2003). The number of childless couples has *doubled* from what it was 20 years ago. As you can see from Figure 6, this percentage varies by racial-ethnic group, with whites and Latinas representing the extremes. Some couples are infertile, but most childless couples have made a *choice* to not have children. Why do they make this choice? Some women believe they would be stuck at home—bored, lonely, with dwindling career opportunities. Some couples perceive their marriage as too fragile to withstand the strains that a child would bring (Gerson 1985). A common reason is to attain a sense of freedom—to pursue a career, to be able to change jobs, to travel, and to have less stress (Lunneborg 1999; Letherby 2002).

With trends firmly in place—more education and careers for women, advances in contraception, legal abortion, the high cost of rearing children, and an emphasis on possessing more material things—the proportion of women who never bear children is likely to increase. Consider this statement in a newsletter:

> We are DINKS (Dual Incomes, No Kids). We are happily married. I am 43; my wife is 42. We have been married for almost twenty years. . . . Our investment strategy has a lot to do with our personal philosophy: "You can have kids—or you can have everything else!"

Many childless couples, in contrast, are not childless by choice. Desperately wanting to have children, they keep trying to do so. Coming to the soul-searching conclusion that they can never bear children, the most common solution is adoption. As featured in the Sociology and the New Technology box on the next page, some turn to solutions not available to previous generations.

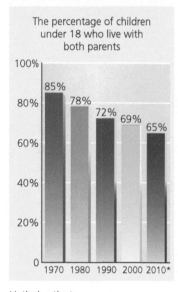

Figure 5 **The Decline of Two-Parent Families**

The percentage of children under 18 who live with both parents

*Author's estimate

Source: By the author. Based on *Statistical Abstract* 1995:Table 79; 2007:Table 62.

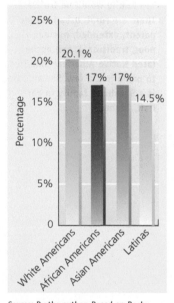

Figure 6 **What Percentage of U.S. Married Women Never Give Birth?**

Source: By the author. Based on Bachu and O'Connell 2000:Table A.

The Brave New World of High-Tech Reproduction: Where Technology Outpaces Law and Sometimes Common Sense

JAYCEE HAS FIVE PARENTS—or none, depending on how you look at it. The story goes like this. Luanne and John Buzzanca were infertile. Although they spent more than $100,000 on treatments, nothing worked. Then a fertility clinic mixed a man's sperm with a woman's egg. Both the man and the woman remained anonymous. Pamela Snell agreed to be a surrogate mother, and a surgeon implanted the fertilized egg in Pamela, who gave birth to Jaycee (Davis 1998a; Foote 1998).

At Jaycee's birth, Pamela handed Jaycee over to Luanne, who was waiting at her bedside. Luanne's husband, John, decided not to be there. He had filed for divorce just a month before.

Luanne asked John for child support. John refused, and Luanne sued. The judge ruled that John didn't have to pay. He said that because Jaycee had been conceived in a petri dish with an egg and sperm from anonymous donors, John wasn't the baby's father. The judge added that Luanne wasn't the baby's mother either.

Five parents—or none? Welcome to the brave—and very real—new world of high-tech reproduction. Reproductive technologies have laid a trap for the unsuspecting, calling into question even what a mother is. Although Pamela Snell gave birth to Jaycee, she is not a mother. How about the donor of the egg? Biologically, yes, but legally, no. Is Luanne a mother? Fortunately, for Jaycee's sake, a higher court ruled that she is.

What is a father? Consider this case. Elizabeth Higgins of Jacksonville, Indiana, had difficulty conceiving. She gave eggs to Memorial Hospital. Her husband gave sperm. A hospital technician mistakenly mixed someone else's sperm with Mrs. Higgins' eggs. The fertilized eggs were implanted in Mrs. Higgins, who gave birth to twin girls. Mrs. Higgins is white, her husband black. Mr. Higgins was bothered because the girls had only Caucasian features, and he couldn't bond with them. Mr. and Mrs. Higgins separated. They sued the hospital for child support, arguing that the hospital, not Mr. Higgins, is the father (Davis 1998b).

If a hospital can be a father in this brave new world, then what's a grandparent? A man in New Orleans donated sperm to a fertility clinic. He died, and his girlfriend decided to be artificially inseminated with his sperm. The grieved parents of the man were upset that their son, although dead, could still father children. They also feared that those children, who would be their grandchildren, would have a legal claim to their estate (Davis 1998b).

How would you apply common sense to these situations?

for your Consideration

With artificial insemination becoming more common, many children are aware of their conception and want to meet the other children from the same sperm donor. To help locate their (half) brothers and sisters, they can consult a Web site, the Donor Sibling Registry. If your biological father were a sperm donor, would you want to meet him? How about your biological siblings? Why or why not?

The Chukwu septuplets of Houston, Texas; Jioke, Ebuka, Echerem, Chidi, Chima, Gorem, and Ikem.

blended family a family
whose members were once
part of other families

Blended Families

The **blended family,** one whose members were once part of other families, is an increasingly significant type of family in the United States. Two divorced people who marry and each bring their children into a new family unit become a blended family. With divorce common, millions of children spend some of their childhood in blended families. One result is more complicated family relationships. Consider this description written by one of my students:

> I live with my dad. I should say that I live with my dad, my brother (whose mother and father are also my mother and father), my half sister (whose father is my dad, but whose mother is my father's last wife), and two stepbrothers and stepsisters (children of my father's current wife). My father's wife (my current stepmother, not to be confused with his second wife who, I guess, is no longer my stepmother) is pregnant, and soon we all will have a new brother or sister. Or will it be a half brother or half sister?
>
> If you can't figure this out, I don't blame you. I have trouble myself. It gets very complicated around Christmas. Should we all stay together? Split up and go to several other homes? Who do we buy gifts for, anyway?

Gay and Lesbian Families

In 1989, Denmark became the first country to legalize marriage between people of the same sex. Since then, several European countries have passed such laws. In 2004, Massachusetts became the first of the U.S. states to legalize same-sex marriages. Walking a fine conceptual tightrope, other states have passed laws that give legal rights to "registered domestic partnerships." This is an attempt to give legal status to same-sex unions and yet sidestep controversy by not calling them marriages.

At this point, most gay and lesbian couples lack both legal marriage and the legal protection of registered "partnerships." Although these couples live throughout the United States, about half are concentrated in just twenty cities. The greatest concentrations are in San Francisco, Los Angeles, Atlanta, New York City, and Washington, D.C. About one-fifth of gay and lesbian couples were previously married to heterosexuals. Twenty-two percent of female couples and 5 percent of male couples have children from their earlier heterosexual marriages (Bianchi and Casper 2000).

What are same-sex relationships like? Like everything else in life, these couples cannot be painted with a single brush stroke. As with opposite-sex couples, social class is significant, and orientations to life differ according to education, occupation, and income. Sociologists Philip Blumstein and Pepper Schwartz (1985) interviewed same-sex couples and found their main struggles to be housework, money, careers, problems with relatives, and sexual adjustment—the same problems that face heterosexual couples. Some also confront discrimination at work, which can add stress to their relationship (Todosijevic et al. 2005). Same-sex couples are more likely to break up, and one argument for legalizing gay marriages is that the marriage contract will make these relationships more stable. If they were surrounded by laws, same-sex marriages would be like opposite-sex marriages—to break them would require negotiating around legal obstacles.

Tim Boyle/Getty Images

A major issue that has caught the public's attention is whether same-sex couples should have the right of legal marriage. This issue will be decided not by public protest but by legislation and the courts.

Trends in U.S. Families

As is apparent from this discussion, marriage and family life in the United States is undergoing a fundamental shift. Let's examine other indicators of this change.

Postponing Marriage and Childbirth

Figure 7 below illustrates one of the most significant changes in U.S. marriages. As you can see, the average age of first-time brides and grooms declined from 1890 to about 1950. In 1890, the typical first-time bride was 22, but by 1950, she had just left her teens. For about twenty years, there was little change. Then in 1970, the average age started to increase sharply. *Today's average first-time bride and groom are older than at any other time in U.S. history.*

Since postponing marriage is today's norm, it may come as a surprise to many readers to learn that *most* U.S. women used to be married by the time they reached age 24. To see this remarkable change, look at Figure 8 on the next page. Postponing marriage has become so extensive that the percentage of women of this age who are unmarried is now more than *double* what it was in 1970. Another consequence of postponing marriage is that the average age at which U.S. women have their first child is also the highest in U.S. history (Mathews and Hamilton 2002).

Why have these changes occurred? The primary reason is cohabitation (Michael et al. 2004). Although Americans have postponed the age at which they first marry, they have *not* postponed the age at which they first set up housekeeping with someone of the opposite sex. Let's look at this trend.

Cohabitation

Figure 9 on the next page shows the increase in **cohabitation,** adults living together in a sexual relationship without being married. This figure is one of the most remarkable in

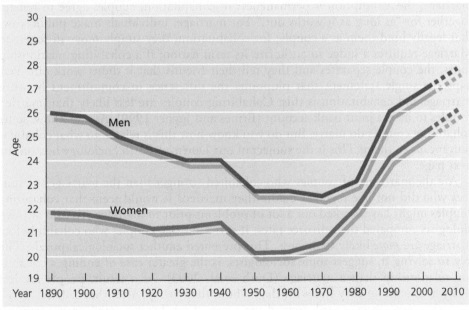

Figure 7   The Median Age at Which Americans Marry for the First Time

Note: The broken lines indicate the author's estimate.

Source: By the author. Based on *Statistical Abstract* 1999:Table 158 (table dropped in later editions); U.S. Bureau of the Census 2003; Fields 2004.

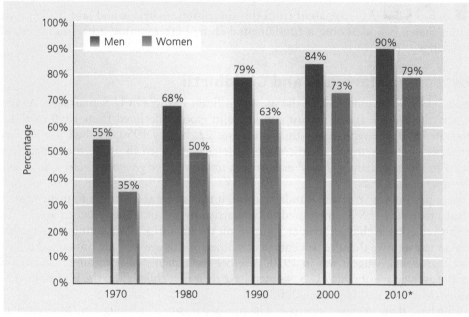

Figure 8 **Americans Ages 20–24 Who Have Never Married**

*Author's estimate.

Source: By the author. Based on *Statistical Abstract* 1993:Table 60; 2002:Table 48; 2007:Table 55.

Figure 9

Cohabitation in the United States

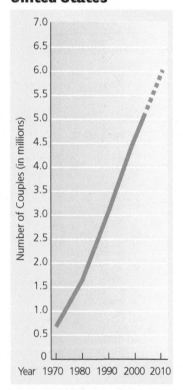

Note: Broken line indicates author's estimate.

Source: By the author. Based on *Statistical Abstract* 1995:Table 60; 2007:Table 61.

sociology. Hardly ever do we have totals that rise this steeply and consistently. Cohabitation is *almost ten times* more common today than it was 30 years ago. Today, 60 percent of the couples who marry for the first time have lived together before marriage. A generation ago, it was just 8 percent (Bianchi and Casper 2000; Batalova and Cohen 2002). Cohabitation has become so common that about 40 percent of U.S. children will spend some time in a cohabiting family (Scommegna 2002).

Commitment is the essential difference between cohabitation and marriage. In marriage, the assumption is permanence; in cohabitation, couples agree to remain together for "as long as it works out." For marriage, individuals make public vows that legally bind them as a couple; for cohabitation, they simply move in together. Marriage requires a judge to authorize its termination; if a cohabiting relationship sours, the couple separates and they tell their friends that it didn't work out. Perhaps the single statement that pinpoints the difference in commitment between marriage and cohabitation is this: Cohabiting couples are less likely than married couples to have a joint bank account (Brines and Joyner 1999). As you know, some cohabiting couples do marry. But do you know how this is related to what cohabitation means to them? This is the subject of our Down-to-Earth Sociology box on the next page.

Are the marriages of couples who cohabited stronger than the marriages of couples who did not live together before they married? It would seem that cohabiting couples might have worked out a lot of problems prior to marriage. To find out, sociologists compared their divorce rates. It turns out that couples who cohabit before marriage are *more* likely to divorce. This presented another sociological puzzle. The key to solving it, suggest some sociologists, is the greater ease of ending a cohabiting relationship than a marriage (Dush et al. 2003). As a result, people are less picky about whom they live with than whom they marry. After they cohabit, however, they experience a push toward marriage—from having common possessions, pets, and children to pressures from friends and family. Many end up marrying a partner that they would not otherwise have chosen.

"You Want Us to Live Together? What Do You Mean By That?"

WHAT HAS LED TO the surge of cohabitation in the United States? Let's consider two fundamental changes in U.S. culture.

The first is changed ideas of sexual morality. It is difficult for today's college students to grasp the sexual morality that prevailed before the 1960s sexual revolution. Almost everyone used to consider sex before marriage to be immoral. Premarital sex existed, to be sure, but it took place furtively and often with guilt. To live together before marriage was called "shacking up," and the couple was said to be "living in sin." A double standard prevailed. It was the woman's responsibility to say no to sex before marriage. Consequently, she was considered to be the especially sinful one in cohabitation.

The second cultural change is the high U.S. divorce rate. Although the rate has declined since 1980, today's young adults have seen more divorce than any prior generation. This makes marriage seem fragile, as if it is something that is not likely to last regardless of how much you devote yourself to it. This is scary. Cohabitation reduces the threat by offering a relationship of intimacy in which divorce is impossible. You can break up, but you can't get divorced.

From the outside, all cohabitation may look the same, but not to the people who are living together. As you can see from Table 3, for about 10 percent of couples, cohabitation is a substitute for marriage. These couples consider themselves married but for some reason don't want a marriage certificate. Some object to marriage on philosophical grounds ("What difference does a piece of paper make?"); others do not yet have a legal divorce from a spouse. Almost half of cohabitants (46 percent) view cohabitation as a step on the path to marriage. For them, cohabitation is more than "going steady" but less than engagement. Another 15 percent of couples are simply "giving it a try." They want to see what marriage to one another might be like. For the least committed, about 29 percent, cohabitation is a form of dating. It provides a dependable source of sex and emotional support.

Do these distinctions make a difference in whether couples marry? Let's look at these couples a half dozen years after they began to live together. As you can see from Table 3, couples who view cohabitation as a substitute for marriage are the least likely to marry and the most likely to continue to cohabit. For couples who see cohabitation as a step toward marriage, the outcome is just the opposite: They are the most likely to marry and the least likely to still be cohabiting. Couples who are the most likely to break up are those who "tried" cohabitation and those for whom cohabitation was a form of dating.

for your Consideration

Can you explain why the meaning of cohabitation makes a difference in whether couples marry? Can you classify cohabiting couples you know into these four types? Do you think there are other types? If so, what would they be?

Table 3	Commitment in Cohabitation: Does It Make a Difference?				
			After 5 to 7 years		
				Of those still together	
Level of Commitment	Percent of Couples	Split Up	Still Together	Married	Cohabiting
Substitute for Marriage	10%	35%	65%	37%	63%
Step toward Marriage	46%	31%	69%	73%	27%
Trial Marriage	15%	51%	49%	66%	34%
Coresidential Dating	29%	46%	54%	61%	39%

Source: Recomputed from Bianchi and Casper 2000.

Unmarried Mothers

Births to single women in the United States have increased steadily during the past decades, going from 10 percent in 1970 to 36 percent today (*Statistical Abstract* 1995:Table 94; 2007:Table 84). Let's place these births in global perspective. As Figure 10 shows, the

Figure 10 Births to Unmarried Women in Ten Industrialized Nations

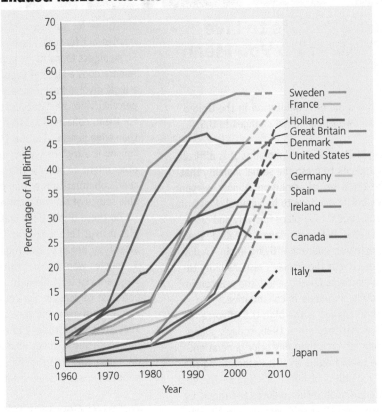

Note: The broken lines indicate the author's estimates.

Source: By the author. Based on *Statistical Abstract* 1993:Table 1380; 2001:Table 1331; 2007:Table 1311.

United States is not alone in its increase. Of the twelve nations for which we have data, all except Japan have experienced sharp increases in births to unmarried mothers. As you can see, the U.S. rate falls higher than average but not at the extreme.

From this figure, it would seem fair to conclude that industrialization sets in motion social forces that encourage out-of-wedlock births. There are several problems with this conclusion, however. Why was the rate so much lower in 1960? Industrialization had been in process for many decades before that time. Why are the rates of Japan and Italy so much lower than the other nations? Why does Japan's rate remain low? Why is Sweden's rate so high? Why have the rates of some nations leveled off—and all at about the same time? Industrialization is too simple an answer. A fuller explanation must focus on customs and values embedded within these cultures. For those answers, we will have to await further research.

Grandparents as Parents

It is becoming more common for grandparents to rear their grandchildren. About 4 percent of white children, 7 percent of Latino children, and 14 percent of African American children are being reared by their grandparents (Waldrop and Weber 2001). The main reason for these *skipped-generation families* is that the parents are incapable of caring for their children (Goldberg-Glen et al. 1998). Some of the parents have died, but the most common reasons are that the parents are ill, homeless, addicted to drugs, or in prison. In other instances, the grandparents stepped in when the parents neglected or abused their children.

Caring for grandchildren can bring great satisfaction. The grandparents know that their grandchildren are in loving hands, they build strong emotional bonds with them, and they are able to transmit their family values. But taking over as parents also brings stress: the unexpected responsibilities of parenthood, the squeezed finances, the need to continue working when they were anticipating retirement, and conflict with the parents of the children (Waldrop and Weber 2001). This added wear and tear takes its toll, and these grandmothers are 55 percent more likely to have heart disease (Lee et al. 2003). (We don't have these data for the grandfathers.)

The "Sandwich Generation" and Elder Care

The *"sandwich generation"* refers to people who find themselves sandwiched between two generations, responsible for both their children and their own aging parents. Typically between the ages of 40 and 55, these people find themselves pulled in two compelling directions. Overwhelmed by two sets of competing responsibilities, they are plagued with guilt and anger because they can be only in one place at a time and have little time to pursue personal interests.

Concerns about elder care have gained the attention of the corporate world, and half of the 1,000 largest U.S. companies offer elder care assistance to their employees (Hewitt Associates 2004). This assistance includes seminars, referral services, and flexible work schedules to help employees meet their responsibilities without missing so much work. Why are companies responding more positively to the issue of elder care than to child care? Most CEOs are older men whose wives stayed home to take care of their children, so they don't understand the stresses of balancing work and child care. In contrast, nearly all have aging parents, and many have faced the turmoil of trying to cope with both their parents' needs and those of work and their own family.

With people living longer, this issue is likely to become increasingly urgent.

Divorce and Remarriage

The topic of family life would not be complete without considering divorce. Let's first try to determine how much divorce there really is.

Problems in Measuring Divorce

You probably have heard that the U.S. divorce rate is 50 percent, a figure that is popular with reporters. The statistic is true in the sense that each year about half as many divorces are granted as there are marriages performed. The totals are 2.2 million marriages and about 1.1 million divorces (*Statistical Abstract* 2007:Tables 17, 76, 119).

What is wrong, then, with saying that the divorce rate is about 50 percent? Think about it for a moment. Why should we compare the number of divorces and marriages that take place during the same year? The couples who divorced do not—with rare exceptions—come from the group that married that year. The one number has *nothing* to do with the other, so these statistics in no way establish the divorce rate.

What figures should we compare, then? Couples who divorce are drawn from the entire group of married people in the country. Since the United States has 60,000,000 married couples, and only about 1 million of them obtain divorces in a year, the divorce rate for any given year is less than 2 percent. A couple's chances of still being married at the end of a year are over 98 percent—not bad odds—and certainly much better odds than the mass media would have us believe. As the Social Map on the next page shows, the "odds"—if we want to call them that—depend on where you live.

Over time, of course, each year's small percentage adds up. A third way of measuring divorce, then, is to ask, "Of all U.S. adults, what percentage are divorced?" Figure 12 on the next page answers this question. You can see how divorce has

Figure 11 **The "Where" of U.S. Divorce**

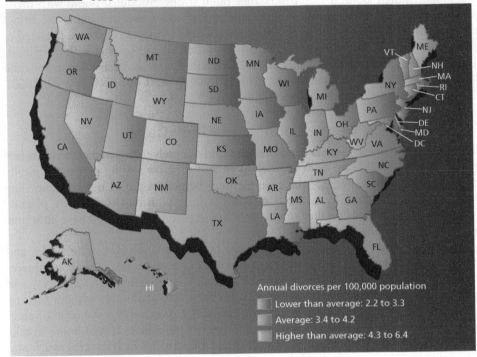

Annual divorces per 100,000 population

Lower than average: 2.2 to 3.3

Average: 3.4 to 4.2

Higher than average: 4.3 to 6.4

Note: Data for California, Georgia, Hawaii, Indiana, and Louisiana, based on the earlier editions in the source, have been decreased by the average decrease in U.S. divorce.

Source: By the author. Based on *Statistical Abstract* 1995:Table 149; 2002:Table 111; 2007:Table 119.

increased over the years and how race-ethnicity makes a difference for the likelihood that couples will divorce. If you look closely, you can also see that the rate of divorce has slowed down.

Figure 12 shows us the percentage of Americans who are currently divorced, but we get yet another answer if we ask the question, "What percentage of Ameri-cans have *ever* been divorced?" This percentage increases with each age group, peaking when people reach their 50s. Forty percent of women in their 50s have been divorced at some point in their lives; for men, the total is 43 percent ("Marital History . . ." 2004).

Figure 12 **What Percentage of Americans Are Divorced?**

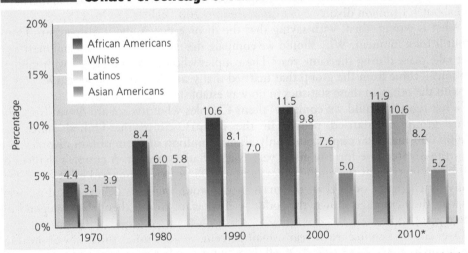

Note: This figure shows the percentage who are divorced and have not remarried, not the percentage who have *ever* divorced. Only these racial-ethnic groups are listed in the source. The source only recently added data on Asian Americans. *Author's estimate

Source: By the author. Based on *Statistical Abstract* 1995:Table 58; 2007:Table 54.

What most of us want to know is what *our* chances of divorce are. It is one thing to know that a certain percentage of Americans are divorced, but have sociologists found out anything that will tell me about *my* chances of divorce? This is the topic of the Down-to-Earth Sociology box below.

Children of Divorce

Each year, more than 1 million U.S. children learn that their parents are divorcing. Numbers like this are cold. They don't tell us what divorce feels like, what the children experience. In the Down-to-Earth Sociology box on the next page, we try to catch a glimpse of this.

Down-to-Earth Sociology

"What Are Your Chances of Getting Divorced?"

IT IS PROBABLY TRUE that over a lifetime about half of all marriages fail (Whitehead and Popenoe 2004). If you have that 50 percent figure dancing in your head, you might as well make sure that you have an escape door open even while you're saying "I do."

Not every group carries the same risk of divorce. Some have a much higher risk, and some much lower. Let's look at some factors that reduce people's risk. As Table 4 shows, sociologists have worked out percentages that you might find useful (Whitehead and Popenoe 2004).

As you can see, people who go to college, participate in a religion, wait to get married before having children and earn more, have a much better chance that their marriage will last. You can also see that having parents who did not divorce is significant. If you reverse these factors, you will see how the likelihood of divorce increases for people who have a baby before they marry, who marry in their teens, and so on. It is important to note, however, that these factors reduce the risk of divorce for groups of people, not for any certain individual.

Here are two other factors that increase the risk for divorce (Aberg 2003). For these, sociologists have not computed percentages. Having co-workers who are of the opposite sex (I'm sure you can figure out why) and working with people who are recently divorced increase the risk of divorce. Apparently, divorce is "contagious," following a pattern like measles. Perhaps being around divorced people makes divorce more acceptable. This would increase the likelihood that married people will act on their inevitable dissatisfactions and attractions. Or it could be that divorced people are more likely to "hit" on their fellow workers—and human nature being what it is . . .

for your Consideration

Why do you think that people who go to college have a lower risk of divorce? How would you explain the other factors

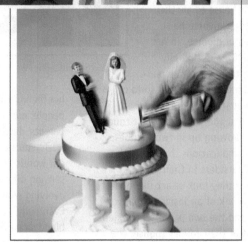

Peter Dazeley/Photographer's Choices/Getty Images

shown in Table 4? What other factors discussed in this chapter indicate a greater or lesser risk of divorce?

Why can't you figure your own chances of divorce by starting with some percentage (say 30 percent likelihood of divorce for the first 10 years of marriage) and then reducing it according to this table (subtracting 13 percent of the 30 percent for going to college, and so on)? To better understand this, you might want to read the section on the misuse of statistics later in this chapter.

Table 4 — What Reduces the Risk of Divorce?

Factors that Reduce People's Chances of Divorce	How Much Does This Decrease the Risk of Divorce?
Some college (vs. high-school dropout)	−13%
Affiliated with a religion (vs. none)	−14%
Parents not divorced	−14%
Age 25 or over at marriage (vs. under 18)	−24%
Having a baby 7 months or longer after marriage (vs. before marriage)	−24%
Annual income over $50,000 (vs. under $25,000)	−30%

Note: These percentages apply to the first ten years of marriage.

Caught Between Two Worlds: The Children of Divorce

THE STATISTICS CAN TELL you how many couples divorce, how many children these couples have, and other interesting information. But the numbers can't tell what divorce is like—how children feel that their world is falling apart when they learn their parents are going to get a divorce. Or how torn apart they feel when they shuffle from one house to another.

Elizabeth Marquardt, a child of divorce herself, did a national study of children of divorce. In her book, *Between Two Worlds* (2005), she skillfully weaves her own experiences with those of the people she interviewed, taking us into the thought world of children who are being pulled apart by their parents.

It's the many little things that the statistics don't touch. The children feel like they are growing up in two families, not one. This creates painful complications that make the children feel like insiders *and* outsiders in their parents' worlds. They are outsiders when they look or act like one of the parents. This used to be a mark of an insider, a part of the family to which the child and the two parents belonged. But now it reminds one parent of their former spouse, the one they want to forget. And those children who end up with different last names than one of their parents—what a dramatic symbol of *outsider* that is. And when children learn something about one parent that they can't tell the other parent—which happens often—how uncomfortable they feel at being unable to share this information. Outsider-insider again.

What information do you share, anyway—or what do you *not* dare to share—as you travel from one world to the other? What do you say when dad asks if mom has a boyfriend? Is this supposed to be a secret? Will dad get mad if you tell him? Will he feel hurt? You don't want him to get angry or to

©Ford Smith/Corbis

feel hurt. Yet you don't want to keep secrets. And will mom get mad if you tell dad? It's all so complicated for a kid.

Marquardt says that as a child of divorce she tried to keep her two worlds apart, but they sometimes collided forcefully. At her mom's house, she could say that things were "screwed up." But if she used "screwed up" at her dad's house, he would correct her, saying, "*Messed* up." He meant the best for her, teaching her better language, but this left her feeling silly and ashamed. Things like this, little to most people, are significant to kids who feel pinched between their parents' differing values, beliefs, and ways of living.

To shuttle between two homes is to enter and leave different worlds—feeling things in common with each, but also sensing differences from each. And then come the strangely evolving relationships—their parent's girlfriends or boyfriends. Eventually, come the new blended families, which may not blend so easily, those that bring the new stepmom or stepdad, and perhaps their children. And then there are the new break-ups, with a recurring cycle of supposedly permanent relationships. What a complicated world for a child to traverse.

Marquardt pinpoints the dilemma for the child of divorce when she says: Being with one parent always means *not* being with the other.

for your Consideration

If you are a child of divorce, did you have two worlds of experience? Were your experiences like those mentioned here? If you lived with both parents, how do you think your life has been different because your parents didn't divorce?

Children whose parents divorce are more likely than children reared by both parents to experience emotional problems, both during childhood and after they grow up (Amato and Sobolewski 2001; Weitoft et al. 2003). They are also more likely to become juvenile delinquents (Wallerstein et al. 2001), and less likely to complete high school, to attend college, and to graduate from college (McLanahan and Schwartz 2002). Finally, the children of divorce are themselves more likely to divorce (Wolfinger 2003), perpetuating a marriage-divorce cycle.

Is the greater maladjustment of the children of divorce a serious problem? This question initiated a lively debate between two researchers, both psychologists. Judith Wallerstein claims that divorce scars children, making them depressed and leaving them with insecurities that follow them into adulthood (Wallerstein et al. 2001). Mavis Hetherington

It is difficult to capture the anguish of the children of divorce, but when I read these lines by the fourth-grader who drew these two pictures, my heart was touched:

Me alone in the park . . .
All alone in the park.
My Dad and Mom are divorced
that's why I'm all alone.

This is me in the picture with my son.
We are taking a walk in the park.
I will never be like my father.
I will never divorce my wife and kid.

replies that 75 to 80 percent of children of divorce function as well as children who are reared by both of their parents (Hetherington and Kelly 2003).

Without meaning to weigh in on either side of this debate, it doesn't seem to be a simple case of the glass being half empty or half full. If 75 to 80 percent of children of divorce don't suffer long-term harm, this leaves one-fourth to one-fifth who do. Any way you look at it, one-fourth or one-fifth of a million children each year is a lot of kids who are having a lot of problems.

What helps children adjust to divorce? Children of divorce who feel close to both parents make the best adjustment, and those who don't feel close to either parent make the worst adjustment (Richardson and McCabe 2001). Other studies show that children adjust well if they experience little conflict, feel loved, live with a parent who is making a good adjustment, and have consistent routines. It also helps if their family has adequate money to meet its needs. Children also adjust better if a second adult can be counted on for support (Hayashi and Strickland 1998). Urie Bronfenbrenner (1992) says this person is like the third leg of a stool, giving stability to the smaller family unit. Any adult can be the third leg, he says—a relative, friend, or even a former mother-in-law—but the most powerful stabilizing third leg is the father, the ex-husband.

As mentioned, when the children of divorce grow up and marry, they are more likely to divorce than are adults who grew up in intact families. Have researchers found any factors that increase the chances that the children of divorce will have successful marriages? Actually, they have. They are more likely to have a lasting marriage if they marry someone whose parents did not divorce. In these marriages, the level of trust is higher and the amount of conflict is less. If both husband and wife come from broken families, however, it is not good news. Those marriages are likely to be marked by high distrust and conflict, leading to a higher chance of divorce (Wolfinger 2003).

Grandchildren of Divorce

Paul Amato and Jacob Cheadle (2005), the first sociologists to study the grandchildren of divorced parents, found that the effects of divorce continue across generations. Using a national sample, they compared children whose grandparents divorced with those whose grandparents did not divorce. Their findings are astounding. The grandchildren of divorce have weaker ties to their parents, they don't go as far in school, and they don't get along as well with their spouses. As these researchers put it, when parents divorce, the consequences ripple through the lives of children who are not yet born.

The Absent Father and Serial Fatherhood

With divorce common and mothers usually granted custody of the children, a new fathering pattern has emerged. In this pattern, known as **serial fatherhood,** a divorced father maintains high contact with his children during the first year or two after the divorce. As the man develops a relationship with another woman, he begins to play a fathering role with the woman's children and reduces contact with his own children. With another breakup, this pattern may repeat. Only about one-sixth of children who live apart from their fathers see their dad as often as every week. Actually, *most* divorced fathers stop seeing their children altogether (Ahlburg and De Vita 1992; Furstenberg and Harris 1992; Seltzer 1994). Apparently, for many men, fatherhood has become a short-term commitment.

The Ex-Spouses

Anger, depression, and anxiety are common feelings at divorce. But so is relief. Women are more likely than men to feel that divorce is giving them a "new chance" in life. A few couples manage to remain friends through it all—but they are the exception. The spouse who initiates the divorce usually gets over it sooner (Kelly 1992; Wang and Amato 2000). This spouse also usually remarries sooner (Sweeney 2002).

Divorce does not necessarily mean the end of a couple's relationship. Many divorced couples maintain contact because of their children (Fischer et al. 2005). For others, the "continuities," as sociologists call them, represent lingering attachments (Vaughan 1985; Masheter 1991; author's file 2005). The former husband may help his former wife hang a picture, paint a room, or move furniture; she may invite him over for a meal or to watch television. They might even go to dinner or to see a movie together. Some couples even continue to make love after their divorce.

After divorce, the ex-spouses' cost of living increases—two homes, two utility bills, and so forth. But the financial impact hits women the hardest. For them, divorce often spells economic hardship. This is especially true for mothers of small children, whose standard of living drops about a third (Seltzer 1994). Finally, as you would expect, women with more education cope better financially.

Remarriage

Despite the number of people who emerge from divorce court swearing "Never again!" many do remarry. The rate at which they remarry, however, has slowed, and today only half of women who divorce remarry (Bramlett and Mosher 2002). Figure 13 shows how significant race-ethnicity is in determining whether women remarry. Comparable data are not available for men.

As Figure 14 shows, most divorced people marry other divorced people. You may be surprised that the women who are most likely to remarry are young mothers and those with less education (Glick and Lin 1986; Schmiege et al. 2001). Apparently women who are more educated and more independent (no children) can afford to be more selective. Men are more likely than women to remarry, perhaps because they have a larger pool of potential mates.

How do remarriages work out? The divorce rate of remarried people *without* children is the same as that of first marriages. Those who bring children into a new marriage, however, are more likely to divorce again (MacDonald and DeMaris 1995). Certainly these relationships are more complicated and stressful. A lack of clear norms to follow may also play a role (Coleman

" I NOW PRONOUNCE YOU SECOND HUSBAND AND FOURTH WIFE."

This fanciful depiction of marital trends may not be too far off the mark.

©Sidney Harris

Reprinted with special permission of King Features Syndicate et al. 2000). As sociologist Andrew Cherlin (1989) noted, we lack satisfactory names for stepmothers, stepfathers, stepbrothers, stepsisters, stepaunts, stepuncles, stepcousins, and stepgrandparents. At the very least, these are awkward terms to use, but they also represent ill-defined relationships.

Two Sides of Family Life

Let's first look at situations in which marriage and family have gone seriously wrong and then try to answer the question of what makes marriage work.

The Dark Side of Family Life: Battering, Child Abuse, Marital Rape, and Incest

The dark side of family life involves events that people would rather keep in the dark. We shall look at spouse battering, child abuse, rape, and incest.

Spouse Battering To study spouse abuse, some sociologists have studied just a few victims in depth (Goetting 2001), while others have interviewed nationally representative samples of U.S. couples (Straus and Gelles 1988; Straus 1992). Although not all sociologists agree (Dobash et al. 1992, 1993; Pagelow 1992), Murray Straus concludes that husbands and wives are about equally likely to attack one another. If gender equality exists here, however, it certainly vanishes when it comes to the effects of violence—85 percent of the injured are women (Rennison 2003). A good part of the reason, of course, is that most husbands are bigger and stronger than their wives, putting women at a physical disadvantage in this literal battle of the sexes. The Down-to-Earth Sociology box on the next page discusses why some women remain with their abusive husbands.

Violence against women is related to the sexist structure of society. Because they grew up with norms that encourage aggression and the use of violence, some men feel that it is their right to control women. When frustrated in a relationship—or even by events outside it—some men become violent. The basic sociological question is how to socialize males to handle frustration and disagreements without resorting to violence (Rieker et al. 1997). We do not yet have this answer.

Child Abuse

I answered an ad about a lakeside house in a middle-class neighborhood that was for sale by owner. As the woman showed me through her immaculate house, I was surprised to see a plywood box in the youngest child's bedroom. About 3 feet high, 3 feet wide, and 6 feet long, the box was perforated with holes and had a little door with a padlock. Curious, I asked what it was. The woman replied matter-of-factly that her son had a behavior problem, and this was where they locked him for "time out." She added that other times they would tie him to a float, attach a line to the dock, and put him in the lake.

I left as soon as I could. With thoughts of a terrorized child filling my head, I called the state child abuse hotline.

As you can tell, what I saw upset me. Most of us are bothered by child abuse—helpless children being victimized by their parents and other adults who are supposed to love, protect, and nurture them. The most gruesome of these cases make the evening news:

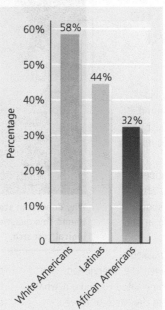

Figure 13 The Probability that Divorced Women Will Remarry in Five Years

Note: Only these groups are listed in the source.

Source: By the author. Based on Bramlett and Mosher 2002.

Figure 14 The Marital History of U.S. Brides and Grooms

- First marriage of bride and groom
- Remarriage of bride and groom
- First marriage of bride, remarriage of groom
- First marriage of groom, remarriage of bride

Source: By the author. Based on *Statistical Abstract* 2000:Table 145. Table dropped in later editions.

"Why Doesn't She Just Leave?" The Dilemma of Abused Women

"WHY WOULD SHE EVER put up with violence?" is a question on everyone's mind. From the outside, it looks so easy. Just pack up and leave. "I know I wouldn't put up with anything like that."

Yet this is not what typically happens. Women tend to stay with their men after they are abused. Some stay only a short while, to be sure, but others remain in abusive situations for years. Why?

Sociologist Ann Goetting (2001) asked this question, too. To learn the answer, she interviewed women who had made the break. She wanted to find out what it was that set them apart. How were they able to leave, when so many women couldn't seem to? She found that

1. They had a positive self-concept.
   Simply put, they believed that they deserved better.
2. They broke with traditional values.
   They did not believe that a wife had to stay with her husband no matter what.
3. They found adequate finances.
   For some, this was easy. But to move out, others had to save for years, putting away just a dollar or two a week.
4. They had supportive family and friends.
   A support network served as a source of encouragement to help them rescue themselves.A support network served as a source of encouragement to help them rescue themselves.

If you take the opposite of these four characteristics, you can understand why some women put up with abuse: They don't think they deserve anything better, they believe it is their duty to stay, they don't think they can make it financially, and they lack a supportive network. These four factors are not of

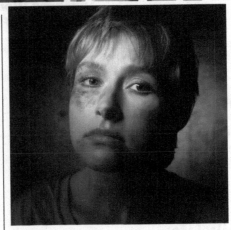

©James W. Porter/Corbis

Why do women stay with husbands who abuse them? This question has been a topic of sociological research.

equal importance to all women, of course. For some, the lack of finances is the most important, while for others, it is their low self-concept. The lack of a supportive network is also significant.

There are two additional factors: The woman must define that what her husband is doing is abuse that warrants her leaving, and she must decide that he is not going to change. If she defines her husband's acts as normal, or perhaps as deserved in some way, she does not have a motive to leave. If she defines his acts as temporary, thinking that her husband will change, she is likely to stick around to try to change her husband.

Sociologist Kathleen Ferraro (2006) reports that when she was a graduate student, her husband "monitored my movements, eating, clothing, friends, money, make-up, and language. If I challenged his commands, he slapped or kicked me or pushed me down." Ferraro was able to leave only after she defined her husband's acts as intolerable abuse—not simply that she was caught up in an unappealing situation that she had to put up with—and after she decided that her husband was not going to change. Fellow students formed the supportive network that Ferraro needed to act on her new definition. Her graduate mentor even hid her from her husband after she left him.

for your Consideration

On the basis of these findings, what would you say to a woman whose husband is abusing her? How do you think battered women's shelters fit into this explanation? What other parts of this puzzle can you think of—such as the role of love?

The 4-year-old girl who was beaten and raped by her mother's boyfriend, who passed into a coma and then three days later passed out of this life; the 6- to 10-year-old children whose stepfather videotaped them engaging in sex acts. Unlike these cases, which made headlines in my area, most child abuse is never brought to our attention: the children who live in filth, who are neglected—left alone for hours or even days at a time—or who are beaten with extension cords—cases like the little boy I learned about when I went house hunting.

Child abuse is extensive. Each year, about 3 million U.S. children are reported to the authorities as victims of abuse or neglect. About 900,000 of these cases are substantiated (*Statistical Abstract* 2007:Table 333). The excuses that parents make are incredible. Of those I have read, one I can only describe as fantastic is this statement, made by a mother to a Manhattan judge, "I slipped in a moment of anger, and my hands accidentally wrapped around my daughter's windpipe" (LeDuff 2003).

Marital or Intimacy Rape   Sociologists have found that marital rape is more common than is usually supposed. For example, between one-third and one-half of women who seek help at shelters for battered women are victims of marital rape (Bergen 1996). Women at shelters, however, are not representative of U.S. women. To get a better answer of how common marital rape is, sociologist Diana Russell (1990) used a sampling technique that allows generalization. She found that 14 percent of married women report that their husbands have raped them. Similarly, 10 percent of a representative sample of Boston women interviewed by sociologists David Finkelhor and Kersti Yllo (1985, 1989) reported that their husbands had used physical force to compel them to have sex. Compared with victims of rape by strangers or acquaintances, victims of marital rape are less likely to report the rape (Mahoney 1999).

With the huge numbers of couples who are cohabiting, the term marital rape needs to include sexual assault in these relationships. Perhaps, then, we should use the term *intimacy rape.* And intimacy rape is not limited to men who sexually assault women. In pathbreaking research, sociologist Lori Girshick (2002) interviewed lesbians who had been sexually assaulted by their partners. In these cases, both the victim and the offender were women. Girshick points out that if the pronoun "he" were substituted for "she" in her interviews, a reader would believe that the events were being told by women who had been battered and raped by their husbands (Bergen 2003). Like wives who have been raped by their husbands, these victims, too, suffered from shock, depression, and self-blame.

Incest   Sexual relations between certain relatives (for example, between brothers and sisters or between parents and children) constitute **incest.** Incest is most likely to occur in families that are socially isolated (Smith 1992). Sociologist Diana Russell (n.d.) found that incest victims who experience the greatest trauma are those who were victimized the most often, whose assaults occurred over longer periods of time, and whose incest was "more intrusive," for example, sexual intercourse as opposed to sexual touching.

Who are the offenders? The most common incest is apparently between brothers and sisters, with the sex initiated by the brother (Canavan et al. 1992; Carlson et al. 2006). With no random samples, however, we do not know how common incest is, and researchers report different results. Russell found that uncles are the most common offenders, followed by first cousins, fathers (stepfathers especially), brothers, and, finally, other relatives ranging from brothers-in-law to stepgrandfathers. From the studies we have, we can conclude that incest between mothers and their children is rare, more so than between fathers and their children.

The Bright Side of Family Life: Successful Marriages

Successful Marriages   After examining divorce and family abuse, one could easily conclude that marriages seldom work out. This would be far from the truth, however, for about three of every five married Americans report that they are "very happy" with their marriages (Whitehead and Popenoe 2004). (Keep in mind that each year divorce removes the most unhappy marriages from this population.) To find out what makes marriage successful, sociologists Jeanette and Robert Lauer (1992) interviewed 351 couples who had been married fifteen years or longer. Fifty-one of these marriages were unhappy, but the couples stayed together for religious reasons, because of family tradition, or "for the sake of the children."

Of the others, the 300 happy couples, all:

1. Think of their spouse as their best friend
2. Like their spouse as a person
3. Think of marriage as a long-term commitment
4. Believe that marriage is sacred
5. Agree with their spouse on aims and goals

incest sexual relations between specified relatives, such as brothers and sisters or parents and children

6. Believe that their spouse has grown more interesting over the years

7. Strongly want the relationship to succeed

8. Laugh together

Sociologist Nicholas Stinnett (1992) used interviews and questionnaires to study 660 families from all regions of the United States and parts of South America. He found that happy families:

1. Spend a lot of time together

2. Are quick to express appreciation

3. Are committed to promoting one another's welfare

4. Do a lot of talking and listening to one another

5. Are religious

6. Deal with crises in a positive manner

Sociologists have uncovered two other factors: Marriages are happier when couples get along with their in-laws (Bryant et al. 2001) and when they do leisure activities that they both enjoy (Crawford et al. 2002).

Symbolic Interactionism and the Misuse of Statistics   Many students express concerns about their own marital future, a wariness born out of the divorce of their parents, friends, neighbors, relatives—even their pastors and rabbis. They wonder about their chances of having a successful marriage. Because sociology is not just about abstract ideas, but is really about our lives, it is important to stress that you are an individual, not a statistic. That is, if the divorce rate were 33 percent or 50 percent, this would *not* mean that if you marry, your chances of getting divorced are 33 percent or 50 percent. That is a misuse of statistics—and a common one at that. Divorce statistics represent all marriages and have absolutely *nothing* to do with any individual marriage. Our own chances depend on our own situations—especially the way we approach marriage.

To make this point clearer, let's apply symbolic interactionism. From a symbolic interactionist perspective, we create our own worlds. That is, because our experiences don't come with built-in meanings, we interpret our experiences, and act accordingly. As we do so, we can create a self-fulfilling prophecy. For example, if we think that our marriage might fail, we are more likely to run when things become difficult. If we think that our marriage is going to work out, we are more likely to stick around and to do things to make the marriage successful. The folk saying "There are no guarantees in life" is certainly true, but it does help to have a vision that a good marriage is possible and that it is worth the effort to achieve.

The Future of Marriage and Family

What can we expect of marriage and family in the future? Despite its many problems, marriage is in no danger of becoming a relic of the past. Marriage is so functional that it exists in every society. Consequently, the vast majority of Americans will continue to find marriage vital to their welfare.

Certain trends are firmly in place. Cohabitation, births to single women, age at first marriage, and parenting by grandparents will increase. As more married women join the work force, wives will continue to gain marital power. The number of elderly will increase, and more couples will find themselves sandwiched between caring for their parents and rearing their own children.

Our culture will continue to be haunted by distorted images of marriage and family: the bleak ones portrayed in the mass media and the rosy ones perpetuated by cultural myths. Sociological research can help to correct these distortions and allow us to see how our own family experiences fit into the patterns of our culture. Sociological research can also help to answer the big question: How can we help formulate social policy that will support and enhance family life?

To conclude this chapter, in the Down-to-Earth Sociology box on the next page we look at a subtle but fundamental change that may have begun to impact the family.

Down-to-Earth Sociology

When Work Becomes Home and Home Becomes Work

WORKERS CAN'T STAND THEIR bosses, and almost everyone would quit work and stay home if they had the chance, right? Don't be too sure.

As sociologist Arlie Hochschild (1997, 2006) did participant observation at a company she calls Amerco, she found that both work and family are changing. The family has become harried, with two working parents juggling their schedules around their work and personal lives as well as their children's school and after-school activities. As with Sharon and Tom in this chapter's opening vignette, parents can feel overwhelmed by responsibilities that come flying at them from several directions at once. Hochschild puts it this way:

[A]t home . . . the emotional demands have become more baffling and complex. In addition to teething, tantrums and the normal developments of growing children, the needs of elderly parents are creating more tasks for the modern family—as are the blending, unblending, reblending of new stepparents, stepchildren, exes and former in-laws.

At the same time that pressures at home have increased, work for many has become less demanding and more rewarding. As Hochschild says,

[N]ew management techniques so pervasive in corporate life have helped transform the workplace into a more appreciative, personal sort of social world . . . many companies now train workers to make their own work decisions, and . . . [many workers] feel recognized for job accomplishments. Amerco regularly strengthens the family-like ties of co-workers by holding "recognition ceremonies" . . . Amerco employees speak of "belonging to the Amerco family". . . . The education-and-training division offers free courses (on company time) in "Dealing with Anger," "How to Give and Accept Criticism," and "How to Cope with Difficult People."

What sort of "recognition ceremonies" do family members have? Or free courses on "How to Cope with Mom" or "How to Understand Your Two-Year-Old—or Unruly Teenager"? With pressures increasing at home and decreasing at work, Hochschild found that some workers volunteer for overtime "just to get away from the house." As Linda, one of the women Hochschild talked to, said,

When I get home, and the minute I turn the key, my daughter is right there. Granted she needs somebody to talk to about her day. . . . The baby is still up. He should have been in bed two hours ago, and that upsets me. The dishes are piled in the sink. My daughter comes right up to the door and complains about anything her stepfather said or did, and she wants to talk about her job. My husband is in the other room hollering to my daughter, "Tracy, I don't ever get any time to talk to your mother, because you're always monopolizing her time before I even get a chance!" They all come at me at once.

Reflecting on what she observed, Hochschild says that for many people, the worlds of home and work have begun to reverse places. Home is becoming more like work, and work is becoming more like home. The key phrase, of course, is "for many people"—because many workplaces are not supportive, and workers still find them disagreeable places (Ducharme et al. 2004).

for your Consideration

It is difficult to pinpoint changes as they first occur, although some sociologists have been able to do so. Sociologist William Ogburn noted in 1933 that personality was becoming more important in mate selection, and in 1945 sociologists Ernest Burgess and Harvey Locke observed that mutual affection and compatibility were becoming more important in marriage. The change has been so complete that today it is difficult to conceive of getting married apart from affection and compatibility.

Could Hochschild have also put her finger on a historical shift just as it has begun to occur? Are the ways we view home and work in the process of reversing? In 50 years or so, will this be the taken-for-granted life for most of us? What do you think?

The cartoonist has aptly picked up the findings of sociologist Arlie Hochschild on the reversal of home and work.

Summary *and* Review

Marriage and Family in Global Perspective

What is a family—and what themes are universal?

Family is difficult to define. There are exceptions to every element that one might consider essential. Consequently, **family** is defined broadly—as people who consider themselves related by blood, marriage, or adoption. Universally, **marriage** and family are mechanisms for governing mate selection, reckoning descent, and establishing inheritance and authority.

Marriage and Family in Theoretical Perspective

What is a functionalist perspective on marriage and family?

Functionalists examine the functions and dysfunctions of family life. Examples include the **incest taboo** and how weakened family functions increase divorce.

What is a conflict perspective on marriage and family?

Conflict theorists focus on inequality in marriage, especially unequal power between husbands and wives.

What is a symbolic interactionist perspective on marriage and family?

Symbolic interactionists examine the contrasting experiences and perspectives of men and women in marriage. They stress that only by grasping the perspectives of wives and husbands can we understand their behavior.

The Family Life Cycle

What are the major elements of the family life cycle?

The major elements are love and courtship, marriage, childbirth, child rearing, and the family in later life. Most mate selection follows predictable patterns of age, social class, race-ethnicity, and religion. Childbirth and child-rearing patterns also vary by social class.

Diversity in U.S. Families

How significant is race-ethnicity in family life?

The primary distinction is social class, not race-ethnicity. Families of the same social class are likely to be similar, regardless of their race-ethnicity.

What other diversity in U.S. families is there?

Also discussed are one-parent, childless, **blended,** and gay and lesbian families. Each has its unique characteristics, but social class is significant in determining their primary characteristics. Poverty is especially significant for single-parent families, most of which are headed by women.

Trends in U.S. Families

What major changes characterize U.S. families?

Three changes are postponement of first marriage, an increase in **cohabitation,** and more grandparents serving as parents to their grandchildren. With more people living longer, many middle-aged couples find themselves sandwiched between rearing their children and taking care of their aging parents.

Divorce and Remarriage

What is the current divorce rate?

Depending on what numbers you choose to compare, you can produce almost any rate you wish, from 50 percent to less than 2 percent.

How do children and their parents adjust to divorce?

Divorce is difficult for children, whose adjustment problems often continue into adulthood. Most divorced fathers do not maintain ongoing relationships with their children. Financial problems are usually greater for the former wives. Although most divorced people remarry, their rate of remarriage has slowed.

Two Sides of Family Life

What are the two sides of family life?

The dark side is abuse—spouse battering, child abuse, marital rape, and **incest.** All these are acts that revolve around the misuse of family power. The bright side is that most people find marriage and family to be rewarding.

The Future of Marriage and Family

What is the likely future of marriage and family?

We can expect cohabitation, births to unmarried women, age at first marriage, and parenting by grandparents to increase. The growing numbers of women in the work force are likely to continue to shift the balance of marital power.

Thinking Critically

1. Functionalists stress that the family is universal because it provides basic functions for individuals and society. What functions does your family provide? Hint: In addition to the section "The Functionalist Perspective," also consider the section "Common Cultural Themes."

2. Explain why social class is more important than race-ethnicity in determining a family's characteristics.

3. Apply this chapter's contents to your own experience with marriage and family. What social factors affect your family life? In what ways is your family life different from that of your grandparents when they were your age?

Additional Resources

What can you use MySocLab for?  www.mysoclab.com

- **Study and Review:** Pre- and Post-Tests, Practice Tests, Flash Cards, Individualized Study Plans.

- **Current Events:** *Sociology in the News,* the daily *New York Times,* and more.

- **Research and Writing:** *Research Navigator, Writing About Sociology,* and more.

Where Can I Read More on This Topic?

Agger, Ben, and Beth Anne Shelton. *Fast Families, Virtual Children: A Critical Sociology of Families and Schooling.* Boulder, Colo.: Paradigm Publishers, 2007. The authors analyze how technology has changed the way families conduct their lives, raise their children, and try to maintain a boundary between work and home.

Bianchi, Suzanne M., John P. Robinson, and Melissa A. Milkie. *Changing Rhythms of American Family Life.* New York: Russell Sage, 2006. Based on time-diaries, the authors conclude that despite their greater participation in the paid labor force U.S. mothers spend just as much time with their children as the previous generation of women did.

Contreras, Josefina M., Kathryn A. Kerns, and Angela M. Neal-Barnett. *Latino Children and Families in the United States: Current Research and Future Directions.* New York: Praeger, 2003. The authors consider how parenting beliefs and practices of Latinos differ by socioeconomic and cultural backgrounds and try to identify family values that can be considered "Latino."

Coontz, Stephanie. *Marriage, a History: From Obedience to Intimacy or How Love Conquered Marriage.* New York: Viking, 2005. This analysis of how the fundamental orientations to marriage have changed contains enlightening excerpts from the past.

Edin, Kathryn, and Maria Kefalas. *Promises I Can Keep: Why Poor Women Put Motherhood Before Marriage.* Berkeley: University of California Press, 2005. The author's interviews provide insight into how low-income single mothers think about marriage and family.

Epstein, Cynthia Fuchs, and Arne L. Kalleberg, eds. *Fighting for Time: Shifting Boundaries of Work and Social Life.* New York: Russell Sage, 2005. Explores changes in the time people spend at work and the consequences of those changes for individuals and families.

Johnson, Leonor Boulin, and Robert Staples. *Black Families at the Crossroads: Challenges and Prospects.* New York: Jossey-Bass, 2005. After placing today's black families in historical context, the authors analyze the impact of economic policies and social change.

Marquardt, Elizabeth. *Between Two Worlds: The Inner Lives of Children of Divorce.* New York: Crown, 2005. The author deftly weaves her own experiences as a child of divorce into her summary of interviews with children who have had this experience.

Romano, Renee Christine. *Race Mixing: Black-White Marriage in Postwar America.* Cambridge, Mass.: Harvard University Press, 2003. Provides the legislative background on these marriages, plus social trends, accompanied by first-person accounts.

Wallace, Harvey. *Family Violence,* 4th ed. Boston: Allyn and Bacon, 2005. This overview examines family violence through three perspectives: legal, medical, and social.

Journals

Family Relations, The History of the Family, International Journal of Sociology of the Family, Journal of Comparative Family Studies, Journal of Divorce, Journal of Divorce and Remarriage, Journal of Family and Economic Issues, Journal of Family Issues, Journal of Family Violence, Journal of Marriage and the Family, and *Marriage and Family Review* publish articles on almost every aspect of marriage and family life.

Religion

From Chapter 18 of *Sociology: A Down-to-Earth Approach*, 9/e. James M. Henslin. Copyright © 2008 by Pearson Education.

Religion

Mural on South Street, *Philadelphia*, PA

The first report was stunning. About a hundred armed agents of the Bureau of Alcohol, Tobacco, and Firearms (ATF) had attacked the compound of the Branch Davidians, an obscure religious group in Waco, Texas. Four of the agents were shot to death. So were six men who tried to defend the compound. Then came a fifty-one-day standoff, televised to the U.S. public, in which the ATF and FBI did such strange things as bombarding the compound with loud music day and night.

At 6 A.M. on the fifty-first day of the siege, following on-again, off-again negotiations with David Koresh, the 33-year-old leader of the group, tanks appeared. One rammed the compound's main building, pumping in gas consisting of chemicals

The government removed the bodies, sealed off the area, and bulldozed the charred remains of the building.

Time Magazine, Copyright Time Inc./Time & Life Pictures/Getty Images

that, according to international law, the U.S. military was forbidden to use against Iraqi soldiers. As a second tank punched holes in the walls, the women and children fled to the second floor. The men shot futilely at the tanks. An explosion rocked the compound, and the buildings burst into flames. Eighty men, women, and children were burned to death. Some of the charred bodies of the twenty-five children were found huddled next to their mothers.

The government removed the bodies, sealed off the area, and bulldozed the charred remains of the buildings. Survivors claimed that the government had set the fire. The government said the Branch Davidians had set it, that they had committed suicide by fire.

sacred Durkheim's term for things set apart or forbidden, that inspire fear, awe, reverence, or deep respect

profane Durkheim's term for common elements of everyday life

religion according to Durkheim, beliefs and practices that separate the profane from the sacred and unite its adherents into a moral community

church according to Durkheim, one of the three essential elements of religion—a moral community of believers; also refers to a type of religious organization, to a large, highly organized group with formal, sedate worship services and little emphasis on personal conversion

Seldom do governments turn this viciously against a religious group, but it does happen. One of the topics we shall consider in this chapter is the relationship of the dominant culture to new religions. Let's begin by asking what religion is.

What Is Religion?

All human societies are organized by some form of the family, as well as by some kind of economic system and political order. As we have seen, these key social institutions touch on aspects of life that are essential to human welfare. This chapter examines religion, another universal social institution.

Sociologists who do research on religion analyze the relationship between society and religion, and study the role that religion plays in people's lives. They do not try to prove that one religion is better than another. Nor is it their goal to verify or disprove anyone's faith. Sociologists have no tools for deciding that one course of action is more moral than another, much less for determining that one religion is "the" correct one. Religion is a matter of faith—and sociologists deal with empirical matters, things they can observe or measure. When it comes to religion, then, sociologists study the effects of religious beliefs and practices on people's lives. They also analyze how religion is related to stratification systems. Unlike theologians, however, sociologists cannot evaluate the truth of a religion's teachings.

In 1912 Emile Durkheim published an influential book, *The Elementary Forms of the Religious Life,* in which he tried to identify the elements that are common to all religions. After surveying religions around the world, Durkheim could find no specific belief or practice that all religions share. He did find, however, that all religions develop a community around their practices and beliefs. All religions also separate the sacred from the profane. By **sacred,** Durkheim referred to aspects of life having to do with the supernatural that inspire awe, reverence, deep respect, even fear. By **profane,** he meant aspects of life that are not concerned with religion or religious purposes but, instead, are part of ordinary, everyday life. Durkheim (1912/1965) summarized his conclusions by saying:

A religion is a unified system of beliefs and practices relative to sacred things, that is to say, things set apart and forbidden—beliefs and practices which unite into one single moral community called a Church, all those who adhere to them.

Religion, then, has three elements:

1. *Beliefs* that some things are sacred (forbidden, set apart from the profane)
2. *Practices* (rituals) centering on the things considered sacred
3. *A moral community* (a church) resulting from a group's beliefs and practices

Durkheim used the word **church** in an unusual sense, to refer to any "moral community" centered on beliefs and practices regarding the sacred. In Durkheim's sense, *church* refers to Buddhists bowing before a shrine, Hindus dipping in the Ganges River, and Confucians offering food to their ancestors. Similarly, the term *moral community* does not imply morality in the sense familiar to most of us—of ethical conduct. Rather, a moral community is simply a group of people who are united by their religious practices—and that would include sixteenth-century Aztec priests who each day gathered around an altar to pluck out the beating heart of a virgin.

To better understand the sociological approach to religion, let's see what pictures emerge when we apply the three theoretical perspectives.

When I visited a Hindu temple in Chattisgargh, India, I was impressed by the colorful and expressive statues on its roof. Here is a close-up of some of those figures, which represent some of the millions of gods that Hindus worship.

©James M. Henslin

The Functionalist Perspective

Functionalists stress that religion is universal because it meets basic human needs. Let's look at some of the functions—and dysfunctions—of religion.

Functions of Religion

Questions about Ultimate Meaning   Around the world, religions provide answers to perplexing questions about ultimate meaning—such as the purpose of life, why people suffer, and the existence of an afterlife. Those answers give followers a sense of purpose, a framework in which to live. Instead of seeing themselves buffeted by random events in an aimless existence, believers see their lives as fitting into a divine plan.

Emotional Comfort   The answers that religion provides about ultimate meaning also comfort people by assuring them that there is a purpose to life, even to suffering. Similarly, religious rituals that enshroud crucial events such as illness and death provide emotional comfort at times of crisis. The individual knows that others care and can find consolation in following familiar rituals.

Social Solidarity   Religious teachings and practices unite believers into a community that shares values and perspectives ("we Jews," "we Christians," "we Muslims"). The religious rituals that surround marriage, for example, link the bride and groom with a broader community that wishes them well. So do other religious rituals, such as those that celebrate birth and mourn death.

Guidelines for Everyday Life   The teachings of religion are not all abstractions. They also provide practical instructions. For example, four of the Ten Commandments delivered by Moses to the Israelites concern God, but the other six contain instructions on how to live everyday life, from how to get along with parents and neighbors to warnings about lying, stealing, and having affairs.

The consequences for people who follow these guidelines can be measured. People who attend church are less likely to abuse alcohol, nicotine, and illegal drugs than are people who don't go to church (Gillum 2005; Wallace et al 2007). This holds true for both adults and teens. In general, churchgoers follow a healthier lifestyle, and they live longer than those who don't go to church. How religion affects health is discussed in the Down-to-Earth Sociology box on the next page.

One of the many functions of religion is social solidarity. Can you see instances of this function in this photo of a Hindu service in Baltimore, Maryland.

Religion and Health: What We Know and Don't Know

DOES RELIGION MAKE A DIFFERENCE in people's health? Although scientists cannot determine the truth of any religion, they can study the effects of religion on people's lives—and health is one of those areas that can be measured.

"After seeing the data, I think I should go to church," said Lynda Powell, an epidemiologist at Rush University Medical Center in Chicago (Helliker 2005). What could prompt such a response?

Powell, along with two colleagues, evaluated the research articles that had been published on the effects of religion on health. They evaluated only research that met solid scientific criteria. For example, they threw out studies that didn't control for age, gender, or race-ethnicity, which are significant variables in health (Powell et al. 2003). Their most outstanding finding is this: People who attend religious services at least once a week have 25 percent fewer deaths than people who don't go to church. Think about it: For every hundred deaths of non-churchgoers, there are only 75 deaths of people who attend church weekly.

How could this possibly be? Perhaps the churchgoers were already healthier. This wasn't the reason, though, for the researchers compared people who were at the same levels of health or illness.

How about healthier lifestyles? Churchgoers are less likely to smoke, to get drunk, and so on. Not this either. The researchers also controlled for lifestyle. Actually, the weekly churchgoers had 30 percent less mortality. When the researchers adjusted for lifestyle and social class, the difference in mortality dropped to 25 percent (Powell et al. 2003).

What explanation could there be, then? Remember that the researchers are scientists, so they aren't going to say: "God." Here are three mechanisms that they suggest might account for the lower mortality of churchgoers: involvement in social statuses that produce a sense of self-worth and purpose in life; experiencing positive emotions; and

This boy is being prayed for at a Pentecostal church in Harlem, New York.

©Barry Lewis/Corbis

learning from compassionate role models calming ways of coping with crises. (The first two sound similar to the sense of community that I suggested might be a reason for the possible longer life of the Abkhasians.)

The explanations suggested by the researchers could be correct, but we need further research to find out.

Is there anything about religion itself that could account for this remarkable reduction in mortality? Some researchers think they've put their finger on it: prayer. Apparently, prayer (or meditation) changes people's brain activity and improves their immune response. Scientists are investigating this hypothesis (Kalb 2003).

One researcher points to something else about religion—the practice of forgiveness. It turns out that people who forgive easily are more likely to be in good psychological health. They are especially less likely to be depressed (Krause and Ellison 2003). To forgive someone who has done you wrong apparently brings release from feelings of resentment, bitterness, and hatred—but holding on to grudges rips you apart inside.

What have researchers found about praying for people who are sick? Does this help them get better? So far, most researchers haven't found any difference between people who are prayed for and those who are not (Benson et al. 2006). But researchers have encountered a problem. How do they find a control group of people who are not being prayed for? There is so much prayer—from parents, siblings, aunts and uncles, friends and neighbors—that some people don't even know they are being prayed for. I'm sure that the researchers will solve this.

We are just at the initial stages of research on religion and health. At this point, we have hardly any answers, but we do have this remarkable statistic about mortality and weekly attendance at religious services.

So, if you want to live longer . . .

Social Control Religion not only provides guidelines for everyday life but also sets limits on people's behaviors. Most norms of a religious group apply only to its members, but nonmembers also feel a spillover. Religious teachings, for example, are incorporated into criminal law. In the United States, blasphemy and adultery were once crimes for which people could be arrested, tried, and sentenced. Some states still have laws that prohibit the sale of alcohol before noon on Sunday, laws whose purpose was to get people out of the saloons and into the churches.

Adaptation Religion can help people adapt to new environments. For example, it isn't easy for immigrants to adjust to the customs of a new land. By keeping their native language alive within a community of people who are going through similar experiences, religion serves as a bridge between the old and new: It provides both continuity with the immigrants' cultural past and encouragement to adapt to the new culture. This was the case for earlier immigrants from Europe, and it remains true today for immigrants from all over the globe. The thousands of Spanish-speaking churches around the United States are an outstanding example.

Support for the Government Most religions provide support for the government. An obvious example is the way some churches so prominently display the U.S. flag. Some fly it in front of the church building, and many display both the U.S. flag and a church flag on stands at the front of their worship center. Regions that become hostile to the government run into trouble, as in the example of our opening vignette.

For their part, governments reciprocate by supporting God. In the extreme, some governments sponsor a particular religion, ban all others, provide financial support for building churches and seminaries, and even pay salaries to the clergy. These religions are known as **state religions.** During the sixteenth and seventeenth centuries in Sweden, the government sponsored Lutheranism; in Switzerland, Calvinism; and in Italy, Roman Catholicism.

In some instances, even though the government sponsors no particular religion, religious beliefs are embedded in a nation's life. This is called **civil religion** (Bellah 1970). For example, U.S. presidents—regardless of whether they are believers—invariably ask God to bless the nation in their inaugural speeches. U.S. officials take office by swearing that they will, in the name of God, fulfill their duty. Similarly, Congress opens each session with a prayer led by its own chaplain. The pledge of allegiance includes the phrase "one nation under God," and coins bear the inscription "In God We Trust."

Social Change Although religion is often so bound up with the prevailing social order that it resists social change, religion occasionally spearheads change. In the 1960s, for example, the civil rights movement, whose goal was to desegregate public facilities and abolish racial discrimination at southern polls, was led by religious leaders, especially leaders of African American churches such as Martin Luther King, Jr. Churches also served as centers at which demonstrators were trained and rallies were organized.

state religion a government-sponsored religion; also called *ecclesia*

civil religion Robert Bellah's term for religion that is such an established feature of a country's life that its history and social institutions are intertwined with the group's teachings about God

functional equivalent in this context, a substitute that serves the same functions (or meets the same needs) as religion; examples are psychotherapy and deep participation in "causes" or social movements

©Bob Henriques/Magnum Photos

Religion can promote social change, as was evident in the U.S. civil rights movement. Dr. Martin Luther King, Jr., a Baptist minister, shown here in his famous "I have a dream" speech, was the foremost leader of this movement.

Functional Equivalents of Religion

If some component of society other than religion answers questions about ultimate meaning and provides emotional comfort and guidelines for daily life, sociologists call it a **functional equivalent** of religion. For some people, Alcoholics Anonymous is a functional equivalent of religion (Chalfant 1992). For others, psychotherapy, humanism, transcendental meditation, or even a political party perform similar functions.

Some functional equivalents are difficult to distinguish from a religion (Brinton 1965; Luke 1985). For example, communism had its prophets (Marx and Lenin), sacred writings (everything written by Marx, Engels, and Lenin, but especially the *Communist Manifesto*), high priests (the heads of the Communist party), sacred buildings (the Kremlin), shrines (Lenin's body on display in Red Square), rituals (the annual May Day parade in Red Square), and even martyrs (Cuba's Ché Guevara). Soviet communism was avowedly atheistic and tried to wipe out all traces of Christianity, Judaism, and Islam from its midst. It even replaced baptisms and circumcisions with state-sponsored rituals that dedicated the child to the state. The Communist party also devised its own rituals for weddings and funerals.

As sociologist Ian Robertson (1987) pointed out, however, there is a fundamental distinction between a religion and its functional equivalent. Although the substitute may perform similar functions, its activities are not directed toward God, gods, or the supernatural.

Dysfunctions of Religion

Functionalists also examine ways in which religion is *dysfunctional,* that is, how it can bring harmful results. Two dysfunctions are religious persecution and war and terrorism.

Religion as Justification for Persecution   Beginning in the 1200s and continuing into the 1800s, in what has become known as the Inquisition, special commissions of the Roman Catholic Church tortured women to make them confess that they were witches, and then burned them at the stake. In 1692, Protestant leaders in Salem, Massachusetts, executed 21 women and men who were accused of being witches. In 2001, in the Democratic Republic of the Congo, about 1,000 alleged witches were hacked to death (Jenkins 2002). Similarly, it seems fair to say that the Aztec religion had its dysfunctions—at least for the virgins who were offered to appease angry gods. In short, religion has been used to justify oppression and any number of brutal acts.

War and Terrorism   History is filled with wars based on religion—commingled with politics. Between the eleventh and fourteenth centuries, for example, Christian monarchs conducted nine bloody Crusades in an attempt to wrest control of the region they called the Holy Land from the Muslims. Terrorist acts, too, are sometimes committed in the name of religion, as discussed in the Down-to-Earth Sociology box on the next page.

The Symbolic Interactionist Perspective

Symbolic interactionists focus on the meanings that people give their experiences, especially how they use symbols. Let's apply this perspective to religious symbols, rituals, and beliefs to see how they help to forge a community of like-minded people.

Religious Symbols

Suppose that it is about two thousand years ago and you have just joined a new religion. You have come to believe that a recently crucified Jew named Jesus is the Messiah, the Lamb of God offered for your sins. The Roman leaders are persecuting the followers of Jesus. They hate your religion because you and your fellow believers will not acknowledge Caesar as God.

Christians are few in number, and you are eager to have fellowship with other believers. But how can you tell who is a believer? Spies are everywhere. The government has sworn to destroy this new religion, and you do not relish the thought of being fed to lions in the Coliseum.

You use a simple technique. While talking with a stranger, as though doodling absentmindedly in the sand or dust, you casually trace the outline of a fish. Only fellow believers know the meaning—that, taken together, the first letter of each word in the Greek sentence "Jesus (is) Christ the Son of God" spell the Greek word for fish. If the other person gives no response, you rub out the outline and continue the interaction as usual. If there is a response, you eagerly talk about your new faith.

All religions use symbols to provide identity and social solidarity for their members. For Muslims, the primary symbol is the crescent moon and star; for Jews, the Star of David; for Christians, the cross. For members, these are not ordinary

Symbolic interactionists stress that a basic characteristic of humans is that they attach meaning to objects and events and then use representations of those objects or events to communicate with one another. Michaelangelo's *Pietà,* depicting Mary tenderly holding her son, Jesus, after his crucifixion, is one of the most acclaimed symbols in the Western world. It is admired for its beauty by believers and nonbelievers alike.

©Scala/Art Resource, NY

Terrorism and the Mind of God

> **WARNING: The "equal time" contents of this box are likely to offend just about everyone.**

AFTER 9/11, THE QUESTION on many people's minds was some form of, "How can people do such evil in the name of God?"

To answer this question, we need to broaden the context. The question is fine, but it cannot be directed solely at Islamic terrorists. If it is, it misses the point.

We need to consider other religions, too. For Christians, we don't have to go back centuries to the Inquisition or to the Children's Crusades. We only have to look at Ireland, and the bombings in Belfast. There, Protestants and Catholics slaughtered each other in the name of God.

In the United States, we can consider the killing of abortion doctors. Paul Hill, a minister who was executed for killing a doctor in Florida, was convinced that his act was good, that he had saved the lives of unborn babies. Before his execution, he said that he was looking forward to heaven. His friend, Reverend Michael Bray, took no lives; instead, he burned abortion clinics.

Since I want to give equal time to the major religions, we can't forget the Jews. Dr. Baruch Goldstein was convinced that Yahweh wanted him to take a Galil assault rifle, go to the Tomb of the Patriarchs, and shoot into a crowd of praying Palestinian men and boys. His admirers built a monument on his grave (Juergensmeyer 2000).

Finally, for the sake of equality, let's not let the Hindus, Buddhists, and Sikhs off the hook. In India, they continue to slaughter one another. In the name of their gods, they attack the houses of worship of the others and blow one another up. (The Hindus are actually equal opportunists—they kill Christians, too. I visited a state in India where Hindus had doused a jeep with gasoline and burned alive an Australian missionary and his two sons.)

None of these terrorists—Islamic, Christian, Jew, Sikh, Buddhist, or Hindu—represent the mainstream of their religion, but they do commit violence for religious reasons. How can they do so? Here are five elements that religious terrorists seem to have in common. (I have extrapolated these principles from the acts of individuals and small groups. Terrorism by the state is another matter.)

First, the individuals believe that they are under attack. Evil forces are bent on destroying the good of their world—whether that be their religion, their way of life, or unborn babies.

Second, they become convinced that God wants the evil destroyed.

HIP/Art Resource, NY

Violence and killing are a dysfunction of religion. The execution of John Rogers took place at Smithfield, England, in 1555, during the reign of Mary I.

Third, they conclude that only violence will resolve the situation, and that violence in this case is good.

Fourth, they become convinced that God has chosen them for this task. They don't necessarily want to kill or to die, but they reluctantly accept their fate. Dying for God's cause is greater than living as a coward who won't stand up for what is right.

Fifth, these perspectives are nurtured by a community, a group in which the individuals find identity. This group may realize that most members of their faith do not support their views, but that is because the others are uninformed, even brainwashed by the enemy or by the liberal, secularized media. The smaller community holds the truth.

For those groups that have scriptures, there are enough references to violence that they are able to interpret selective passages as "God's mandated" solution to the threat they feel.

If these orientations are accompanied by the view that we are in a final confrontation between good and evil, they become even more powerful. If we are in the end times and this is the final battle, there is no retreat. Some Christians, Jews, Muslims, and Sikhs hold such a view (Juergensmeyer 2000).

Under these conditions, morality is turned upside down. Killing becomes a moral act, a good done for a greater cause. This greater good may require self-sacrifice—the most notable example being a suicide bombing.

There is just enough truth in these points of view to keep the delusion alive. After all, wouldn't it have been better for the millions of Jews and the millions of other victims if someone had had the nerve and foresight to kill Hitler? Wouldn't his death and one's own self-sacrifice have been a greater good? Today, there are those bad Protestants, those bad Catholics, those bad Jews, those bad Palestinians, those bad abortionists, those bad Americans—an endless list. And the violence is for the Greater Good: what God wants.

Once people buy into this closed system of thought, discussion in which contrasting views are shared and considered flies out the window. The individuals become convinced that they have access to the mind of God.

This analysis would not be complete without stressing that religious terrorism is often a political instrument. There are those who exploit the conditions analyzed here to enforce their political agenda. Religious riots in India, for example, are usually not spontaneous, but, rather, are "produced" by leaders who benefit from them (Brass 2003).

This photo of people having a religious experience is from Billy Graham's last crusade, held in New York City in 2005, when Graham was 86 years old. Here is the caption from the *New York Times* where this photo first appeared: "The altar call is the moment at the end of an evangelical Protestant church service when the minister urges audience members to step forward, make a public decision to accept Jesus Christ as their savior and be born anew."

©James Estrin/The New York Times

symbols, but sacred emblems that evoke feelings of awe and reverence. In Durkheim's terms, religions use symbols to represent what the group considers sacred and to separate the sacred from the profane.

A symbol is a condensed way of communicating. Worn by a fundamentalist Christian, for example, the cross says, "I am a follower of Jesus Christ. I believe that He is the Messiah, the promised Son of God, that He loves me, that He died to take away my sins, that He rose from the dead and is going to return to earth, and that through Him I will receive eternal life."

That is a lot to pack into one symbol—and it is only part of what the symbol means to a fundamentalist believer. To people in other traditions of Christianity, the cross conveys somewhat different meanings—but to all Christians, the cross is a shorthand way of expressing many meanings. So it is with the Star of David, the crescent moon and star, the cow (expressing to Hindus the unity of all living things), and the various symbols of the world's many other religions.

Rituals

Rituals, ceremonies or repetitive practices, are also symbols that help to unite people into a moral community. Some rituals, such as the bar mitzvah of Jewish boys and the Holy Communion of Christians, are designed to create in devout believers a feeling of closeness with God and unity with one another. Rituals include kneeling and praying at set times; bowing; crossing oneself; singing; lighting candles and incense; reading scripture; and following prescribed traditions at processions, baptisms, weddings, and funerals.

Beliefs

Symbols, including rituals, develop from beliefs. The belief may be vague ("God is") or highly specific ("God wants us to prostrate ourselves and face Mecca five times each day"). Religious beliefs include not only *values* (what is considered good and desirable in life— how we ought to live) but also a **cosmology,** a unified picture of the world. For example, the Jewish, Christian, and Muslim belief that there is only one God, the Creator of the universe, who is concerned about the actions of humans and who will hold us accountable for what we do, is a cosmology. It presents a unifying picture of the universe.

Religious Experience

The term **religious experience** refers to a sudden awareness of the supernatural or a feeling of coming into contact with God. Some people undergo a mild version, such as feeling closer to God when they look at a mountain or listen to a certain piece of music. Others report a life-transforming experience. St. Francis of Assisi, for example, said that he became aware of God's presence in every living thing.

Some Protestants use the term **born again** to describe people who have undergone such a life-transforming religious experience. These people say that they came to the realization that they had sinned, that Jesus had died for their sins, and that God wants them to live a new life. Their worlds become transformed. They look forward to the Resurrection and to a new life in heaven, and they see relationships with spouses, parents, children, and even bosses in a new light. They also report a need to make changes in how they interact with others so that their lives reflect their new, personal commitment to Jesus as their "Savior and Lord." They describe a feeling of beginning life anew; hence the term *born again*.

Community

Finally, the shared meanings that come through symbols, rituals, and beliefs (and for some, a religious experience) unite people into a moral community. People in a moral community feel a bond with one another, for their beliefs and rituals bind them together—and at the same time separate them from those who do not share their unique symbolic world. Mormons, for example, feel

One of the functions of religion is to create community—a sense of being connected with one another and, in this case, also a sense of being connected with God. To help accomplish this, religions often use rituals. Shown here are Javanese Muslim women in Surinam as they celebrate Id al Fatr at the end of Rammadan.

©Stapleton Collection/Corbis

a "kindred spirit" (as it is often known) with other Mormons. Baptists, Jews, Jehovah's Witnesses, and Muslims feel similar bonds with members of their respective faiths.

As a symbol of their unity, members of some religious groups address one another as "brother" or "sister." "Sister Luby, we are going to meet at Brother and Sister Maher's on Wednesday" is a common way of expressing a message. The terms *brother* and *sister* are intended to symbolize a relationship so close that the individuals consider themselves members of the same family.

Community is powerful. Not only does it provide the basis for mutual identity but also it establishes norms that govern the behavior of its members. Members either conform or they lose their membership. In Christian churches, for example, an individual whose adultery becomes known, and who refuses to admit wrongdoing and ask forgiveness, may be banned from the church. He or she may be formally excommunicated, as in the Catholic tradition, or more informally "stricken from the rolls," as is the usual Protestant practice.

Removal from the community is a serious matter for people whose identity is bound up in that community. Sociologists John Hostetler (1980), William Kephart, and William Zellner (2001) describe the Amish practice of *shunning*—ignoring an offender in all situations. Persons who are shunned are treated as though they do not exist (for if they do not repent by expressing sorrow for their act, they have ceased to exist as members of the community). The shunning is so thorough that even family members, who themselves remain in good standing in the congregation, are not allowed to talk to the person being shunned. This obviously makes for some interesting times at the dinner table.

The Conflict Perspective

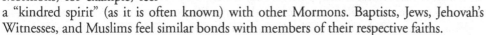 The conflict perspective has an entirely different focus. Conflict theorists examine how religion supports the status quo and helps to maintain social inequalities.

Opium of the People

In general, conflict theorists are highly critical of religion. Karl Marx, an avowed atheist who believed that the existence of God was impossible, set the tone for conflict theorists with his most famous statement on this subject: "Religion is the sigh of the oppressed creature, the sentiment of a heartless world. . . . It is the opium of the people" (Marx 1844/1964). By this statement, Marx meant that oppressed workers find escape in religion. For them, religion is like a drug that helps them to forget their misery. By diverting their thoughts toward future happiness in an afterlife, religion takes their eyes off their suffering in this world, thereby greatly reducing the possibility that they will rebel against their oppressors.

A Legitimation of Social Inequalities

Conflict theorists say that religion legitimates the social inequalities of the larger society. By this, they mean that religion teaches that the existing social arrangements of a society represent what God desires. For example, during the Middle Ages, Christian theologians decreed the *divine right of kings*. This doctrine meant that God determined who would become king, and set him on the throne. The king ruled in God's place, and it was the duty of a king's subjects to be loyal to him (and to pay their taxes). To disobey the king was to disobey God.

In what was perhaps the supreme technique of legitimating the social order (and one that went even a step farther than the divine right of kings), the religion of ancient Egypt held that the Pharaoh himself was a god. The Emperor of Japan was similarly declared divine. If this were so, who could ever question his decisions? Today's politicians would give their right arm for such a religious teaching.

Conflict theorists point to many other examples of how religion legitimates the social order. In India, Hinduism supports the caste system by teaching that an individual who tries to change caste will come back in the next life as a member of a lower caste—or even as an animal. In the decades before the American Civil War, Southern ministers used scripture to defend slavery, saying that it was God's will—while Northern ministers legitimated *their* region's social structure by using scripture to denounce slavery as evil (Ernst 1988; Nauta 1993; White 1995).

This engraving is of a Quaker meeting in the 1700s when women sat on one side of the church, and men on the other. Some Jewish and Muslim groups continue this practice today. Do you think that sex-segregated seating supports the conflict perspective that religion reflects and legitimates social inequalities? Why or why not?

QUAKERS MEETING.

Religion and the Spirit of Capitalism

Max Weber disagreed strongly with the conflict perspective that religion merely reflects and legitimates the social order, and that it impedes social change by encouraging people to focus on the afterlife. In contrast, Weber said that religion's focus on the afterlife is a source of profound social change.

Like Marx, Weber observed the early industrialization of European countries. Weber became intrigued with the question of why some societies embraced capitalism while others clung to their traditional ways. Tradition is strong and tends to hold people in check; yet some societies had been transformed by capitalism, while others remained untouched. As he explored this puzzle, Weber concluded that religion held the key to **modernization**—the transformation of traditional societies to industrial societies.

To explain his conclusions, Weber wrote *The Protestant Ethic and the Spirit of Capitalism* (1904–1905/1958).

1. Capitalism is not just a superficial change. Rather, capitalism represents a fundamentally different way of thinking about work and money. *Traditionally, people worked just enough to meet their basic needs, not so that they could have a surplus to invest.* To accumulate money (capital) as an end in itself, not just to spend it, was a radical departure from traditional thinking. People even came to consider it a duty to invest money in order to make profits, which, in turn, they reinvested to make more profits. Weber called this new approach to work and money the **spirit of capitalism.**

2. Why did the spirit of capitalism develop in Europe, and not, for example, in China or India, where the people had similar material resources and education? According to Weber, *religion was the key.* The religions of China and India, and indeed Roman Catholicism in Europe, encouraged a traditional approach to life, not thrift and investment. Capitalism appeared when Protestantism came on the scene.

3. What was different about Protestantism, especially Calvinism? John Calvin taught that God had predestined some people to go to heaven, and others to hell. Neither church membership nor feelings about your relationship with God could assure you that you were saved. You wouldn't know your fate until after you died.

4. This doctrine created intense anxiety among Calvin's followers: "Am I predestined to hell or to heaven?" they wondered. As Calvinists wrestled with this question, they concluded that church members have a duty to prove that they are one of God's elect, and to live as though they are predestined to heaven—for good works are a demonstration of salvation.

5. This conclusion motivated Calvinists to lead moral lives *and* to work hard, to not waste time, and to be frugal—for idleness and needless spending were signs of worldliness. Weber called this self-denying approach to life the **Protestant ethic.**

6. As people worked hard and spent money only on necessities (a pair of earrings or a second pair of dress shoes would have been defined as sinful luxuries), they had money left over. Because it couldn't be spent, this capital was invested, which led to a surge in production.

7. Weber's analysis can be summed up this way: The change in religion (from Catholicism to Protestantism, especially Calvinism) led to a fundamental change in thought and behavior (the *Protestant ethic*). The result was the *spirit of capitalism.* For this reason, capitalism originated in Europe and not in places where religion did not encourage capitalism's essential elements: the accumulation of capital and its investment and reinvestment.

Although Weber's analysis has been influential, it has not lacked critics (Kalberg 2002). Hundreds of scholars have attacked it, some for overlooking the lack of capitalism in Scotland (a Calvinist country), others for failing to explain why the Industrial Revolution was born in England (not a Calvinist country). Hundreds of other scholars

modernization the transformation of traditional societies into industrial societies

spirit of capitalism Weber's term for the desire to accumulate capital as a duty—not to spend the money, but as an end in itself—and to constantly reinvest it

Protestant ethic Weber's term to describe the ideal of a self-denying, highly moral life accompanied by hard work and frugality

"We're thinking maybe it's time you started getting some religious instruction. There's Catholic, Protestant, and Jewish—any of those sound good to you?"

For some Americans, religion is an "easy-going, makes-little-difference" matter, as expressed in this cartoon. For others, religious matters are firmly held, and followers find even slight differences of faith to be significant.

have defended Weber's argument. There is currently no historical evidence that can definitively prove or disprove Weber's thesis.

At this point in history, the Protestant ethic and the spirit of capitalism are not confined to any specific religion or even to any one part of the world. Rather, they have become cultural traits that have spread to societies around the globe (Greeley 1964; Yinger 1970). U.S. Catholics have about the same approach to life as do U.S. Protestants. In addition, Hong Kong, Japan, Malaysia, Singapore, South Korea, and Taiwan—not exactly Protestant countries—have embraced capitalism (Levy 1992). China is in the midst of doing so.

The World's Major Religions

The largest of the thousands of religions in the world are listed in Figure 1. Let's briefly review six of them.

Judaism

The origin of Judaism is traced to Abraham, who lived about four thousand years ago in Mesopotamia. Jews believe that God (Jahweh) made a covenant with Abraham, selecting his descendants as a chosen people—promising to make them "as numerous as the sands of the seashore" and to give them a special land that would be theirs forever. The sign of this covenant was the circumcision of males, which was to be performed when a boy was eight days old. Descent is traced through Abraham and his wife, Sarah, their son Isaac, and their grandson Jacob (also called Israel).

Religion, which provides community and identity, is often passed from the older to the younger. Shown here are Hasidic Jews in Brooklyn. Differences among religious groups are often incomprehensible to outsiders. The man on the left is carrying a pouch under his left arm, considered by the men on the right to be a violation of the Sabbath.

AP Images

RELIGION

Joseph, a son of Jacob, was sold by his brothers into slavery and taken to Egypt. Following a series of hair-raising adventures, Joseph became Pharaoh's right-hand man. When a severe famine hit Canaan, where Jacob's family was living, Jacob and his eleven other sons fled to Egypt. Under Joseph's leadership, they were welcome. A subsequent Pharaoh, however, enslaved the Israelites. After about four hundred years, Moses, an Israelite who had been adopted by Pharaoh's daughter, confronted Pharaoh. He persuaded Pharaoh to release the slaves, who at that time numbered about 2 million. Moses led them out of Egypt, but before they reached their Promised Land, the Israelites spent forty years wandering in the desert. Sometime during those years, Moses delivered the Ten Commandments from Mount Sinai. Abraham, Isaac, Jacob, and Moses hold revered positions in Judaism. The events of their lives and the recounting of the early history of the Israelites are contained in the first five books of the Bible, called the Torah.

The founding of Judaism marked a fundamental change in religion, for it was the first religion based on **monotheism,** the belief that there is only one God. Prior to Judaism, religions were based on **polytheism,** the belief that there are many gods. In Greek religion, for example, Zeus was the god of heaven and earth, Poseidon the god of the sea, and Athena the goddess of wisdom. Other groups followed **animism,** believing that all objects in the world have spirits, some of which are dangerous and must be outwitted.

Contemporary Judaism in the United States comprises three main branches: Orthodox, Reform, and Conservative. Orthodox Jews adhere to the laws espoused by Moses. They eat only foods prepared in a designated manner (kosher), observe the Sabbath in a traditional way, and segregate males and females in their religious services. During the 1800s, a group that wanted to make their practices more compatible with U.S. culture broke from this tradition. This liberal group, known as Reform Judaism, mostly uses English in its religious ceremonies and has reduced much of the use of ritual. The third branch, Conservative Judaism, falls somewhere between the other two. No branch has continued polygyny (allowing a man to have more than one wife), the original marriage custom of the Jews, which was outlawed by rabbinic decree about a thousand years ago.

The history of Judaism is marked by conflict and persecution. The Israelites were conquered by the Babylonians, and were again made slaves. After returning to Israel and rebuilding the temple, they were later conquered by the Romans, and, after their rebellion at Masada in A.D. 70 failed, they were exiled for almost two thousand years into other nations. During those centuries, they faced prejudice, discrimination, and persecution (called **anti-Semitism**) by many peoples and rulers. The most horrendous example was the Nazi Holocaust of World War II, when Hitler attempted to eliminate the Jews as a people. Under the Nazi occupation of Europe and North Africa, about 6 million Jews were slaughtered. Many died in gas ovens that were constructed for just this purpose.

Central to Jewish teaching is the requirement to love God and do good deeds. Good deeds begin in the family, where each member has an obligation toward the others. Sin is a conscious choice to do evil, and must be atoned for by prayers and good works. Jews consider Jerusalem a holy city and believe that the Messiah will one day appear there, bringing redemption for them all.

Christianity

Christianity, which developed out of Judaism, is also monotheistic. Christians believe that Jesus Christ is the Messiah whom God promised the Jews.

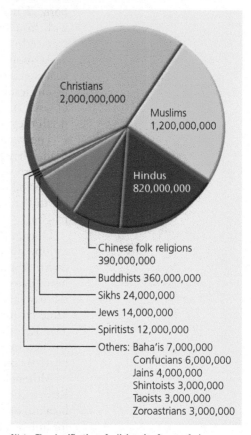

Figure 1 **The World's Largest Religions**[a]

- Christians 2,000,000,000
- Muslims 1,200,000,000
- Hindus 820,000,000
- Chinese folk religions 390,000,000
- Buddhists 360,000,000
- Sikhs 24,000,000
- Jews 14,000,000
- Spiritists 12,000,000
- Others: Baha'is 7,000,000
  Confucians 6,000,000
  Jains 4,000,000
  Shintoists 3,000,000
  Taoists 3,000,000
  Zoroastrians 3,000,000

[a]*Note:* The classification of religions is often confusing. Animists, for example, although numerous, are not listed as a separate group in the source. It is sometimes difficult to tell what groups are included in what categories.

Sources: "Adherents of . . . " 2003.

monotheism the belief that there is only one God

polytheism the belief that there are many gods

animism the belief that all objects in the world have spirits, some of which are dangerous and must be outwitted

anti-Semitism prejudice, discrimination, and persecution directed against Jews

Jesus was born in poverty, and traditional Christians believe his mother was a virgin. Within two years of his birth, Herod—named king of Palestine by Caesar, who had conquered Israel—was informed that people were saying a new king had been born. When they realized Herod had sent soldiers to kill the baby, Jesus' parents fled with him to Egypt. After Herod died, they returned, settling in the small town of Nazareth.

At about the age of 30, Jesus began a preaching and healing ministry. His teachings challenged the contemporary religious establishment, and as his popularity grew, the religious leaders plotted to have him killed by the Romans. Christians interpret the death of Jesus as a blood sacrifice made to atone for their sins. They believe that through his death they have peace with God and will inherit eternal life.

The twelve main followers of Jesus, called *apostles,* believed that Jesus rose from the dead. They preached the need to be "born again," that is, to accept Jesus as Savior, give up selfish ways, and live a devout life. The new religion spread rapidly, and after an initial period of hostility on the part of imperial Rome—during which time believers were fed to the lions in the Coliseum—in A.D. 317 Christianity became the empire's official religion.

During the first thousand years of Christianity, there was only one church organization, directed from Rome. During the eleventh century, after disagreement over doctrine and politics, Greek Orthodoxy was declared independent of Rome. It was headquartered in Constantinople (now Istanbul, Turkey). During the Middle Ages, the Roman Catholic Church, which was aligned with the political establishment, became corrupt. Some Church offices, such as that of bishop, were sold for a set price. The Reformation, which was led by Martin Luther in the sixteenth century, was sparked by Luther's outrage that the forgiveness of sins (including those not yet committed) could be purchased by buying an "indulgence."

Although Martin Luther's original goal was to reform the Church, not divide it, the Reformation began a splintering of Christianity. The Reformation coincided with the breakup of feudalism, and as the ancient political structure came apart, people clamored for independence in both political and religious thought. Today, Christianity is the most popular religion in the world, with about 2 billion adherents. Christians are divided into hundreds of groups, some with doctrinal differences so slight that only members of the group can appreciate the extremely fine distinctions that they feel significantly separate them from others. The Social Map on the next page shows how some of these groups are distributed in the United States.

Islam

Islam, whose followers are known as Muslims, began in the same part of the world as Judaism and Christianity. Islam, the world's third monotheistic religion, has over a billion followers. It was founded by Muhammad, who was born in Mecca (now in Saudi Arabia) in about A.D. 570. Muhammad married Khadija, a wealthy widow. About the age of 40, he reported that he had had visions from God. These, and his teachings, were later written down in a book called the Qur'an (Koran). Few paid attention to Muhammad, although Ali, his son-in-law, believed him. When he found out that there was a plot to murder him, Muhammad fled to Medina, where he found a more receptive audience. There he established a *theocracy* (a government based on the principle that God is king, God's laws are the statutes of the land, and priests are the earthly administrators of God). In A.D. 630 he returned to Mecca, this time as a conqueror (Bridgwater 1953).

After Muhammad's death, a struggle for control over the empire he had founded split Islam into two branches that remain today, the Sunni and the Shi'ite. The Shi'ites believe that the *imam* (the religious leader) is inspired as he interprets the Qur'an. They are generally more conservative and are inclined to **fundamentalism,** the belief that modern ways of life threaten religion and that the faith as it was originally practiced should

fundamentalism the belief that true religion is threatened by social change and that the faith as it was originally practiced should be restored

Figure 2 Church Membership: Dominant Religion, by County

When no religious group has 25 percent of the total membership in a county, that county is left blank. When two or more religious groups have 25–49 percent of the membership in a county, the largest is shown.

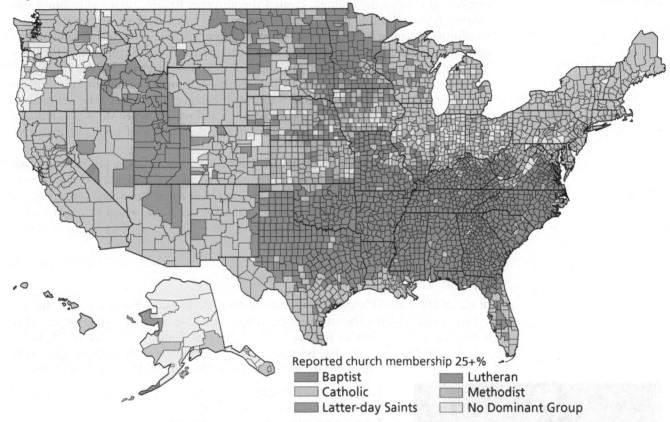

Reported church membership 25+%

- Baptist
- Catholic
- Latter-day Saints
- Lutheran
- Methodist
- No Dominant Group

be restored. The Sunnis, who do not share this belief, are generally more liberal, more accepting of social change.

Like the Jews, Muslims trace their ancestry to Abraham. Abraham fathered a son, Ishmael, by Hagar, his wife Sarah's Egyptian maid (Genesis 25:12). Ishmael had twelve sons, from whom a good portion of today's Arab world is descended. For them also, Jerusalem is a holy city. The Muslims consider the Bibles of the Jews and the Christians to be sacred, but they take the Qur'an as the final word. They believe that the followers of Abraham and Moses (Jews) and Jesus (Christians) changed the original teachings and that Muhammad restored these teachings to their initial purity. It is the duty of each Muslim to make a pilgrimage to Mecca during his or her lifetime. Unlike the Jews, the Muslims continue to practice polygyny. They limit a man to four wives, however.

Hinduism

Unlike the other religions just described, Hinduism has no specific founder. Going back about four thousand years, Hinduism was the chief religion of India. The term *Hinduism,* however, is Western, and in India the closest term is *dharma* (law). Unlike Judaism, Christianity, and Islam, Hinduism has no canonical scripture, that is, no texts thought to be inspired by God. Instead, several books, including the *Brahmanas,*

Bhagavad-Gita, and *Upanishads,* expound on the moral qualities that people should strive to develop. They also delineate the sacrifices people should make to the gods.

Hindus are *polytheists;* that is, they believe that there are many gods. They believe that one of these gods, Brahma, created the universe. Brahma, along with Shiva (the Destroyer) and Vishnu (the Preserver), form a triad that is at the center of modern Hinduism. A central belief is *karma,* spiritual progress. There is no final judgment, but, instead, **reincarnation,** a cycle of life, death, and rebirth. Death involves only the body. The soul continues its existence, coming back in a form that matches the individual's moral progress in the previous life (which centers on proper conduct in following the rules of one's caste). If an individual reaches spiritual perfection, he or she has attained *nirvana.* This marks the end of the cycle of death and rebirth, when the soul is reunited with the universal soul. When this occurs, *maya,* the illusion of time and space, has been conquered.

Some Hindu practices have been modified as a consequence of social protest—especially child marriage and *suttee,* the practice of cremating a surviving widow along with her deceased husband (Bridgwater 1953). Other ancient rituals remain unchanged, however, and include *kumbh mela,* a purifying washing in the Ganges River, which takes place every twelve years, and in which many millions participate.

Buddhism

In about 600 B.C., Siddhartha Gautama founded Buddhism. (Buddha means the "enlightened one," a term Gautama was given by his disciples.) Gautama was the son of an upper-caste Hindu ruler in an area north of Benares, India. At the age of 29, he renounced his life of luxury and became an ascetic. Through meditation, he discovered the "four noble truths," which emphasize self-denial and compassion.

1. Existence is suffering.
2. The origin of suffering is desire.
3. Suffering ceases when desire ceases.
4. The way to end desire is to follow the "noble eightfold path."

The noble eightfold path consists of

1. Right belief
2. Right resolve (to renounce carnal pleasure and to harm no living creature)
3. Right speech
4. Right conduct
5. Right occupation or living
6. Right effort
7. Right-mindedness (or contemplation)
8. Right ecstasy

Depictions of Buddha are found throughout the world. Many Buddhists keep small statues in their homes and businesses, at which they make daily offerings of food. This golden Buddha statue is in Bangkok, Thailand.

The central symbol of Buddhism is the eight-spoked wheel. Each spoke represents one aspect of the path. As with Hinduism, the ultimate goal of Buddhism is the cessation of rebirth and thereby of suffering. Buddhists teach that all things are temporary, even the self. Because all things are destined to pass away, there is no soul (Reat 1994).

Buddhism spread rapidly. In the third century B.C., the ruler of India adopted Buddhism and sent missionaries throughout Asia to spread the new teaching (Bridgwater 1953). By the fifth century A.D., Buddhism reached the height of its popularity in India, after which it died out. Buddhism, however, had spread to Ceylon, Burma, Tibet, Laos, Cambodia, Thailand, China, Korea, and Japan, where it flourishes today. With increased immigration from Asian nations, vigorous communities of Buddhists have also developed in the United States (Cadge and Bender 2004).

©Redlink/Corbis

Confucianism

About the time that Gautama lived, K'ung Fu-tsu (551–479 B.C.) was born in China. Confucius (his name strung together in English), a public official, was distressed by the corruption that he saw in government. Unlike Gautama, who urged withdrawal from social activities, Confucius urged social reform and developed a system of moral principles based on peace, justice, and universal order. His teachings were incorporated into writings called the *Analects*.

The basic moral principle of Confucianism is to maintain *jen,* sympathy or concern for other humans. The key to *jen* is to sustain right relationships—being loyal and placing morality above self-interest. In what is called the "Confucian Golden Rule," Confucius stated a basic principle for *jen:* to treat those who are subordinate to you as you would like to be treated by people superior to yourself. Confucius taught that right relationships within the family (loyalty, respect) should be the model for society. He also taught the "middle way," an avoidance of extremes.

Confucianism was originally atheistic, simply a set of moral teachings without reference to the supernatural. As the centuries passed, however, local gods were added to the teachings, and Confucius himself was declared a god. Confucius' teachings became the basis for the government of China. About A.D. 1000, the emphasis on meditation gave way to a stress on improvement through acquiring knowledge. This emphasis remained dominant until the twentieth century. By this time, the government had become rigid, and respect for the existing order had replaced respect for relationships (Bridgwater 1953). Following the Communist revolution of 1949, political leaders attempted to weaken the people's ties with Confucianism. They succeeded in part, but Confucianism remains embedded in Chinese culture.

Types of Religious Groups

Sociologists have identified four types of religious groups: cult, sect, church, and ecclesia. Why do some of these groups meet with hostility, while others are more accepted? For an explanation, look at Figure 3.

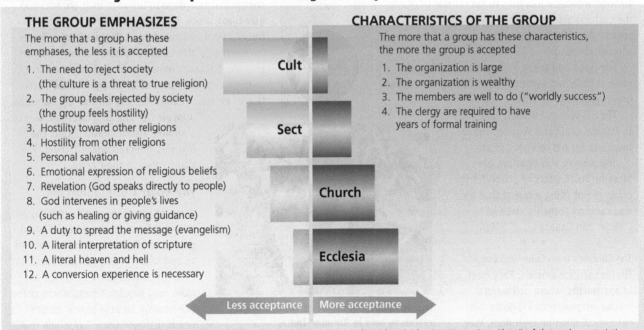

Figure 3 **Religious Groups: From Hostility to Acceptance**

THE GROUP EMPHASIZES

The more that a group has these emphases, the less it is accepted

1. The need to reject society (the culture is a threat to true religion)
2. The group feels rejected by society (the group feels hostility)
3. Hostility toward other religions
4. Hostility from other religions
5. Personal salvation
6. Emotional expression of religious beliefs
7. Revelation (God speaks directly to people)
8. God intervenes in people's lives (such as healing or giving guidance)
9. A duty to spread the message (evangelism)
10. A literal interpretation of scripture
11. A literal heaven and hell
12. A conversion experience is necessary

CHARACTERISTICS OF THE GROUP

The more that a group has these characteristics, the more the group is accepted

1. The organization is large
2. The organization is wealthy
3. The members are well to do ("worldly success")
4. The clergy are required to have years of formal training

Cult

Sect

Church

Ecclesia

Less acceptance — More acceptance

Note: Any religious organization can be placed somewhere on this continuum, based on its having "more" or "less" of these characteristics and emphases. The varying proportions of the rectangles are intended to represent the group's relative characteristics and emphases.

Sources: By the author. Based on Troeltsch 1931; Pope 1942; and Johnson 1963.

cult a new religion with few followers, whose teachings and practices put it at odds with the dominant culture and religion

charismatic leader literally, someone to whom God has given a gift; more commonly, someone who exerts extraordinary appeal to a group of followers

charisma literally, an extraordinary gift from God; more commonly, an outstanding or "magnetic" personality that draws people to the individual

Let's explore what sociologists have found about these four types of religious groups. The summary that follows is a modification of analyses by sociologists Ernst Troeltsch (1931), Liston Pope (1942), and Benton Johnson (1963).

Cult

The word *cult* conjures up bizarre images—shaven heads, weird music, brainwashing—even ritual suicide may come to mind. Cults, however, are not necessarily weird, and few practice "brainwashing" or bizarre rituals. In fact, *all religions began as cults* (Stark 1989). A **cult** is simply a new or different religion whose teachings and practices put it at odds with the dominant culture and religion. Because the term cult arouses such negative meanings in the public mind, however, some scholars prefer to use the term *new religion* instead. As is evident from the Cultural Diversity box below, "new" can mean that an older, unfamiliar religion from one culture has made its appearance in another culture.

Cults often originate with a **charismatic leader,** an individual who inspires people because he or she seems to have extraordinary qualities. **Charisma** refers to an outstanding gift or to some exceptional quality. People feel drawn to both the person and the message because they find something highly appealing about the individual—in some instances, almost a magnetic charm.

The most popular religion in the world began as a cult. Its handful of followers believed that an unschooled carpenter who preached in remote villages in a backwater

---

Cultural Diversity *in the* United States

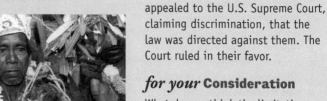

Human Heads and Animal Blood: The Toleration of Religion

AS THE CUSTOMS OFFICIALS LOOKED over the line of people who had just gotten off the plane from Haiti, there was nothing to make this particular woman stand out. She would have passed through without a problem, except for one thing: As the customs agents gave her luggage a routine search, they found something that struck them as somewhat unusual—a human head.

The head had teeth, hair, pieces of skin, and some dirt. It had evidently been dug up from some grave, probably in Haiti.

The 30-year old woman, who lives in Florida, practiced Voodoo. The head was for her religious rituals.

The woman was arrested. She faces up to 15 years in prison for the crime of not filing a report that she was carrying "organic material" ("Mujer con Cabeza . . ." 2006).

• • •

The Santeros from Cuba who live in Florida sacrifice animals. They meet in apartments, where, following a Yoruba religion, they kill goats and chickens. Calling on their gods, they first ask permission to sacrifice the animals. After sacrificing them, they pour

Human skulls dug up for gajan, a religious ceremony held in Kurmun, India.

©Reuters/Corbis

out the animals' blood, which opens and closes the doors of their destiny. They also cut off the animals' heads and place them at locations in the city that represent the four directions of a compass. This is done to terrorize their enemies and give them safety. The sacrificed heads also protect the city from hurricanes and other destructive forces.

When city officials in Hialeah, Florida, learned that the Santeros were planning to build a church in their city, they passed a law against the sacrifice of animals within the city limits. The Santeros appealed to the U.S. Supreme Court, claiming discrimination, that the law was directed against them. The Court ruled in their favor.

for your Consideration

What do you think the limitations on religious freedom should be? Should people be allowed to sacrifice animals as part of their religious practices?

If the Santeros can sacrifice animals, why shouldn't people who practice voodoo be able to use human heads if they want to? (Assume that the relatives of the dead person have given their permission.)

country was the Son of God, that he was killed and came back to life. Those beliefs made the early Christians a cult, setting them apart from the rest of their society. Persecuted by both religious and political authorities, these early believers clung to one another for support. Many cut off associations with their friends who didn't accept the new message. To others, the early Christians must have seemed deluded and brainwashed.

So it was with Islam. When Muhammad revealed his visions and said that God's name was really Allah, only a few people believed him. To others, he must have seemed crazy, deranged.

Each cult (or new religion) is met with rejection on the part of society. Its message is considered bizarre, its approach to life strange. Its members antagonize the majority, who are convinced that they have a monopoly on the truth. The new religion may claim messages from God, visions, visits from angels—some form of enlightenment or seeing the true way to God. The cult demands intense commitment, and its followers, who are confronting a hostile world, pull together in a tight circle, separating themselves from nonbelievers.

Most cults fail. Not many people believe the new message, and the cult fades into obscurity. Some, however, succeed and make history. Over time, large numbers of people may come to accept the message and become followers of the religion. If this happens, the new religion changes from a cult to a sect.

Sect

A **sect** is larger than a cult, but its members still feel tension between their views and the prevailing beliefs and values of the broader society. A sect may even be hostile to the society in which it is located. At the very least, its members remain uncomfortable with many of the emphases of the dominant culture; in turn, nonmernbers tend to be uncomfortable with members of the sect.

Ordinarily, sects are loosely organized and fairly small. They emphasize personal salvation and an emotional expression of one's relationship with God. Clapping, shouting, dancing, and extemporaneous prayers are hallmarks of sects. Like cults, sects also stress **evangelism,** the active recruitment of new members.

If a sect grows, its members tend to gradually make peace with the rest of society. To appeal to a broader base, the sect shifts some of its doctrines, redefining matters to remove some of the rough edges that create tension between it and the rest of society. As the members become more respectable in the eyes of the society, they feel less hostility and little, if any, isolation. If a sect follows this course, as it grows and becomes more integrated into society, it changes into a church.

Church

At this point, the religious group is highly bureaucratized—probably with national and international headquarters that give direction to the local congregations, enforce rules about who can be ordained, and control finances. The relationship with God has grown less intense. The group is likely to have less emphasis on personal salvation and emotional expression. Worship services are likely to be more sedate, with sermons more formal, and written prayers read before the congregation. Rather than being recruited from the outside by fervent, personal evangelism, most new members now come from within, from children born to existing members. Rather than joining through conversion—seeing the new truth—children may be baptized, circumcised, or dedicated in some other way. At some designated age, children may be asked to affirm the group's beliefs in a confirmation or bar mitzvah ceremony.

Ecclesia

Finally, some groups become so well integrated into a culture, and so strongly allied with their government, that it is difficult to tell where one leaves off and the other takes over. In these *state religions,* also called **ecclesia,** the government and religion work together to try to shape society. There is no recruitment of members, for citizenship makes everyone

sect a religious group larger than a cult that still feels substantial hostility from and toward society

evangelism an attempt to win converts

ecclesia a religious group so integrated into the dominant culture that it is difficult to tell where the one begins and the other leaves off; also called a *state religion*

a member. For most people in the society, the religion provides little meaning: The religion is part of a cultural identity, not an eye-opening experience. Sweden provides a good example of how extensively religion and government intertwine in an ecclesia. In the 1860s, all citizens had to memorize Luther's *Small Catechism* and be tested on it yearly (Anderson 1995). Today, Lutheranism is still the state religion, but most Swedes come to church only for baptisms, marriages, and funerals.

Unlike cults and sects, which perceive God as personally involved with and concerned about an individual's life, ecclesias envision God as more impersonal and remote. Church services reflect this view of the supernatural, for they tend to be highly formal, directed by ministers or priests who, after undergoing rigorous training in approved schools or seminaries, follow prescribed rituals.

Examples of ecclesia include the Church of England (whose very name expresses alignment between church and state), the Lutheran church in Norway and Denmark, Islam in Iran and Iraq, and, during the time of the Holy Roman Empire, the Roman Catholic Church, which was the official religion for the region that is now Europe.

Variations in Patterns

Obviously, not all religious groups go through all these stages—from cult to sect to church to ecclesia. Some die out because they fail to attract enough members. Others, such as the Amish, remain sects. And, as is evident from the few countries that have state religions, very few religions ever become ecclesias.

In addition, these classifications are not perfectly matched in the real world. For example, although the Amish are a sect, they place little or no emphasis on recruiting others. The early Quakers, another sect, shied away from emotional expressions of their beliefs. They would quietly meditate in church, with no one speaking, until God gave someone a message to share with others. Finally, some groups that become churches may retain a few characteristics of sects, such as an emphasis on evangelism or a personal relationship with God.

Although all religions began as cults, not all varieties of a particular religion begin that way. For example, some **denominations**—"brand names" within a major religion, such as Methodism or Reform Judaism—begin as splinter groups. Some members of a church disagree with *particular* aspects of the church's teachings (not its major message), and they break away to form their own organization. An example is the Southern Baptist Convention, which was formed in 1845 to defend the right to own slaves (Ernst 1988; Nauta 1993; White 1995).

When Religion and Culture Conflict

As we have seen, cults and sects represent a break with the past. This division presents a challenge to the social order, and often generates hostility. When religion and the culture in which it is embedded find themselves in conflict, how do they adapt?

First, the members of a religion may reject the dominant culture and have as little as possible to do with nonmembers of their religion. Like the Amish, they may withdraw into closed communities. The Amish broke away from Swiss-German Mennonites in 1693. They try to preserve the culture of their ancestors, who lived in a simpler time when there were no televisions, movies, automobiles, or even electricity. To do so, they emphasize family life and traditional male and female roles. They continue to wear the style of clothing that their ancestors wore three hundred years ago, to light their homes with oil lamps, and to speak German at home and in church. They also continue to reject radio, television, motorized vehicles, and education beyond the eighth grade. They do mingle with non-Amish when they shop in town—where they are readily distinguishable by their form of transportation (horse-drawn carriages), clothing, and speech.

©James M. Henslin

Like other aspects of culture, religion is filled with background assumptions that usually go unquestioned. In this photo, which I took outside a Boston theater in midwinter, what background assumption of religion is this man violating?

In the *second* pattern, a cult or sect rejects only specific elements of the prevailing culture. For example, religious teachings may dictate that immodest clothing—short skirts, skimpy swimsuits, low-cut dresses, and so on—is immoral, or that wearing makeup or going to the movies is wrong. Most elements of the main culture, however, are accepted. Although specific activities are forbidden, members of the religion are able to participate in most aspects of the broader society. They resolve this mild tension either by adhering to the religion or by "sneaking," doing the forbidden acts on the sly.

In the *third* pattern, the society rejects the religious group. In the extreme, as with the early Christians, political leaders may even try to destroy it. The Roman emperor declared the followers of Jesus to be enemies of Rome and ordered them to be hunted down and destroyed. In the United States, after mobs hounded the new Mormons out of several communities and then killed Joseph Smith, the founder of their religion, the Mormons decided to escape the dominant culture altogether. In 1847, they settled in a wilderness, in what is today Utah's Great Salt Lake Valley (Bridgwater 1953). Our opening vignette focused on another example, the destruction of the Branch Davidians by the U.S. government.

Religion in the United States

With its hundreds of denominations and sects, how can we generalize about religion in the United States? What do these many religious groups have in common? It certainly isn't doctrine (church teaching), but doctrine is not the focus of sociology. Sociologists, rather, are interested in the relationship between society and religion, and the role that religion plays in people's lives. To better understand religion in U.S. society, then, let's first find out who belongs to religious groups, and then look at the groups they belong to.

Characteristics of Members

About 65 percent of Americans belong to a church, synagogue, or mosque. What are the characteristics of people who hold formal membership in a religion?

Social Class   Religion in the United States is stratified by social class. As you can see from Figure 4 on the next page, some religious groups are "top-heavy," and others are "bottom-heavy." The most top-heavy are Jews and Episcopalians; the most bottom-heavy are Assembly of God, Southern Baptists, and Jehovah's Witnesses. This figure provides further confirmation that churchlike groups tend to appeal to people who are more economically successful, while the more sectlike groups attract the less successful.

From this figure, you can see how *status consistency* applies to religious groups. If a group ranks high (or low) on education, it is also likely to rank high (or low) on income and occupational prestige. Jews, for example, rank the highest on education, income, and occupational prestige, while Jehovah's Witnesses rank the lowest on these three measures of social class. As you can see, the Mormons are status inconsistent. They rank second in income, fourth in education, and tie for sixth in occupational prestige. Even more status inconsistent is the Assembly of God. Their members tie for third in occupational prestige but rank only eighth in income and ninth in education. This inconsistency is so jarring that there could be a problem with the sample.

Americans who change their social class also have a tendency to change their religion. Their new social class experiences create changes in their ideas about the world, molding new preferences for music and styles of speech. Upwardly mobile people are likely to seek a religion that draws more affluent people. An upwardly mobile Baptist, for example, may become a Methodist or a Presbyterian. For Roman Catholics, the situation is somewhat different. Because each parish is a geographical unit, Catholics who move into more affluent neighborhoods are also likely to be moving to a congregation that has a larger proportion of affluent members.

Figure 4 **Social Class and Religious Affiliation**

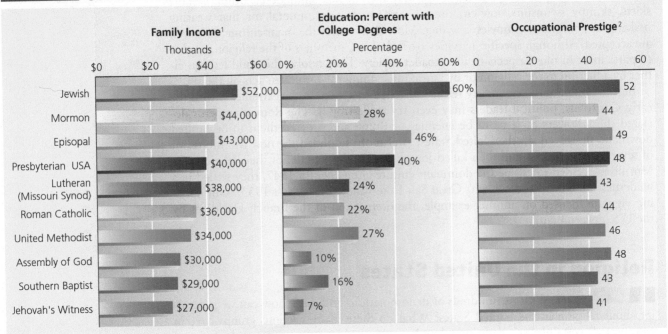

	Family Income[1] Thousands	Education: Percent with College Degrees Percentage	Occupational Prestige[2]
Jewish	$52,000	60%	52
Mormon	$44,000	28%	44
Episopal	$43,000	46%	49
Presbyterian USA	$40,000	40%	48
Lutheran (Missouri Synod)	$38,000	24%	43
Roman Catholic	$36,000	22%	44
United Methodist	$34,000	27%	46
Assembly of God	$30,000	10%	48
Southern Baptist	$29,000	16%	43
Jehovah's Witness	$27,000	7%	41

[1]Since the income data were reported, inflation has run approximately 24 percent.

[2]Higher numbers mean that more of the group's members work at occupations that have higher prestige, generally those that require more education and pay more. For more information on occupational prestige.

Source: By the author. Based on Smith and Faris 2005.

Race-Ethnicity It is common for religions around the world to be associated with race-ethnicity: Islam with Arabs, Judaism with Jews, Hinduism with Indians, and Confucianism with Chinese. Sometimes, as with Hinduism and Confucianism, a religion and a particular country are almost synonymous. Christianity is not associated with any one country, although it is associated primarily with Western culture.

In the United States, all major religious groups draw from the nation's many racial-ethnic groups. Like social class, however, race-ethnicity tends to cluster. People of Irish descent are likely to be Roman Catholics; those with Greek ancestors are likely to belong to the Greek Orthodox Church. African Americans are likely to be Protestants—more specifically, Baptists—or to belong to fundamentalist sects.

Although many churches are integrated, it is with good reason that Sunday morning between 10 and 11 A.M. has been called "the most segregated hour in the United States." African Americans tend to belong to African American churches, while most whites see only whites in theirs. The segregation of churches is based on custom, not on law.

Characteristics of Religious Groups

Let's examine features of the religious groups in the United States.

Diversity With its 300,000 congregations and hundreds of denominations, no religious group even comes close to being a dominant religion in the United States (*Statistical Abstract* 2007:Tables 73, 74). Table 1 illustrates some of this remarkable diversity.

Pluralism and Freedom It is the U.S. government's policy not to interfere with religions. The government's position is that its obligation is to ensure an environment in which people can worship as they see fit. Religious freedom is so extensive that anyone can start a church and proclaim himself or herself a minister, revelator, or any other desired term. If officials feel threatened by a religious group, however, the government grossly violates its hands-off policy, as with the Branch Davidians featured in our opening vignette. Since 9/11, the government has infiltrated mosques to monitor the activities of Arab immigrants (Elinson 2004). The Cultural Diversity box five pages back discusses other limits to this policy.

Competition and Recruitment The many religious groups of the United States compete for clients. They even advertise in the Yellow Pages of the telephone directory and insert appealing advertising—under the guise of news—in the religion section of the Saturday or Sunday edition of the local newspapers. Because of this intense competition, some groups modify their message, making it closer to what their successful competitors are offering (Greeley and Hout 1999).

Commitment Americans are a religious people, and 40 percent report that they attend religious services each week (Gallup Poll 2007). Sociologists have questioned this statistic, suggesting that the high totals are due to an *interviewer effect.* Because people want to please interviewers, they stretch the truth a bit. To find out, sociologists Stanley Presser and Linda Stinson (1998) examined people's written reports (no interviewer present) on how they spent their Sundays. They concluded that about 30 percent or so do attend church each week.

Whether the percentage of weekly church attendance is 30 or 40, Americans are a religious people, and they back up their commitment with generous support for religion and its charities. Each year Americans donate about $88 billion to religious causes (*Statistical Abstract* 2007:Table 567). To appreciate the significance of this huge figure, keep in mind that, unlike a country in which there is an ecclesia, those billions of dollars are not forced taxes, but money that people give away.

Toleration The general religious toleration of Americans can be illustrated by three prevailing attitudes: (1) "All religions have a right to exist—as long as they don't try to brainwash or hurt anyone." (2) "With all the religions to choose from, how can anyone tell which one—if any—is true?" (3) "Each of us may be convinced about the truth of our religion—and that is good—but don't be obnoxious by trying to convince others that you have the exclusive truth."

Fundamentalist Revival The fundamentalist Christian churches are undergoing a revival. They teach that the Bible is literally true and that salvation comes only through a personal relationship with Jesus Christ. They also denounce what they see as the degeneration of U.S. culture: flagrant sex on television, in movies, and in videos; abortion; corruption in public office; premarital sex, cohabitation; and drug abuse. Their answer to these problems is firm, simple, and direct: People whose hearts are changed through religious conversion will change their lives. The mainstream churches, which offer a more remote God and less emotional involvement, fail to meet the basic religious needs of large numbers of Americans. For an example, see the Down-to-Earth Sociology box on the next page.

One result is that mainstream churches are losing members while the fundamentalists are gaining them. Figure 5 two pages ahead depicts this change. The exception is the Roman Catholic Church, whose growth in North America is due primarily to heavy immigration from Mexico and other Roman Catholic countries.

The Electronic Church What began as a ministry to shut-ins and those who do not belong to a church blossomed into its own type of church. Its preachers, called "televangelists," reach millions of viewers and raise millions of dollars. Some of its most famous ministries are those of Robert Schuller (the "Crystal Cathedral") and Pat Robertson (the 700 Club).

Table 1 How U.S. Adults Identify with Religion[a]

Christian	160,000,000
Protestant	108,000,000
Baptist	34,000,000
No denomination	21,300,000
Methodist	14,000,000
Lutheran	9,600,000
Pentecostal	7,600,000
Presbyterian	5,600,000
Churches of Christ	4,000,000
Episcopalian/Anglican	3,500,000
Mormon	2,800,000
United Church of Christ	1,400,000
Jehovah's Witness	1,300,000
Evangelical Church	1,000,000
Seventh Day Adventist	700,000
Church of the Nazarene	550,000
Disciples of Christ	500,000
Reformed Churches	500,000
Church of the Brethren	360,000
Mennonite	350,000
Quakers	200,000
Other	350,000
Roman Catholic	51,000,000
Eastern Orthodox	650,000
Other Religions	8,000,000
Jews	2,800,000
Buddhist	1,100,000
Islamic	1,100,000
Hindu	800,000
Unitarian/Universalist	600,000
Pagan	150,000
Wican	150,000
Native American	100,000
Spiritualist	100,000
Other and unclassified	850,000
No Religion	30,000,000
Refused to answer	11,000,000

[a]All totals must be taken as approximate. Some groups ignore reporting forms. Totals are rounded to the nearest 100,000.

Sources: Niebuhr 2001 (for Muslim total); Statistical Abstract 2000:Table 74; 2007:Table 73.

The New Face of Religion: Pentecostals and the Spanish-Speaking Immigrants

THAT MILLIONS OF IMMIGRANTS from Spanish-speaking countries have become part of the U.S. social scene is not news. That most of them are poor isn't news, either. Almost all the immigrants who came before them were poor, too.

What is news is that many of these Latinos are abandoning the Roman Catholic religion and are embracing a form of Protestantism called Pentecostalism. Pentecostals, often referred to by the derisive term, holy rollers, believe that the Bible is the inerrant word of God. Taking the Bible literally, they believe there is a real heaven and hell. They lay hands on each other and pray for healings. They expect God to act in their lives in a very personal way. They speak in tongues.

And they are noisily joyful about their faith.

Go into one of their storefront churches, such as those on Amsterdam Avenue in New York City—or in any of the thousands of little churches that are springing up around the country. You'll hear music and clapping—a lot of it and loud. When the preachers preach, they show their enthusiasm to the message. They talk about a real God who is personally concerned about people's lives and the troubles they are going through, about the heaven God has prepared for them. The preachers warn the congregation, too, about the dangers of sins—the adultery that lurks, seductively beckoning them to fall from a righteous way of life; the downfall of drugs and alcohol; the dead end of laziness and extravagance; the value of thrift and hard work. The congregation breaks out into "Amens." "Amen, brother! Bring it on!" will shout one person, while another says, "Yes, sister. Tell it like it is!"

The preachers know what they are talking about. They, too, work at factory jobs during the day. They know what it is to sweat for a living and that J-O-B is really spelled B-R-O-K-E. Cantankerous bosses, unpaid bills, and paychecks that run out before the month does are part of their own lives. They live what they are preaching.

The music is upbeat. The drums and guitars sound like the salsa music you hear on the radio, but this with religious lyrics. The tempo, though, is the same. People clap and sway to the rhythmic sounds.

Some break out into tongues, strange sounds that some pray silently, that others shout out. Some tongues,

Angel Franco/The New York Times

Prayer and blessing at the Ark of Salvation for the New Milennium, a storefront church in New York City.

they believe, are messages straight from God. But no one can understand them unless someone else is given the interpretation. When this happens, people listen intently for what God has to say to them personally.

This is quite unlike the Roman Catholic religion that most of them have left behind as they adapt to their new land. Here, they say, they find a solidarity that gives them purpose in life, that encourages them to continue to work despite facing one obstacle after another, that strengthens them to resist the drugs and sex that flood their neighborhoods.

It isn't just for an hour on Sunday mornings. These people come night after night, some go every night of the week, for the comfort and encouragement of the message and music—and the opportunity to give expression to their emotions among a like-minded people.

This is the new face of religion. Pentecostalism is not some aberration, some flash in the pan. It is the fastest-growing religion in the United States, and there are perhaps 400 million Pentecostals worldwide. This religion is making such an impact that about 850,000 New Yorkers claim to be Pentecostal. That's one out of every ten (Gonzalez 2007). Not all are Latinos, of course, but about a third of the New York Pentecostals are.

Nor are all Pentecostals poor. This form of Protestantism is also being welcomed by some of the middle class and the educated. But the middle-class arms aren't open as wide. The appeal is primarily to the poor. When the poor make the transition to the middle class—as their religion, with its emphasis on work and thrift will help them do—they are likely to seek new forms of religious expression.

When this happens, we can expect that Pentecostalism will also adapt, that the form will remain recognizable, but the fervor will be lost. For now, though, it is the fervor—the intensity that connects the individuals to God and to one another—that is the driving force of this religion. The Pentecostals would phrase this a little differently. They would say that the fervor is merely the expression of the driving force of their religion, which is the Holy Spirit.

Either way you put it, these people are on fire. And that fire is burning a new imprint on the face of religion.

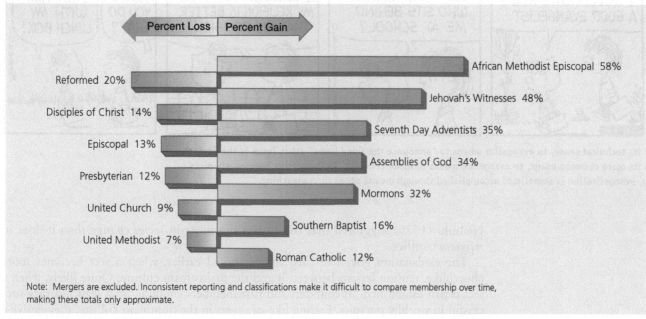

Figure 5 **U.S. Churches: Gains and Losses in Ten Years**

Percent Loss | Percent Gain

African Methodist Episcopal 58%
Reformed 20%
Jehovah's Witnesses 48%
Disciples of Christ 14%
Seventh Day Adventists 35%
Episcopal 13%
Assemblies of God 34%
Presbyterian 12%
Mormons 32%
United Church 9%
Southern Baptist 16%
United Methodist 7%
Roman Catholic 12%

Note: Mergers are excluded. Inconsistent reporting and classifications make it difficult to compare membership over time, making these totals only approximate.

Source: By the author. Recomputed from Jones et al. 2002.

Many local ministers view the electronic church as a competitor. They complain that it competes for the attention and dollars of their members. Leaders of the electronic church reply that the money goes to good causes and that through its conversions, the electronic church feeds members into the local churches, strengthening, not weakening them.

The Internet and Religion   As with so many aspects of life, the Internet is having an impact on religion. We will focus on this change in the concluding section. For now, let's look at secularization.

Secularization of Religion and Culture

The term *secularization* refers to the process by which worldly affairs replace spiritual interests. (The term **secular** means "belonging to the world and its affairs.") As we shall see, both religions and cultures can become secularized.

The Secularization of Religion

As the model, fashionably slender, paused before the head table of African American community leaders, her gold necklace glimmering above the low-cut bodice of her emerald-green dress, the hostess, a member of the Church of God in Christ, said, "It's now OK to wear more revealing clothes—as long as it's done in good taste." Then she added, "You couldn't do this when I was a girl, but now it's OK—and you can still worship God." (Author's files)

When I heard these words, I grabbed a napkin and quickly jotted them down, my sociological imagination stirred by their deep implication. As strange as it may seem, this simple event pinpoints the essence of why the Christian churches in the United States have splintered. Let's see how this could possibly be.

The simplest explanation for why Christians don't have just one church, or at most several, instead of the hundreds of sects and denominations that dot the U.S. landscape, is disagreements about doctrine (church teaching). As theologian and sociologist Richard Niebuhr pointed out, however, there are many ways of settling doctrinal disputes besides splintering off and forming other religious organizations.

secular belonging to the world and its affairs

In its technical sense, to evangelize means to "announce the Good News" (that Jesus is the Savior). In its more common usage, to evangelize means to make converts. As *Peanuts* so humorously picks up, evangelization is sometimes accomplished through means other than preaching.

Niebuhr (1929) suggested that the answer lies more in *social* change than it does in *religious* conflict.

The explanation goes like this. As was noted earlier, when a sect becomes more churchlike, tension lessens between it and the mainstream culture. Quite likely, when a sect is first established, its founders and first members are poor, or at least not very successful in worldly pursuits. Feeling like strangers in the dominant culture, they derive a good part of their identity from their religion. In their church services and lifestyle, they stress how different their values are from those of the dominant culture. They are also likely to emphasize the joys of the coming afterlife, when they will be able to escape from their present pain.

As time passes, the group's values—such as frugality and the avoidance of gambling, alcohol, and drugs—help the members become successful. As their children attain more education and become more middle class, members of this group grow more respectable in the eyes of society. They no longer experience the alienation that was felt by the founders of their group. Life's burdens don't seem as heavy, and the need for relief through an afterlife becomes less pressing. Similarly, the pleasures of the world no longer appear as threatening to the "truth." As is illustrated by the woman at the fashion show, people then attempt to harmonize their religious beliefs with their changing ideas about the culture.

This process is called the **secularization of religion**—shifting the focus from spiritual matters to the affairs of this world. Anyone familiar with today's mainstream Methodists would be surprised to know that they once were a sect. Methodists used to ban playing cards, dancing, and going to movies. They even considered circuses to be sinful. As Methodists grew more middle class, however, they began to change their views on sin. They started to dismantle the barriers that they had constructed between themselves and the outside world (Finke and Stark 1992).

Secularization leads to a splintering of the group, for adjusting to the secular culture displeases some of the group's members, especially those who have had less worldly success. These people still feel a gulf between themselves and the broader culture. For them, tension and hostility continue to be real. They see secularization as a desertion of the group's fundamental truths, a "selling out" to the secular world.

After futile attempts by die-hards to bring the group back to its senses, the group splinters. Those who protested the secularization of Methodism, for example, were kicked out—even though *they* represented the values around which the group had organized in the first place. The dissatisfied—who have come to be viewed as complainers—then form a sect that once again stresses its differences from the world; the need for more personal, emotional religious experiences; and salvation from the pain of living in this world. As time passes, the cycle repeats: adjustment to the dominant culture by some, continued dissatisfaction by others, and further splintering.

This process is not limited to sects, but also occurs in churches. When U.S. Episcopalians elected an openly gay bishop in 2003, some pastors and congregations

secularization of religion the replacement of a religion's spiritual or "other worldly" concerns with concerns about "this world"

splintered from the U.S. church and affiliated with the more conservative African archbishops. In an ironic twist, this made them mission congregations from Africa. Sociologists have not yet compared the income or wealth of those who stayed with the group that elected the gay bishop and those who joined the splinter groups. If such a study is done and it turns out that there is no difference, we will have to modify the secularization thesis.

The Secularization of Culture Just as religion can secularize, so can culture. Sociologists use the term **secularization of culture** to refer to a culture that was once heavily influenced by religion, but no longer retains much of that influence. The United States provides an example.

Despite attempts to reinterpret history, the Pilgrims and most of the founders of the United States were highly religious people. The Pilgrims were even convinced that God had guided them to found a new religious community whose members would follow the Bible. Similarly, many of the framers of the U.S. Constitution felt that God had guided them to develop a new form of government.

The clause in the Constitution that mandates the separation of church and state was *not* an attempt to keep religion out of government, but a (successful) device to avoid the establishment of a state religion like that in England. Here, people were to have the freedom to worship as they wished. The assumption of the founders was even more specific—that Protestantism represented the true religion.

The phrase in the Declaration of Independence, "All men are *created* equal," refers to a central belief in God as the creator of humanity. A member of the clergy opened Congress with prayer. Many colonial laws were based on principles derived explicitly from the Old and New Testaments. In some colonies, blasphemy was a crime, as was failing to observe the Sabbath. Similarly, sexual affairs were a crime; in some places adultery carried the death penalty. Even public kissing between husband and wife was considered an offense, punishable by placement in the public stocks (Frumkin 1967). In other words, religion permeated U.S. culture. It was part and parcel of how the colonists saw life. Their lives, laws, and other aspects of the culture reflected their religious beliefs.

Today, U.S. culture has secularized; the influence of religion on public affairs has greatly diminished. No longer are laws based on religious principles. It has even become illegal to post the Ten Commandments in civic buildings. Overall, ideas of what is "generally good" have replaced religion as an organizing principle for the culture.

Underlying the secularization of culture is *modernization,* a term that refers to a society industrializing, urbanizing, developing mass education, and adopting science and advanced technology. Science and advanced technology bring with them a secular view of the world that begins to permeate society. They provide explanations for many aspects of life that people traditionally attributed to God. As a consequence, people come to depend much less on religion to explain life. Birth and death—and everything in between, from life's problems to its joys—are attributed to natural causes. When a society has secularized thoroughly, even religious leaders may turn to answers provided by biology, philosophy, psychology, sociology, and so on.

Although the secularization of U.S. culture means that religion has become less important in public life, *personal* religious involvement among Americans has not diminished. Rather, it has increased (Finke and Stark 1992). About 86 percent believe there is a God, and 81 percent believe there is a heaven. Not only do 63 percent claim membership in a church or synagogue, but, as we saw, on any given weekend somewhere between 30 and 40 percent of all Americans attend a worship service (Gallup 1990, 2007).

Table 2 underscores the paradox. Look at how religious participation has increased while the culture has secularized. The proportion of Americans who belong to a church or synagogue is now about *four* times higher than it was when the country was founded. Church membership, of course, is only a rough indicator of how significant religion is in people's lives. Some church members are not particularly religious, while many intensely religious people—Lincoln, for one—never join a church.

Table 2 **Growth in Religious Membership**

Americans Who Belong To a Church or Synagogue	
Year	**Percentage Who Claim Membership**
1776	17%
1860	37%
1890	45%
1926	58%
1975	71%
2000	68%
2005	65%

Note: The sources do not contain data on mosque membership.

Sources: Finke and Stark 1992; *Statistical Abstract* 2002:Table 64; Gallup Poll 2005.

The Future of Religion

A group of prominent intellectuals once foresaw an end to religion. As science advanced, they said, it would explain everything. It would transform human thought and replace religion, which was merely superstitious thinking left over from more primitive times. In 1966 Anthony Wallace, one of the world's best-known anthropologists at the time, confidently made the following prediction:

> The evolutionary future of religion is extinction. Belief in supernatural beings . . . will become only an interesting historical memory. . . . doomed to die out, all over the world, as a result of the increasing adequacy and diffusion of scientific knowledge.

Wallace and the many other social analysts who took this position were wrong. Religion thrives in the most advanced scientific nations, in capitalist and in socialist countries. It is evident that these analysts did not understand the fundamental significance of religion in people's lives.

Humans are inquiring creatures. They are aware that they have a past, a present, and a future. They reflect on their experiences to try to make sense of them. One of the questions people ponder as they reflect on life concerns the purpose of it all. Why are we born? Is there an afterlife? If so, where are we going, and what will it be like when we get there? Out of these concerns arises this question: If there is a God, what does God want of us in this life? Does God have a preference about how we should live?

Science, including sociology, cannot answer such questions. By its very nature, science cannot tell us about four main concerns that many people have:

1. *The existence of God.* About this, science has nothing to say. No test tube has either isolated God or refuted God's existence.
2. *The purpose of life.* Although science can provide a definition of life and describe the characteristics of living organisms, it has nothing to say about ultimate purpose.
3. *An afterlife.* Science can offer no information on this at all, for it has no tests to prove or disprove a "hereafter."
4. *Morality.* Science can demonstrate the consequences of behavior, but not the moral superiority of one action compared with another. This means that science cannot even prove that loving your family and neighbor is superior to hurting and killing them. Science can describe death and measure consequences, but it cannot determine the moral superiority of any action, even in such an extreme example.

There is no doubt that religion will last as long as humanity lasts, for what could replace it? And if something did, and answered such questions, would it not be religion under a different name?

To glimpse the cutting edge of religious change, we'll close with a look at the online marketing of religion.

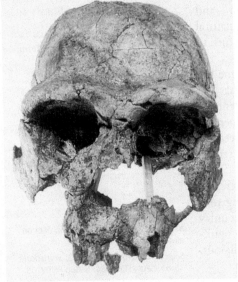

A basic principle of symbolic interactionism is that meaning is not inherent in an object or event, but is determined by people as they interpret the object or event. Old bones and fossils are an excellent illustration of this principle. Does this skull of homo erectus "prove" evolution? Does it "disprove" creation? Such "proof" and "disproof" lie in the eye of the beholder, based on the background assumptions by which it is interpreted.

God on the Net: The Online Marketing of Religion

You want to pray right there at the Holy Land, but you can't leave home? No problem. Buy our special telephone card—now available at your local 7-11. Just record your prayer, and we will broadcast it via the Internet at the site you choose. Press one for the holy site of Jerusalem, press two for the holy site of the Sea of Galilee, press three for the birthplace of Jesus, press four for . . . . (Rhoads 2007)

This service is offered by a company in Israel. No discrimination. Open to Jews and Christians alike. Maybe with expansion plans for Muslims. Maybe to anyone, as long as they can pay $10 for a two-minute card.

Erin Polzin, a 20-year-old college student, listens to a Lutheran worship service on the radio, confesses online, and uses PayPal to tithe. "I don't like getting up early," she says. "This is like going to church without really having to" (Bernstein 2003).

Going to church in your pajamas without even having to comb your hair does have a certain appeal.

And this bothers some religious leaders. They are concerned about what they call the "faithful but lazy." But, then, they always have been. The Internet is just changing the form of the "laziness."

The Internet is doing much more than this. Some say that the Net has put us on the verge of a religious reformation as big as the one set off by Gutenberg's invention of the printing press. This sounds like an exaggeration, but perhaps it is true. We'll see. The Net certainly has become popular for spiritual pursuits (Larsen 2001).

Muslims in France download sermons and join an invisible community of worshippers at virtual mosques. Jews in Sweden type messages that fellow believers in Jerusalem download and insert in the Western Wall. Christians in the United States make digital donations to the Crystal Cathedral. Buddhists in Japan seek enlightenment online. The Internet helps to level the pulpit: On the Net, the leader of a pagan group can compete directly with the Pope.

The Internet is also making religious rebellion easier—and harder for organizations to punish their rebels. Jacques Gaillot is a French Roman Catholic bishop who takes theological positions that upset the church hierarchy. He says that the clergy should marry, women should be ordained, and homosexual partnerships should be blessed. Pope John Paul II exiled him to the Saharan desert of North Africa, a strategy that used to work well to silence dissidents. With our new navigability of space and time, however, in his remote outpost Gaillot logs onto the Internet, where he preaches to a virtual congregation via Real Audio (Huffstutter 1998; Williams 2003).

The Net poses spiritual risks, too. There's always the chance that while you are surfing for religious answers, you'll come across one of those ubiquitous porn sites. But not if you are in the Philippines and using its largest Internet service provider (Sindayen 2001). It is run by the Catholic Bishops' Conference. If someone gives in to temptation and tries to tap into one of the forbidden destinations, up pops this message: "Thank God you're not able to access that bad site."

No one knows the outcome, but the times, they are a-changin'. Because of the Net, we now have:

Churches that exist only in cyberspace

The Internet—and a credit card—can connect believers to holy sites, where prayers can be written out and placed. Shown here is a prayer being inserted in the Western Wall, the last remnant of the Jewish Second Temple, which was destroyed by the Romans in 70 A.D.

©Israel images/Alamy

Chat rooms directed by rabbis, priests, ministers, imams, and leaders of witchcraft

Online donations by credit card and Internet pay providers

Online counseling for spiritual problems

E-mailing of prayers

A virtual church in which you transform yourself into a computer image. You can direct your computer character to walk around the virtual church, to talk to other computer images if you are bored, or if you are there for religious purposes, to kneel and pray (Feder 2004).

for your Consideration

Do you think that virtual religion can satisfy people's religious needs? How can it replace the warm embrace of fellow believers? Can it bring comfort to someone who is grieving for a loved one?

We are gazing into the future. How do you think this new medium will affect our religious lives? How do you think it might change religion?

Summary *and* Review

What Is Religion?
Durkheim identified three essential characteristics of religion: beliefs that set the **sacred** apart from the **profane, rituals**, and a moral community (a **church**).

The Functionalist Perspective
What are the functions and dysfunctions of religion?
Among the functions of religion are answering questions about ultimate meaning, providing emotional comfort, social solidarity, guidelines for everyday life, social control, adaptation, support for the government, and fostering social change. Non-religious groups or activities that provide these functions are called **functional equivalents** of religion. Among the dysfunctions of religion are religious persecution and war and terrorism.

The Symbolic Interactionist Perspective
What aspects of religion do symbolic interactionists study?
Symbolic interactionists focus on the meanings of religion for its followers. They examine religious symbols, rituals, beliefs, **religious experiences,** and the sense of community that religion provides.

The Conflict Perspective
What aspects of religion do conflict theorists study?
Conflict theorists examine the relationship of religion to social inequalities, especially how religion reinforces a society's stratification system.

Religion and the Spirit of Capitalism
What does the spirit of capitalism have to do with religion?
Max Weber saw religion as a primary source of social change. He analyzed how Protestantism gave rise to the **Protestant ethic,** which stimulated what he called the **spirit of capitalism.** The result was capitalism, which transformed society.

The World's Major Religions
What are the world's major religions?
Judaism, Christianity, and Islam, all **monotheistic** religions, can be traced to the same Old Testament roots. Hinduism, the chief religion of India, has no specific founder, but Judaism (Abraham), Christianity (Jesus), Islam (Muhammad), Buddhism (Gautama), and Confucianism (K'ung Fu-tsu) do. Specific teachings and history of these six religions are reviewed in the text.

Types of Religious Groups
What types of religious groups are there?
Sociologists divide religious groups into cults, sects, churches, and ecclesias. All religions began as **cults.** Those that survive tend to develop into **sects** and eventually into **churches.** Sects, often led by **charismatic leaders,** are unstable. Some are perceived as threats and are persecuted by the state. **Ecclesias,** or state religions, are rare.

Religion in the United States
What are the main characteristics of religion in the United States?
Membership varies by social class and race-ethnicity. The major characteristics are diversity, pluralism and freedom, competition, commitment, toleration, a fundamentalist revival, and the electronic church.

What is the connection between secularization of religion and the splintering of churches?
Secularization of religion, a change in a religion's focus from spiritual matters to concerns of "this world," is the key to understanding why churches divide. Basically, as a cult or sect changes to accommodate its members' upward social class mobility, it changes into a church. Left dissatisfied are members who are not upwardly mobile. They tend to splinter off and form a new cult or sect, and the cycle repeats itself. Cultures permeated by religion also secularize. This, too, leaves many people dissatisfied and promotes social change.

The Future of Religion
Although industrialization led to the **secularization of culture,** this did not spell the end of religion, as many social analysts assumed it would. Because science cannot answer questions about ultimate meaning, the existence of God or an afterlife, or provide guidelines for morality, the need for religion will remain. In any foreseeable future, religion will prosper. The Internet is likely to have far-reaching consequences on religion.

Thinking Critically

1. Since 9/11, many people have wondered how anyone can use religion to defend or promote terrorism. How does the Down-to-Earth Sociology box on terrorism and the mind of God help to answer this question?

2. How has secularization affected religion and culture in the United States (or of your country of birth)?

3. Why is religion likely to remain a strong feature of U.S. life—and remain strong in people's lives around the globe?

Additional Resources

What can you use MySocLab for?  www.mysoclab.com

- **Study and Review:** Pre- and Post-Tests, Practice Tests, Flash Cards, Individualized Study Plans.
- **Current Events:** *Sociology in the News,* the daily *New York Times,* and more.

- **Research and Writing:** *Research Navigator, Writing About Sociology,* and more,

Where Can I Read More on This Topic?

Ault, James M. *Spirit and Flesh: Life in a Fundamentalist Baptist Church.* New York: Alfred A. Knopf, 2004. This participant observation study of an independent Baptist congregation provides insight into the initiation and maintenance of faith and relationships.

Cateura, Linda Brandi, and Omid Safi. *Voices of American Muslims.* New York: Hippocrene Books, 2006. U.S. Muslims describe their religion, experiences with suspicion and misunderstandings, and, in this heated period of terrorist attacks by Muslims, their devotion to the United States.

Gilman, Sander. *Jewish Frontiers: Essays on Bodies, Histories, and Identities.* New York: Macmillan, 2003. Analyzes Jewish identity from the framework of living on a frontier, and the representation of this identity in the mass media.

Juergensmeyer, Mark. *Terror in the Mind of God: The Global Rise of Religious Violence,* 3rd ed. Berkeley: University of California Press, 2003. The author's summaries of religious violence provide a rich background for understanding this behavior.

McRoberts, Omar M. *Streets of Glory: Church and Community in a Black Urban Neighborhood.* Chicago: University of Chicago Press, 2003. Four Corners, one of the toughest areas of Boston, contains twenty-nine mostly storefront churches. The author finds most of them are attended and run by people who do not live in the neighborhood and who have little or no attachment to the surrounding area.

Smith, Christian, and Melinda Denton. *Soul Searching: The Religious and Spiritual Life of American Teenagers.* Oxford: Oxford University

Press, 2006. In this survey the spiritual life of U.S. teenagers, the authors let youth express the meaning of their spiritual life in gtheir own words.

Thibodeau, David, and Leon Whiteson. *A Place Called Waco: A Survivor's Story.* New York: Public Affairs, 2000. A first-person account of life inside the Branch Davidian compound, written by one of only four survivors of the fire who were not sentenced to prison.

Wolfe, Alan. *The Transformation of American Religion: How We Actually Live Our Faith.* New York: The Free Press, 2004. The author's thesis is that individualism is changing the shape and substance of religion in the United States, minimizing doctrine and maximizing feelings and personal satisfactions.

Zellner, William W., and William M. Kephart. *Extraordinary Groups: An Examination of Unconventional Lifestyles,* 7th ed. New York: Worth, 2001. This sketch of the history and characteristics of eight groups (the Old Order Amish, Oneida Community, Gypsies, Church of Christ Scientist, Hasidim, Father Divine Movement, Mormons, and Jehovah's Witnesses) illustrates how groups can maintain unconventional beliefs and practices.

Journals

These journals publish articles that focus on the sociology of religion: *Journal for the Scientific Study of Religion, Review of Religious Research,* and *Sociological Analysis: A Journal in the Sociology of Religion.*

Deviance and Social Control

From Chapter 8 of *Sociology: A Down-to-Earth Approach*, 9/e. James M. Henslin. Copyright © 2008 by Pearson Education.

Deviance and Social Control

Vincent Van Gogh, *Prisoners Exercising*, 1890

In just a few moments I was to meet my first Yanomamö, my first primitive man. What would it be like? . . . I looked up (from my canoe) and gasped when I saw a dozen burly, naked, filthy, hideous men staring at us down the shafts of their drawn arrows. Immense wads of green tobacco were stuck between their lower teeth and lips, making them look even more hideous, and strands of dark-green slime dripped or hung from their noses. We arrived at the village while the men were blowing a hallucinogenic drug up their noses. One of the side effects of the drug is a runny nose. The mucus is always saturated with the green powder, and the Indians usually let it run freely from their nostrils. . . . I just sat there holding my notebook, helpless and pathetic . . .

The whole situation was depressing, and I wondered why I ever decided to switch from civil engineering to anthropology in the first place. . . . (Soon) I was covered with red pigment, the result of a dozen or so

They would "clean" their hands by spitting slimy tobacco juice into them.

Corbis Sygma

complete examinations. . . . These examinations capped an otherwise grim day. The Indians would blow their noses into their hands, flick as much of the mucus off that would separate in a snap of the wrist, wipe the residue into their hair, and then carefully examine my face, arms, legs, hair, and the contents of my pockets. I said (in their language), "Your hands are dirty"; my comments were met by the Indians in the following way: they would "clean" their hands by spitting a quantity of slimy tobacco juice into them, rub them together, and then proceed with the examination.

This is how Napoleon Chagnon describes the cultural shock he felt when he met the Yanomamö tribe of the rain forests of Brazil. His ensuing months of fieldwork continued to bring surprise after surprise, and often Chagnon (1977) could hardly believe his eyes—or his nose.

deviance the violation of rules or norms

crime the violation of norms written into law

stigma "blemishes" that discredit a person's claim to a "normal" identity

If you were to list the deviant behaviors of the Yanomamö, what would you include? The way they appear naked in public? Use hallucinogenic drugs? Let mucus hang from their noses? Or the way they rub hands filled with mucus, spittle, and tobacco juice over a frightened stranger who doesn't dare to protest? Perhaps. But it isn't this simple, for as we shall see, deviance is relative.

What Is Deviance?

Sociologists use the term **deviance** to refer to any violation of norms, whether the infraction is as minor as driving over the speed limit, as serious as murder, or as humorous as Chagnon's encounter with the Yanomamö. This deceptively simple definition takes us to the heart of the sociological perspective on deviance, which sociologist Howard S. Becker (1966) described this way: *It is not the act itself, but the reactions to the act, that make something deviant.* What Chagnon saw disturbed him, but to the Yanomamö those same behaviors represented normal, everyday life. What was deviant to Chagnon was *conformist* to the Yanomamö. From their viewpoint, you *should* check out strangers the way they did, and nakedness is good, as are hallucinogenic drugs and letting mucus be "natural."

Chagnon's abrupt introduction to the Yanomamö allows us to see the *relativity of deviance*, a major point made by symbolic interactionists. Because different groups have different norms, *what is deviant to some is not deviant to others.* (See the photo on this page.) This principle holds both *within* a society as well as across cultures. Thus, acts that are acceptable in one culture—or in one group within a society—may be considered deviant in another culture, or by another group within the same society. This idea is explored in the Cultural Diversity box on the next page.

This principle also applies to a specific form of deviance known as **crime,** the violation of rules that have been written into law. In the extreme, an act that is applauded by one group may be so despised by another group that it is punishable by death. Making a huge profit on business deals is one example. Americans who do this are admired. Like Donald Trump, Jack Welch, and Warren Buffet, they may even write books about their exploits. In China, however, until recently this same act was considered a crime called *profiteering.* Anyone who was found guilty was hanged in a public square as a lesson to all.

Unlike the general public, sociologists use the term *deviance* nonjudgmentally, to refer to any act to which people respond negatively. When sociologists use this term, it does not mean that they agree that an act is bad, just that people judge it negatively. To sociologists, then, *all* of us are deviants of one sort or another, for we all violate norms from time to time.

To be considered deviant, a person does not even have to *do* anything. Sociologist Erving Goffman (1963) used the term **stigma** to refer to characteristics that discredit people. These include violations of norms of ability (blindness, deafness, mental handicaps) and norms of appearance (a facial birthmark, obesity). They also include involuntary memberships, such as being a victim of AIDS or the brother of a rapist. The stigma can become a person's master status, defining him or her as deviant. A master status cuts across all other statuses that a person occupies.

©James M. Henslin

I took this photo on the outskirts of Hyderabad, India. Is this man deviant? If this were a U.S. street, he would be. But here? No houses have running water in his neighborhood, and the men, women, and children bathe at the neighborhood water pump. This man, then, would not be deviant in his culture. And yet, he is actually mugging for my camera, making the three bystanders laugh. Does this additional factor make this a scene of deviance?

How Norms Make Social Life Possible

No human group can exist without norms, for *norms make social life possible by making behavior predictable.* What would life be like if you could not predict what others would do? Imagine for a moment that you have gone to a store to purchase milk:

Suppose the clerk says, "I won't sell you any milk. We're overstocked with soda, and I'm not going to sell anyone milk until our soda inventory is reduced."

HUMAN SEXUALITY ILLUSTRATES how a group's *definition* of an act, not the act itself, determines whether it will be considered deviant. Let's look at some examples reported by anthropologist Robert Edgerton (1976).

Human Sexuality in Cross-Cultural Perspective

Norms of sexual behavior vary so widely around the world that what is considered normal in one society may be considered deviant in another. In Kenya, a group called the Pokot place high emphasis on sexual pleasure, and they expect that both a husband and wife will reach orgasm. If a husband does not satisfy his wife, he is in trouble—especially if she thinks that his failure is because of adultery. If this is so, the wife and her female friends will sneak up on her husband when he is asleep. The women will tie him up, shout obscenities at him, beat him, and then urinate on him. As a final gesture of their contempt, before releasing him, they will slaughter and eat his favorite ox. The husband's hours of painful humiliation are intended to make him more dutiful concerning his wife's conjugal rights.

Pokot married man, northern Kenya

Africa Photobank/Alamy

that sexual relations should take place exclusively between husband and wife. Yet the *only* person in one Zapotec community who had not had any extramarital affairs was considered deviant. Evidently, these people have an unspoken understanding that married couples will engage in affairs, but be discreet about them. When a wife learns that her husband is having an affair, she usually has one, too.

One Zapotec wife did not follow this covert norm. Instead, she would praise her own virtue to her husband—and then voice the familiar "headache" excuse. She also told other wives the names of the women their husbands were sleeping with. As a result, this virtuous woman was condemned by everyone in the village. Clearly, real norms can conflict with ideal norms—another illustration of the gap between ideal and real culture.

for your Consideration

How do the behaviors of the Pokot wife and husband look from the perspective of U.S. norms? Are there U.S. norms in the first place? How about

People can also become deviants for failing to understand that the group's ideal norms may not be its real norms. As with many groups, the Zapotec Indians of Mexico profess the Zapotec woman? The rest of the Zapotec community? How does cultural relativity apply?

You don't like it, but you decide to buy a case of soda. At the checkout, the clerk says, "I hope you don't mind, but there's a $5 service charge on every fifteenth customer." You, of course, are the fifteenth.

Just as you start to leave, another clerk stops you and says, "We're not working any more. We decided to have a party." Suddenly a CD player begins to blast, and everyone in the store begins to dance. "Oh, good, you've brought the soda," says a different clerk, who takes your package and passes sodas all around.

Life is not like this, of course. You can depend on grocery clerks to sell you milk. You can also depend on paying the same price as everyone else, and not being forced to attend a party in the store. Why can you depend on this? Because we are socialized to follow norms, to play the basic roles that society assigns to us.

Without norms, we would have social chaos. Norms lay out the basic guidelines for how we should play our roles and interact with others. In short, norms bring about **social order,** a group's customary social arrangements. Our lives are based on these arrangements, which is why deviance often is perceived as threatening: Deviance undermines predictability, the foundation of social life. Consequently, human groups develop a system of **social control**—formal and informal means of enforcing norms.

social order a group's usual and customary social arrangements, on which its members depend and on which they base their lives

social control a group's formal and informal means of enforcing its norms

Sanctions

People do not enforce folkways strictly, but they become upset when people break mores (MORE-rays). Expressions of disapproval of deviance, called **negative sanctions,** range from frowns and gossip for breaking folkways to imprisonment and capital punishment for breaking mores. In general, the more seriously the group takes a norm, the harsher the penalty for violating it. In contrast, **positive sanctions**—from smiles to formal awards—are used to reward people for conforming to norms. Getting a raise is a positive sanction; being fired is a negative sanction. Getting an *A* in intro to sociology is a positive sanction; getting an *F* is a negative one.

Most negative sanctions are informal. You might stare if you observe someone dressed in what you consider to be inappropriate clothing, or you might gossip if a married person you know spends the night with someone other than his or her spouse. Whether you consider the breaking of a norm merely an amusing matter that warrants no severe sanction or a serious infraction that does, however, depends on your perspective. If a woman appears at your college graduation ceremonies in a bikini, you may stare and laugh, but if this is *your* mother, you are likely to feel that different sanctions are appropriate. Similarly, if it is *your* father who spends the night with an 18-year-old college freshman, you are likely to do more than gossip.

Shaming and Degradation Ceremonies

Shaming is another sanction. Shaming is especially effective when members of a primary group use it. For this reason, parents sometimes use it to keep children in line. Shaming is also effective in small communities, where the individual's reputation is at stake. As our society grew large and urban, its sense of community diminished, and shaming lost its effectiveness. Shaming seems to be making a comeback. One Arizona sheriff makes the men in his jail wear pink underwear (Boxer 2001). Digital cameras and camera cell phones have encouraged online shaming sites. They feature bad drivers, older men who leer at teenaged girls, and dog walkers who don't pick up their dog's poop (Saranow 2007). Some sites include photos of the offenders, as well as their addresses and phone numbers.

In small communities, shaming can be the centerpiece of the enforcement of norms, with the violator marked as a deviant and held up for all the world to see. In Nathaniel Hawthorne's *The Scarlet Letter*, town officials forced Hester Prynne to wear a scarlet A sewn on her dress. The A stood for *adulteress*. Wherever she went, Prynne had to wear this badge of shame, and the community expected her to wear it every day for the rest of her life.

Sociologist Harold Garfinkel (1956) gave the name **degradation ceremony** to formal attempts to brand someone as an outsider. The individual is called to account before the group, witnesses denounce him or her, the offender is pronounced guilty, and steps are taken to strip the individual of his or her identity as a group member. In some court martials, officers who are found guilty stand at attention before their peers while the insignia of rank are ripped from their uniforms. This procedure dramatizes that the individual is no longer a member of the group. Although Hester Prynne was not banished from the group physically, she was banished morally; her degradation ceremony proclaimed her a *moral* outcast from the community. The scarlet A marked her as "not one" of them.

Although we don't use scarlet A's today, informal degradation ceremonies still occur. Consider what happened to Joseph Gray (Chivers 2001):

Joseph Gray, a fifteen-year veteran of the New York City police force, was involved in a fatal accident. The *New York Times* and New York television stations reported that Gray had spent the afternoon drinking in a topless bar before plowing his car into a vehicle carrying a pregnant woman, her son, and her sister. All three died. Gray was accused of manslaughter and drunk driving. (He was later convicted on both counts.)

The news media kept hammering this story to the public. Three weeks later, as Gray left police headquarters after resigning from his job, an angry crowd gathered around

Dion Ogust/The Image Works

There is no norm that says, "Do not hang in the air, suspended by flesh hooks," as this woman is doing at a tattoo festival in Woodstock, New York. What sanctions might come into play if she did this at work during her lunch hour? Why the difference?

negative sanction an expression of disapproval for breaking a norm, ranging from a mild, informal reaction such as a frown to a formal reaction such as a prison sentence or an execution

positive sanction a reward or positive reaction for following norms, ranging from a smile to a prize

degradation ceremony a term coined by Harold Garfinkel to describe rituals designed to remake the self by stripping away an individual's particular social identity and stamping a new one in its place

DEVIANCE AND SOCIAL CONTROL

him. Gray hung his head in public disgrace as Victor Manuel Herrera, whose wife and son were killed in the crash, followed him, shouting, "You're a murderer!"

■ ■ ▲ ■
IN SUM In sociology, the term *deviance* refers to all violations of social rules, regardless of their seriousness. The term is not a judgment about the behavior. Deviance is relative, for what is deviant in one group may be conformist in another. Consequently, we must consider deviance from *within* a group's own framework, for it is *their* meanings that underlie their behavior. The following Thinking Critically section focuses on this issue.

Thinking Critically

Is It Rape, Or Is It Marriage? A Study in Culture Clash

Surrounded by cornfields, Lincoln, Nebraska, is about as provincial as a state capital gets. Most of its residents have little experience dealing with people who come from different ways of life. Their baptism into cultural diversity came as a shock.

The wedding was traditional and followed millennia-old Islamic practices (Annin and Hamilton 1996). A 39-year-old immigrant from Iraq had arranged for his two eldest daughters, ages 13 and 14, to marry two fellow Iraqi immigrants, ages 28 and 34. A Muslim cleric flew in from Ohio to perform the ceremony.

Nebraska went into shock. So did the immigrants. What is marriage in Iraq is rape in Nebraska. The husbands were charged with rape, the girls' father with child abuse, and their mother with contributing to the delinquency of minors.

The event made front page news in Saudi Arabia, where people shook their heads in amazement at Americans. Nebraskans shook their heads in amazement, too.

In Fresno, California, a young Hmong immigrant took a group of friends to a local college campus. There, they picked up the Hmong girl whom he had selected to be his wife (Sherman 1988; Lacayo 1993b). The young men brought her to his house, where he had sex with her. The young woman, however, was not in agreement with this plan.

The Hmong call this *zij poj niam*, "marriage by capture." For them, this is an acceptable form of mate selection, one that mirrors Hmong courtship ideals of strong men and virtuous, resistant women. The Fresno District Attorney, however, called it kidnapping and rape.

©UPI/Bettmann/Corbis

Degradation ceremonies are intended to humiliate norm violators and mark them as "not members" of the group. This photo was taken by the U.S. army in 1945 after U.S. troops liberated Cherbourg, France. Members of the French resistance shaved the heads of these women, who had "collaborated" (had sex with) the occupying Nazis. They then marched the shamed women down the streets of the city, while the public shouted insults and spat on them.

Frans Lemmens/Corbis Zefa Collection

Culture conflict centered around parents giving girls like this in marriage to men 15 to 20 years older.

As migration intensifies, other countries are experiencing similar culture shock. Germans awoke one morning to the news that a 28-year-old Turkish man had taken his 11-year-old wife to the registry office in Dusseldorf to get her an ID card. The shocked officials detained the girl and shipped her back to Turkey (Stephens 2006).

In Bishkek, Kyrgystan, a former republic of the Soviet Union, one father said that he wouldn't mind if a man kidnapped his daugher to marry her. "After all," he said, "that's how I got my wife" (Smith 2005).

for your Consideration

To apply *symbolic interactionism* to these real-life dramas, ask how the perspectives of the people involved explain why they did what they did. To apply *functionalism*, ask how the U.S. laws that were violated are "functional" (that is, what are their benefits, and to whom?). To apply *conflict theory*, ask what groups are in conflict in these examples. (Do not focus on the individuals involved, but on the groups to which they belong.)

Understanding events in terms of different theoretical perspectives does not tell us which reaction is "right" when cultures clash. Science can analyze causes and consequences, but it cannot answer questions of what is "right" or moral. Any "ought" that you feel about these cases comes from your values, which brings us, once again, to the initial issue: the relativity of deviance.

Competing Explanations of Deviance: Sociology, Sociobiology, and Psychology

If social life is to exist, norms are essential. So why do people violate them? To better understand the reasons, it is useful to know how sociological explanations differ from biological and psychological ones.

Sociobiologists explain deviance by looking for answers *within* individuals. They assume that **genetic predispositions** lead people to such deviances as juvenile delinquency and crime (Lombroso 1911; Wilson and Herrnstein 1985; Goozen et al. 2007). Among their explanations are the following three theories: (1) intelligence—low intelligence leads to crime; (2) the "XYY" theory—an extra Y chromosome in males leads to crime; and (3) body type—people with "squarish, muscular" bodies are more likely to commit **street crime**—acts such as mugging, rape, and burglary.

How have these theories held up? We should first note that most people who have these supposedly "causal" characteristics do not become criminals. Regarding intelligence, you already know that some criminals are very intelligent, and that most people of low intelligence do not commit crimes. Regarding the extra Y chromosome, most men who commit crimes have the normal XY chromosome combination, and most men with the XYY combination do not become criminals. No women have this combination of genes, so this explanation can't even be applied to female criminals. Regarding body type, criminals exhibit the full range of body types, and most people with "squarish, muscular" bodies do not become street criminals.

Psychologists also focus on abnormalities *within* the individual. They examine what are called **personality disorders.** Their supposition is that deviating individuals have deviating personalities (Barnes 2001; Mayer 2007), and that subconscious motives drive people to deviance. No specific childhood experience, however, is invariably linked with deviance. For example, children who had "bad toilet training," "suffocating mothers," or "emotionally aloof fathers" may become embezzling bookkeepers—or good accountants. Just as college students, teachers, and police officers represent a variety of bad—and good—childhood experiences, so do deviants. Similarly, people with "suppressed anger" can become freeway snipers or military heroes—or anything else. In short, there is no inevitable outcome of any childhood experience. Deviance is not associated with any particular personality.

In contrast with both sociobiologists and psychologists, *sociologists* search for factors *outside* the individual. They look for social influences that "recruit" people to break norms. To account for why people commit crimes, for example, sociologists examine such external influences as socialization, membership in subcultures, and social class.

genetic predisposition inborn tendencies; in this context, to commit deviant acts

street crime crimes such as mugging, rape, and burglary

personality disorders the view that a personality disturbance of some sort causes an individual to violate social norms

Social class refers to people's relative standing in terms of education, occupation, and especially income and wealth.

The point stressed earlier, that deviance is relative, leads sociologists to ask a crucial question: Why should we expect to find something constant within people to account for a behavior that is conforming in one society and deviant in another?

To see how sociologists explain deviance, let's contrast the three sociological perspectives—symbolic interactionism, functionalism, and conflict theory.

The Symbolic Interactionist Perspective

As we examine symbolic interactionism, it will become more evident why sociologists are not satisfied with explanations that are rooted in biology or personality. A basic principle of symbolic interactionism is this: We act according to our interpretations of situations, not according to blind predisposition. Let's consider how our membership in groups influences our views of life and thus affects our behavior.

Differential Association Theory

The Theory Contrary to theories built around biology and personality, sociologists stress that people *learn* deviance. Edwin Sutherland coined the term **differential association** to indicate that we learn to deviate from or conform to society's norms primarily from the *different* groups we *associate* with (Sutherland 1924, 1947; Sutherland et al. 1992). On the most obvious level, some boys and girls join street gangs, while others join the Scouts. As sociologists have repeatedly demonstrated, what we learn influences us toward or away from deviance (Deflem 2006; Chambliss 1973/2007).

Sutherland's theory is actually more complicated than this, but he basically said that deviance is learned. This goes directly against the view that deviance is due to biology or personality. Sutherland stressed that the different groups with which we associate (our "*different*ial association") give us messages about conformity and deviance. We may receive mixed messages, but we end up with more of one than the other (an "excess of definitions," as Sutherland put it). The end result is an imbalance—attitudes that tilt us more toward one direction than another. Consequently, either we conform or we deviate.

Families Since our family is so important for teaching us attitudes, it probably is obvious to you that the family makes a big difference in whether we learn deviance or conformity. Researchers have confirmed this informal observation. They have found that delinquents are more likely to come from families that get in trouble with the law. Of the many studies that show this, one stands out: Of all jail inmates across the United States, almost *half* have a father, mother, brother, sister, or spouse who has served time in prison (*Sourcebook of Criminal Justice Statistics* 2003:Table 6.0011). In short, families that are involved in crime tend to set their children on a lawbreaking path.

Friends, Neighborhoods, and Subcultures Most people don't know the term *differential association,* but they do know how it works. Most parents want to move out of "bad" neighborhoods because they know that if their kids have delinquent friends, they are likely to become delinquent, too. Sociological research supports this common observation (Miller 1958; Chung and Steinberg 2006; Yonas et al. 2006). Some neighborhoods even develop a subculture of violence. In these places, even a teasing remark can mean instant death. If the neighbors feel that a victim deserved to be killed, they refuse to testify because "he got what was coming to him" (Kubrin and Weitzer 2003).

differential association Edwin Sutherland's term to indicate that associating with some groups results in learning an "excess of definitions" of deviance, and, by extension, in a greater likelihood that one will become deviant

To experience a sense of belonging is a basic human need. Membership in groups, especially peer groups, is a primary way that people meet this need. Regardless of the orientation of the group—whether to conformity or to deviance—the process is the same. These members of a street gang in Cali, Colombia, are showing off their homemade guns.

P.Mariani/R.Langlois/Corbis

Some neighborhoods even develop subcultures in which killing is considered an honorable act:

> Sociologist Ruth Horowitz (1983, 2005), who did participant observation in a lower-class Chicano neighborhood in Chicago, discovered how associating with people who have a certain concept of "honor" propels young men to deviance. The formula is simple. "A real man has honor. An insult is a threat to one's honor. Therefore, not to stand up to someone is to be less than a real man."

Now suppose you are a young man growing up in this neighborhood. You likely would do a fair amount of fighting, for you would interpret many things as attacks on your honor. You might even carry a knife or a gun, for words and fists wouldn't always be sufficient. Along with members of your group, you would define fighting, knifing, and shooting quite differently from the way most people do.

Members of the Mafia also intertwine ideas of manliness with violence. For them, *to kill is a measure of their manhood.* Not all killings are accorded the same respect, however, for "the more awesome and potent the victim, the more worthy and meritorious the killer" (Arlacchi 1980). Some killings are done to enforce norms. A member of the Mafia who gives information to the police, for example, has violated *omertá* (the Mafia's vow of secrecy). This offense can never be tolerated, for it threatens the very existence of the group. Mafia killings further illustrate just how relative deviance is. Although killing is deviant to mainstream society, for members of the Mafia, *not* to kill after certain rules are broken—such as when someone "squeals" to the cops—is the deviant act.

Prison or Freedom?   An issue that comes up over and over again in sociology is whether we are prisoners of socialization. Symbolic interactionists stress that we are not mere pawns in the hands of others. We are not destined to think and act as our group memberships dictate. Rather, we *help to produce our own orientations to life.* By joining one group rather than another (differential association), for example, we help to shape the self. For instance, one college student may join a feminist group that is trying to change the treatment of women in college; another may associate with a group of women who shoplift on weekends. Their choice of groups points them in different directions. The one who associates with shoplifters may become even more oriented toward criminal activities, while the one who joins the feminist group may develop an even greater interest in producing social change.

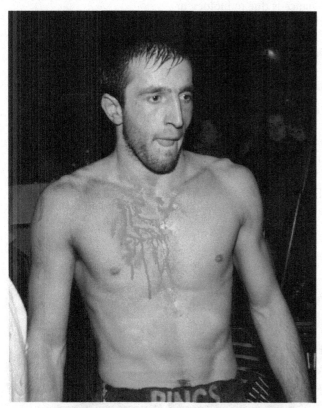

©Boris Kudriavov/R.P.G./Sygma/Corbis

The social control of deviance takes many forms, some rather subtle. With its mayhem, "cage fighting" might look like the opposite of social control, but it is a way to channel aggressive impulses in a way that leaves no vendetta, feud, or "score to settle."

Control Theory

Inside most of us, it seems, are desires to do things that would get us in trouble—inner drives, temptations, urges, hostilities, and so on. Yet most of the time we stifle these desires. Why?

The Theory   Sociologist Walter Reckless (1973), who developed **control theory,** stresses that two control systems work against our motivations to deviate. Our *inner controls* include our internalized morality—conscience, religious principles, ideas of right and wrong. Inner controls also include fears of punishment, feelings of integrity, and the desire to be a "good" person (Hirschi 1969; Rogers 1977; McShane and Williams 2007). Our *outer controls* consist of people—such as family, friends, and the police—who influence us not to deviate.

The stronger our bonds are with society, the more effective our inner controls are (Hirschi 1969). Bonds are based on *attachments* (feeling affection and respect for people who conform to mainstream norms), *commitments* (having a stake in society that you don't want to risk, such as a respected place in your family, a good standing at college, a good job), *involvements* (putting time and energy into approved activities), and *beliefs* (believing that certain actions are morally wrong).

This theory can be summarized as *self*-control, says sociologist Travis Hirschi. The key to learning high self-control is socialization, especially in childhood. Parents help their children to develop self-control by supervising them and punishing their deviant acts (Gottfredson and Hirschi 1990).

Applying the Theory

Suppose that some friends have invited you to a night club. When you get there, you notice that everyone seems unusually happy—almost giddy would be a better word. They seem to be euphoric in their animated conversations and dancing. Your friends tell you that almost everyone here has taken the drug Ecstasy, and they invite you to take some with them.

What do you do? Let's not explore the question of whether taking Ecstasy in this setting is a deviant or a conforming act. That is a separate issue. Instead, concentrate on the pushes and pulls you would feel. The pushes toward taking the drug: your friends, the setting, and your curiosity. Then there are the inner controls: the inner voices of your conscience and your parents, perhaps of your teachers, as well as your fears of arrest and of the dangers of illegal drugs. There are also the outer controls—perhaps the uniformed security guard looking in your direction.

So, what *did* you decide? Which was stronger: your inner and outer controls or the pushes and pulls toward taking the drug? It is you who can best weigh these forces, for they differ with each of us.

Labeling Theory

Symbolic interactionists have developed **labeling theory,** which focuses on the significance of the labels (names, reputations) that we are given. Labels tend to become a part of our self-concept, and help to set us on paths that either propel us into or divert us from deviance. Let's look at how people react to society's labels—from "whore" and "pervert" to "cheat" and "slob."

Rejecting Labels: How People Neutralize Deviance   Most people resist the negative labels that others try to pin on them. Some are so successful that even though they persist in deviance, they still consider themselves conformists. For example, even though they beat up people and vandalize property, some delinquents consider themselves to be conforming members of society. How do they do it?

Sociologists Gresham Sykes and David Matza (1957/1988) studied boys like this. They found that the boys used five **techniques of neutralization** to deflect society's norms.

Denial of Responsibility   Some boys said, "I'm not responsible for what happened because . . ." and then they were quite creative about the "becauses." Some said that what happened was an "accident." Other boys saw themselves as "victims" of society. What else could you expect? They were like billiard balls shot around the pool table of life.

Denial of Injury   Another favorite explanation of the boys was "What I did wasn't wrong because no one got hurt." They would define vandalism as "mischief," gang fights as a "private quarrel," and stealing cars as "borrowing." They might acknowledge that what they did was illegal, but claim that they were "just having a little fun."

Denial of a Victim   Some boys thought of themselves as avengers. Vandalizing a teacher's car was done to get revenge

labeling theory the view that the labels people are given affect their own and others' perceptions of them, thus channeling their behavior either into deviance or into conformity

techniques of neutralization ways of thinking or rationalizing that help people deflect (or neutralize) society's norms

Jerry Springer guides people to publicly reveal their deviances. As Springer parades deviants before the public, the shock and surprise wear off, making the deviance seem "more" normal. What is occurring is the *mainstreaming of deviance*— disapproved behaviors moving into the mainstream, or becoming more socially acceptable.

Ralf-Finn Hestoft/Corbis

DEVIANCE AND SOCIAL CONTROL   147

for an unfair grade, while shoplifting was a way to even the score with "crooked" store owners. In short, even if the boys did accept responsibility and admit that someone had gotten hurt, they protected their self-concept by claiming that the people "deserved what they got."

Condemnation of the Condemners Another technique the boys used was to deny that others had the right to judge them. They might accuse people who pointed their fingers at them of being "a bunch of hypocrites": The police were "on the take," teachers had "pets," and parents cheated on their taxes. In short, they said, "Who are *they* to accuse *me* of something?"

Appeal to Higher Loyalties A final technique the boys used to justify antisocial activities was to consider loyalty to the gang more important than following the norms of society. They might say, "I had to help my friends. That's why I got in the fight." Not incidentally, the boy may have shot two members of a rival group, as well as a bystander!

In sum: These five techniques of neutralization have implications far beyond this group of boys, for it is not only delinquents who try to neutralize the norms of mainstream society. Look again at these five techniques—don't they sound familiar? (1) "I couldn't help myself"; (2) "Who really got hurt?"; (3) "Don't you think she deserved that, after what *she* did?"; (4) "Who are *you* to talk?"; and (5) "I had to help my friends—wouldn't you have done the same thing?" All of us attempt to neutralize the moral demands of society, for neutralization helps us to sleep at night.

Embracing Labels: The Example of Outlaw Bikers Although most of us resist attempts to label us as deviant, some people revel in a deviant identity. Some teenagers, for example, make certain by their clothing, choice of music, hairstyles, and "body art" that no one misses their rejection of adult norms. Their status among fellow members of a subculture—within which they are almost obsessive conformists—is vastly more important than any status outside it.

One of the best examples of a group that embraces deviance is motorcycle gangs. Sociologist Mark Watson (1980/2006) did participant observation with outlaw bikers. He rebuilt Harleys with them, hung around their bars and homes, and went on "runs" (trips) with them. He concluded that outlaw bikers see the world as "hostile, weak, and effeminate." They pride themselves on looking "dirty, mean, and generally undesirable" and take pleasure in provoking shocked reactions to their appearance and behavior. Holding the conventional world in contempt, they also pride themselves on getting into trouble, laughing at death, and treating women as lesser beings whose primary value is to provide them with services—especially sex. Outlaw bikers also regard themselves as losers, a factor that becomes woven into their unusual embrace of deviance.

The Power of Labels: The Saints and the Roughnecks We can see how powerful labeling is by studying the "Saints" and the "Roughnecks." Both groups of high school boys were "constantly occupied with truancy, drinking, wild parties, petty theft, and vandalism." Yet their teachers looked on the Saints as "headed for success" and the Roughnecks as "headed for trouble." By the time they finished high school, not one Saint had been arrested, while the Roughnecks had been in constant trouble with the police.

Why did the members of the community perceive these boys so differently? Chambliss (1973/2007) concluded that this split vision was due to *social class.* As symbolic interactionists emphasize, social class vitally affects our perceptions and behavior. The Saints came from respectable, middle-class families, while the Roughnecks were from less respectable, working-class families. These backgrounds led teachers and the authorities to expect good behavior from the Saints but trouble from the Roughnecks. And, like the rest of us, teachers and police saw what they expected to see.

The boys' social class also affected their visibility. The Saints had automobiles, and they did their drinking and vandalism outside of town. Without cars, the Roughnecks hung around their own street corners, where their drinking and boisterous behavior drew the attention of police and confirmed the negative impressions that the community already had of them.

The boys' social class also equipped them with distinct *styles of interaction*. When police or teachers questioned them, the Saints were apologetic. Their show of respect for authority elicited a positive reaction from teachers and police, allowing the Saints to escape school and legal problems. The Roughnecks, said Chambliss, were "almost the polar opposite." When questioned, they were hostile. Even when they tried to assume a respectful attitude, everyone could see through it. Consequently, while teachers and police let the Saints off with warnings, they came down hard on the Roughnecks.

Although what happens in life is not determined by labels alone, the Saints and the Roughnecks did live up to the labels that the community gave them. As you may recall, all but one of the Saints went on to college. One earned a Ph.D., one became a lawyer, one a doctor, and the others business managers. In contrast, only two of the Roughnecks went to college. They earned athletic scholarships and became coaches. The other Roughnecks did not fare so well. Two of them dropped out of high school, later became involved in separate killings, and were sent to prison. One became a local bookie, and no one knows the whereabouts of the other.

How do labels work? Although the matter is complex, because it involves the self-concept and reactions that vary from one individual to another, we can note that labels open and close doors of opportunity. Unlike its meaning in sociology, the term *deviant* in everyday usage is emotionally charged with a judgment of some sort. This label can lock people out of conforming groups and push them into almost exclusive contact with people who have been similarly labeled.

IN SUM Symbolic interactionists examine how people's definitions of the situation underlie their deviating from or conforming to social norms. They focus on group membership (differential association), how people balance pressures to conform and to deviate (control theory), and the significance of the labels that are given to people (labeling theory).

The label *deviant* involves competing definitions and reactions to the same behavior. This central point of symbolic interactionism is explored in the Mass Media box on the next page.

The Functionalist Perspective

When we think of deviance, its dysfunctions are likely to come to mind. Functionalists, in contrast, are as likely to stress the functions of deviance as they are to emphasize its dysfunctions.

Can Deviance Really Be Functional for Society?

Most of us are upset by deviance, especially crime, and assume that society would be better off without it. The classic functionalist theorist Emile Durkheim (1893/1933, 1895/1964), however, came to a surprising conclusion. Deviance, he said—including crime—is functional for society, for it contributes to the social order. Its three main functions are:

1. *Deviance clarifies moral boundaries and affirms norms.* A group's ideas about how people should think and act mark its *moral boundaries*. Deviant acts challenge those boundaries. To call a member into account is to say, in effect, "You broke an important rule, and we cannot tolerate that." Punishing deviants affirms the group's norms and clarifies what it means to be a member of the group.
2. *Deviance promotes social unity.* To affirm the group's moral boundaries by punishing deviants fosters a "we" feeling among the group's members. In saying, "You can't get away with that," the group collectively affirms the rightness of its own ways.

mass Media in social life

Pornography on the Internet: Freedom Versus Censorship

Pornography vividly illustrates one of the sociological principles discussed in this chapter: the relativity of deviance. It is not the act, but reactions to the act, that make something deviant. Consider one of today's major issues, pornography on the Internet.

Web surfers have such a wide choice of pornography that some sites are indexed by race-ethnicity, hair color, body type, heterosexual or gay, single or group, teenagers, cheerleaders, and older women who "still think they have it." Some offer only photographs, others video. There also are live sites. After signing in and agreeing to the hefty per-minute charges, you can command your "model" to do anything your heart desires. The Internet sex industry even has an annual trade show, Internext. Predictions at Internext are that hotels will soon offer not just sex videos on demand but also live images of people having sex (Johnston 2007).

What is the problem? Why can't people exchange nude photos electronically if they want to? Or watch others having sex online, if someone offers that service?

Although some people object to any kind of sex site, what disturbs many are the sites that feature bondage, torture, rape, bestiality (humans having sex with animals), and sex with children.

The Internet abounds with chat rooms, where people "meet" online to discuss some topic. No one is bothered by the chat rooms where the topic is Roman architecture or rap music or sports. But those whose focus is how to torture women are another matter. So are those that offer lessons on how to seduce grade school children—or that extol the delights of having sex with three-year-olds.

The state and federal governments have passed laws against child pornography, and the police seize computers and search them for illegal pictures. The penalties can be severe. When photos of children in sex acts were found on an Arizona man's computer, he was sentenced to 200 years in prison (Greenhouse 2007). When he appealed his sentence as unconstitutional, his sentence was upheld. To exchange pictures of tortured and sexually abused women, however, remains legal.

©Matt Mahurin

for your Consideration

Some people feel that no matter how much they may disagree with a point of view or find it repugnant, communications about it (including photos and videos) must be allowed. They believe that if we let the government censor the Internet in any way, it will censor other communications. Do you think it should be legal to exchange photos of women being sexually abused or tortured? Should it be legal to discuss ways to seduce children? If not, on what basis should they be banned? If we make these activities illegal, then what other communications should we prohibit? On what basis?

Finally, can you disprove the central point of the symbolic interactionists—that an activity is deviant only because people decide that it is deviant? You may use examples cited in this box, or any others that you wish. You cannot invoke God or moral absolutes in your argument, however, as they are outside the field of sociology. Sociology cannot decide moral issues, even in extreme cases.

---

3. *Deviance promotes social change.* Groups do not always agree on what to do with people who push beyond their accepted ways of doing things. Some group members may even approve of the rule-breaking behavior. Boundary violations that gain enough support become new, acceptable behaviors. Thus, deviance may force a group to rethink and redefine its moral boundaries, helping groups—and whole societies—to change their customary ways.

Strain Theory: How Social Values Produce Deviance

Functionalists argue that crime is a *natural* part of society, not an aberration or some alien element in our midst. Indeed, they say, some mainstream values actually generate crime. To understand what they mean, consider what sociologists Richard Cloward and Lloyd Ohlin (1960) identified as the crucial problem of the industrialized world: the need to locate and train the most talented people of every generation—whether they were born into wealth or into poverty—so that they can take over the key technical jobs of society. When children are born, no one knows which ones will have the ability to become dentists, nuclear physicists, or engineers. To get the most talented people to compete with one another, society tries to motivate *everyone* to strive for success. It does this by arousing discontent—making people feel dissatisfied with what they have so that they will try to "better" themselves.

Most people, then, end up with strong desires to reach **cultural goals** such as wealth or high status, or to achieve whatever other objectives society holds out for them. However, not everyone has equal access to society's **institutionalized means,** the legitimate ways of achieving success. Some people find their path to education and good jobs blocked. These people experience *strain* or frustration, which may motivate them to take a deviant path.

This perspective, known as **strain theory,** was developed by sociologist Robert Merton (1956, 1968). People who experience strain, he said, are likely to feel *anomie,* a sense of normlessness. Because mainstream norms (such as working hard or pursuing higher education) don't seem to be getting them anywhere, people who experience strain find it difficult to identify with these norms. They may even feel wronged by the system, and its rules may seem illegitimate.

Table 1 compares people's reactions to cultural goals and institutionalized means. The first reaction, which Merton said is the most common, is *conformity,* using socially acceptable means to try to reach cultural goals. In industrialized societies most people try to get good jobs, a good education, and so on. If well-paid jobs are unavailable, they take less desirable jobs. If they are denied access to Harvard or Stanford, they go to a state university. Others take night classes and go to vocational schools. In short, most people take the socially acceptable road.

Four Deviant Paths The remaining four responses, which are deviant, represent reactions to strain. Let's look at each. *Innovators* are people who accept the goals of society but use illegitimate means to try to reach them. Crack dealers, for instance, accept the goal of achieving wealth, but they reject the legitimate avenues for doing so. Other examples are embezzlers, robbers, and con artists.

The second deviant path is taken by people who become discouraged and give up on achieving cultural goals. Yet they still cling to conventional rules of conduct. Merton called this response *ritualism.* Although ritualists have given up on getting ahead at work, they survive by following the rules of their job. Teachers whose idealism is shattered (who are said to suffer from "burnout"), for example, remain in the classroom, where they teach without enthusiasm. Their response is considered deviant because they cling to the job even though they have abandoned the goal, which may have been to stimulate young minds or to make the world a better place.

People who choose the third deviant path, *retreatism,* reject both the cultural goals and the institutionalized means of achieving them. Those who drop out of the pursuit of success by way of alcohol or drugs are retreatists. Although their withdrawal takes them on a different path, women who enter a convent or men a monastery are also retreatists.

cultural goals the legitimate objectives held out to the members of a society

institutionalized means approved ways of reaching cultural goals

strain theory Robert Merton's term for the strain engendered when a society socializes large numbers of people to desire a cultural goal (such as success), but withholds from many the approved means of reaching that goal; one adaptation to the strain is crime, the choice of an innovative means (one outside the approved system) to attain the cultural goal

Table 1	How People Match Their Goals to Their Means		
Do They Feel the Strain That Leads to Anomie?	**Mode of Adaptation**	**Cultural Goals**	**Institutionalized Means**
No	Conformity	Accept	Accept
	Deviant Paths:		
	1. Innovation	Accept	Reject
Yes	2. Ritualism	Reject	Accept
	3. Retreatism	Reject	Reject
	4. Rebellion	Reject/Replace	Reject/Replace

Source: Based on Merton 1968.

The final type of deviant response is *rebellion*. Convinced that their society is corrupt, rebels, like retreatists, reject both society's goals and its institutionalized means. Unlike retreatists, however, rebels seek to give society new goals. Revolutionaries are the most committed type of rebels.

In sum: Strain theory underscores the sociological principle that deviants are the product of society. Mainstream social values (cultural goals and institutionalized means to reach those goals) can produce strain (frustration, dissatisfaction). People who feel this strain are more likely than others to take the deviant (nonconforming) paths summarized in Table 1.

Illegitimate Opportunity Structures: Social Class and Crime

One of the more interesting sociological findings in the study of deviance is that the social classes have distinct styles of crime. Let's see how unequal access to the institutionalized means to success helps to explain this.

Street Crime Functionalists point out that industrialized societies have no trouble socializing the poor into wanting to own things. Like others, the poor are bombarded with messages urging them to buy everything from X boxes and iPods to designer jeans and new cars. Television and movies show images of middle-class people enjoying luxurious lives. These images reinforce the myth that all full-fledged Americans can afford society's many goods and services.

In contrast, the school system, the most common route to success, often fails the poor. The middle class runs it, and there the children of the poor confront a bewildering world, one that is at odds with their background. Their speech, with its nonstandard grammar, is often sprinkled with what the middle class considers obscenities. Their ideas of punctuality, as well as their poor preparation in paper-and-pencil skills, are also a mismatch with their new environment. Facing such barriers, the poor are more likely than their more privileged counterparts to drop out of school. Educational failure, in turn, closes the door on many legitimate avenues to financial success.

Not infrequently, however, a different door opens to the poor, one that Cloward and Ohlin (1960) called **illegitimate opportunity structures.** Woven into the texture of life in urban slums, for example, are robbery, burglary, drug dealing, prostitution, pimping, gambling, and other crimes, commonly called "hustles" (Liebow 1967/1999; Sanchez-Jankowski 2003; Anderson 1978, 1990/2006). For many of the poor, the "hustler" is a role model—glamorous, in control, the image of "easy money," one of the few people in the area who comes close to attaining the cultural goal of success. For such reasons, then, these activities attract disproportionate numbers of the poor. As is discussed in the Down-to-Earth Sociology box on the next page, gangs are one way that the illegitimate opportunity structure beckons disadvantaged youth.

White-Collar Crime The more privileged social classes are not crime-free, of course, but for them different illegitimate opportunities beckon. They find *other forms* of crime to be functional. Physicians, for example, don't hold up cabbies, but many do cheat Medicare. You've heard about bookkeepers who embezzle from their employers and corporate officers who manipulate stock prices. In other words, rather than mugging, pimping, and committing burglary, the more privileged encounter "opportunities" for evading income tax, bribing public officials, embezzling, and so on. Sociologist Edwin Sutherland (1949) coined the term **white-collar crime** to refer to crimes that people of respectable and high social status commit in the course of their occupations.

A special form of white-collar crime is **corporate crime,** crimes committed by executives in order to benefit their corporation. For example, to increase corporate profits, Sears executives defrauded the poor of over $100 million. Their victims were so poor that they had filed for bankruptcy. To avoid a

Lynne Fernandes/The Image Works

Social class divides people into such distinct ways of life that even crimes differ by social class. Jeffrey Skilling, former CEO of Enron Corporation, was convicted of 19 counts of fraud, conspiracy, and insider trading. The poor have neither the opportunity to commit these types of crimes nor the chance to make the huge profits they offer. In addition to his sentence of 24 years in prison, Skilling also had to pay back $45 million to victims of his crimes.

Islands in the Street: Urban Gangs in the United States

FOR MORE THAN TEN YEARS, sociologist Martín Sánchez Jankowski (1991) did participant observation of thirty-seven African American, Chicano, Dominican, Irish, Jamaican, and Puerto Rican gangs in Boston, Los Angeles, and New York City. The gangs earned money through gambling, arson, mugging, armed robbery, and selling moonshine, drugs, guns, stolen car parts, and protection. Jankowski ate, slept, and sometimes fought with the gangs, but by mutual agreement he did not participate in drug dealing or other illegal activities. He was seriously injured twice during the study.

Contrary to stereotypes, Jankowski did not find that the motive for joining was to escape a broken home (there were as many members from intact families as from broken homes) or to seek a substitute family (the same number of boys said they were close to their families as those that said they were not). Rather, the boys joined to gain access to money, to have recreation (including girls and drugs), to maintain anonymity in committing crimes, to get protection, and to help the community. This last reason may seem surprising, but in some neighborhoods,

A. Ramey/PhotoEdit, Inc.

gangs protect residents from outsiders and spearhead political change (Kontos et al. 2003). The boys also saw the gang as an alternative to the dead-end—and deadening—jobs held by their parents.

Neighborhood residents are ambivalent about gangs. On the one hand, they fear the violence. On the other hand, many of the adults once belonged to gangs, some gangs provide better protection than the police, and gang members are the children of people who live in the neighborhood.

Particular gangs will come and go, but gangs will likely always remain part of the city. As functionalists point out, gangs fulfill needs of poor youth who live on the margins of society.

for your Consideration

What are the functions that gangs fulfill (the needs they meet)? Suppose that you have been hired as an urban planner by the City of Los Angeles. How could you arrange to meet the needs that gangs fulfill in ways that minimize violence and encourage youth to follow mainstream norms?

---

criminal trial, Sears pleaded guilty. This frightened the parent companies of Macy's and Bloomingdales, which had similar deceptive practices, and they settled with their debtors out of court (McCormick 1999). Similarly, Citigroup had to pay $70 million for preying on the poor (O'Brien 2004). None of the corporate thieves at Sears, Macy's, Bloomingdales, or Citigroup spent a day in jail.

Seldom is corporate crime taken seriously, even when it results in death. One of the most notorious corporate crimes involved the decision by Firestone executives to allow faulty tires to remain on U.S. vehicles—even though they were recalling the tires in Saudi Arabia and Venezuela. These tires cost the lives of about 200 Americans (White et al. 2001). No Firestone executive went to jail.

Consider this: Under federal law, causing the death of a worker by willfully violating safety rules is a misdemeanor punishable by up to six months in prison. Yet harassing a wild burro on federal lands is punishable by a year in prison (Barstow and Bergman 2003).

At $400 billion a year (Reiman 2004), "crime in the suites" actually costs more than "crime in the streets." This refers only to dollar costs. No one has yet figured out a way to compare, for example, the suffering experienced by a rape victim with the pain felt by an elderly couple who have lost their life savings to white-collar fraud.

The greatest concern of Americans, however, is street crime. They fear the violent stranger who will change their life forever. As the Social Map on the next page shows, the chances of such an encounter depend on where you live. From this map, you can see that entire regions are safer or more dangerous than others. In general, the northern states are the safest, and the southern states the most dangerous.

Figure 1 — Some States Are Safer: Violent Crime in the United States

Violent crimes are murder, rape, robbery, and aggravated assault. As this figure illustrates, violent crime varies widely among the states. The chances of becoming a victim of these crimes are ten times higher in South Carolina, the most dangerous state, than in North Dakota, the safest state. Washington, D.C., not a state, is in a class by itself. Its rate of 1,371 is three times the national average and over 17 times North Dakota's rate.

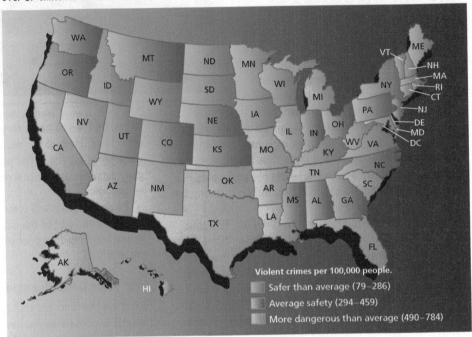

Violent crimes per 100,000 people.
- Safer than average (79–286)
- Average safety (294–459)
- More dangerous than average (490–784)

Source: By the author. Based on *Statistical Abstract of the United States* 2007:Table 297.

Gender and Crime A major change in the nature of crime is the growing number of female offenders. As Table 2 shows, women are committing a larger proportion of crime—from car theft to possession of illegal weapons. The basic reason for this increase is women's changed social location. As more women work in factories, corporations, and

Table 2 — Women and Crime: What a Difference a Dozen Years Make

Of all those arrested, what percentage are women?

Crime	1992	2004	Change
Car Theft	10.8%	17.1%	+58%
Burglary	9.2%	14.2%	+54%
Stolen Property	12.5%	18.6%	+49%
Aggravated Assault	14.8%	20.6%	+39%
Drunken Driving	13.8%	18.6%	+35%
Robbery	8.5%	11.0%	+29%
Arson	13.4%	16.2%	+21%
Larceny/Theft	32.1%	38.2%	+19%
Illegal Drugs	16.4%	18.9%	+15%
Forgery and Counterfeiting	34.7%	39.7%	+14%
Illegal Weapons	7.5%	8.2%	+9%
Fraud	42.1%	45.0%	+7%

Source: By the author. Based on *Statistical Abstract of the United States* 2007:Table 317.

the professions, their opportunities for crime increase. Like men, women are also enticed by illegitimate opportunities.

IN SUM Functionalists conclude that much street crime is the consequence of socializing everyone into equating success with owning material possessions, while denying many in the lower social classes the legitimate means to attain that success. People from higher social classes encounter different opportunities to commit crimes. The growing crime rates of women illustrate how changing gender roles are giving more women access to illegitimate opportunities.

The Conflict Perspective

Class, Crime, and the Criminal Justice System

Two leading U.S. aerospace companies, Hughes Electronics and Boeing Satellite Systems, were accused of illegally exporting missile technology to China. The technology places the United States at risk, for it allowed China to improve its delivery system for nuclear weapons. The two companies pleaded guilty and paid fines. No executives went to jail. (Gerth 2003)

Contrast this corporate crime—which places you in danger—with stories in newspapers about people who are sentenced to several years in prison for stealing cars. How can a legal system that is supposed to provide "justice for all" be so inconsistent? According to conflict theorists, this question is central to the analysis of crime and the **criminal justice system**—the police, courts, and prisons that deal with people who are accused of having committed crimes. Let's see what conflict theorists have to say about this.

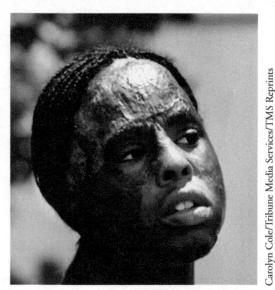

Most white-collar crime is a harmless nuisance, but some brings horrible costs. Shown here is Alisha Parker, who, with three siblings, was burned when the gas tank of her 1979 Chevrolet Malibu exploded after a rear-end collision. Although General Motors executives knew about the problem with the Malibu gas tanks, they had ignored it. Outraged at the callousness of GM's conduct, the jury awarded these victims the staggering sum of $4.9 billion.

The Granger Collection, New York

This 1871 wood engraving depicts children as they are being paid for their day's work in a London brickyard. In early capitalism, most street criminals came from the *marginal working class*, as did these children. It is the same today.

criminal justice system the system of police, courts, and prisons set up to deal with people who are accused of having committed a crime

"If you want justice, it's two hundred dollars an hour. Obstruction of justice runs a bit more."

The cartoonist's hyperbole makes an excellent commentary on the social class disparity of our criminal justic system. Not only are the crimes of the wealthy not as likely to come to the attention of authorities as are the crimes of the poor, but when they do, the wealthy can afford legal expertise that the poor cannot.

Power and Inequality

Conflict theorists regard power and social inequality as the main characteristics of society. They stress that the power elite that runs society also controls the criminal justice system. This group makes certain that laws are passed that will protect its position in society. Other norms, such as those that govern informal behavior (chewing with a closed mouth, appearing in public with combed hair, and so on), may come from other sources, but they are not as important. Such norms influence our everyday behavior, but they do not determine who has power or who gets sent to prison.

Conflict theorists see the most fundamental division in capitalist society as that between the few who own the means of production and the many who sell their labor. Those who buy labor, and thereby control workers, make up the **capitalist class;** those who sell their labor form the **working class.** Toward the most depressed end of the working class is the **marginal working class:** people who have few skills, who are subject to layoffs, and whose jobs are low paying, part time, or seasonal. This class is marked by unemployment and poverty. From its ranks come most of the prison inmates in the United States. Desperate, these people commit street crimes, and because their crimes threaten the social order that keeps the elite in power, they are punished severely.

The Law as an Instrument of Oppression

According to conflict theorists, the idea that the law operates impartially and administers a code that is shared by all is a cultural myth promoted by the capitalist class. These theorists see the law as an instrument of oppression, a tool designed by the powerful to maintain their privileged position (Spitzer 1975; Reiman 2004; Chambliss 2000, 2007). Because the working class has the potential to rebel and overthrow the current social order, when its members get out of line, the law comes down hard on them.

For this reason, the criminal justice system does not focus on the owners of corporations and the harm they do through manufacturing unsafe products, creating pollution, and manipulating prices—or the crimes of Hughes and Boeing mentioned on the previous page. Instead, it directs its energies against violations by the working class. The violations of the capitalist class cannot be ignored totally, however, for if they become too outrageous or oppressive, the working class might rise up and revolt. To prevent this, a flagrant violation by a member of the capitalist class is occasionally prosecuted. The publicity given to the case helps to stabilize the social system by providing evidence of the "fairness" of the criminal justice system.

Usually, however, the powerful are able to bypass the courts altogether, appearing instead before an agency that has no power to imprison (such as the Federal Trade Commission). People from wealthy backgrounds who sympathize with the intricacies of the corporate world direct these agencies. It is they who oversee most cases of manipulating the price of stocks, insider trading, violating fiduciary duty, and so on. Is it surprising, then, that the typical sanction for corporate crime is a token fine?

When groups that have been denied access to power gain that access, we can expect to see changes in the legal system. This is precisely what is occurring now. Racial-ethnic minorities and homosexuals, for example, have more political power today than ever before. In line with conflict theory, a new category called *hate crime* has been formulated.

capitalist class the wealthy who own the means of production and buy the labor of the working class

working class those people who sell their labor to the capitalist class

marginal working class the most desperate members of the working class, who have few skills, little job security, and are often unemployed

DEVIANCE AND SOCIAL CONTROL

IN SUM From the perspective of conflict theory, the small penalties that are imposed for crimes committed by the powerful are typical of a legal system that has been designed by the elite (capitalists) to keep themselves in power, to control workers, and, ultimately, to stabilize the social order. From this perspective, law enforcement is a cultural device through which the capitalist class carries out self-protective and repressive policies.

Reactions to Deviance

Whether it involves cheating on a sociology quiz or holding up a liquor store, any violation of norms invites reaction. Reactions, though, vary with culture. Before we examine reactions in the United States, let's take a little side trip to Greenland, an island nation three times the size of Texas located between Canada and Denmark. I think you'll enjoy this little excursion in cultural diversity.

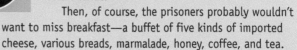

Cultural Diversity *around the* World

"What Kind of Prison Is This?"

THE PRISON IN NUUK, the capital of Greenland, has no wall around it. It has no fence. It doesn't even have bars.

The other day, Meeraq Lendenhann, a convicted rapist, walked out of prison. He didn't run or hide. He just walked out. Meeraq went to a store he likes to shop at, bought a CD of his favorite group, U2, and then walked back to the prison.

If Meeraq tires of listening to music, he can send e-mail and play games on a computer. Like other prisoners, he also has a personal TV with satellite hookup.

The prison holds 60 prisoners—the country's killers, rapists, and a few thieves. The prisoners leave the prison to work at regular jobs, where they average $28,000 or so a year. But they have to return to the prison after work. And they are locked into their rooms at 9:30.

The prisoners have to work, because the prison charges them $150 a week for room and board. The extra money goes into their savings accounts, or to help support their families.

And, of course, the prisoners can have guns. At least during the summer. A major summer sport for Greenlanders is hunting reindeer and seals. Prisoners don't want to miss out on the fun, so if they ask, they are given shotguns.

But gun use isn't as easy as it sounds. Judges have set a severe requirement: The prisoners have to be accompanied by armed guards. If that isn't bad enough, the judges have added another requirement—that the prisoners not get drunk while they hunt.

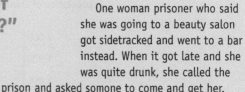

One woman prisoner who said she was going to a beauty salon got sidetracked and went to a bar instead. When it got late and she was quite drunk, she called the prison and asked somone to come and get her.

If someone from another culture asks about the prisoners running away, the head of the prison says, "Where would they run? It's warm inside, and cold outside."

Then, of course, the prisoners probably wouldn't want to miss breakfast—a buffet of five kinds of imported cheese, various breads, marmalade, honey, coffee, and tea.

—Based on Naik 2004.

for your Consideration

Greenland's unique approach arose out of its history of hunting and fishing for a living. If men were locked up, they wouldn't be able to hunt or fish, and their families would suffer. From this history has come the main goal of Greenland's prison—to integrate offenders into society. This treatment helps prisoners slip back into village life after they have served their sentence. The incorrigibles, those who remain dangerous, about 20 men—are sent to a prison in Copenhagen, Denmark. Meeraq, the rapist, is given injections of androcur, a testosterone-reducing drug that lowers his sex drive. Alcoholics are given antabuse, a drug that triggers nasty reactions if someone drinks alcohol.

How do you think we could apply Greenland's approach to the United States?

Street Crime and Prisons

Let's turn back to the United States. Figure 2 illustrates the remarkable growth in the U.S. prison population. The number of prisoners is actually higher than the total shown in this figure. If we add jail inmates, the total comes to over two million people—one out of every 143 citizens. Not only does the United States have more prisoners than any other nation, but it also has a larger percentage of its population in prison as well. The number of prisoiners has grown so fast that the states have had to hire private companies to operate jails for them. About 110,000 prisoners are in these "private" jails (*Sourcebook of Criminal Justice Statistics* 2006:Table 6.32).

To better understand U.S. prisoners, let's compare them with the U.S. population. As you look at Table 3 on the next page, several things may strike you. Almost all prisoners (87 percent) are ages 18 to 44, and almost all of them are men. Then there is this remarkable statistic: Although African Americans make up just 12.8 percent of the U.S. population, close to half of all prisoners are African Americans. On any given day, about

Figure 2 **How Much Is Enough? The Explosion in the Number of U.S. Prisoners**

To better understand how remarkable this change is, compare the increase in U.S. prisoners with the increase in the U.S. population. Between 1970 and 2004, the U.S. population increased 43 percent, while the number of prisoners increased 764 percent, *18 times greater*. If the number of prisoners had grown at the same rate as the U.S. population, there would be about 280,000 prisoners, only 13 percent of today's total. (Or, if the U.S. population had increased at the same rate as that of U.S. prisoners, the U.S. population would be 3,650,000,000—more than the population of China, India, Canada, Mexico, and all of Europe combined.)

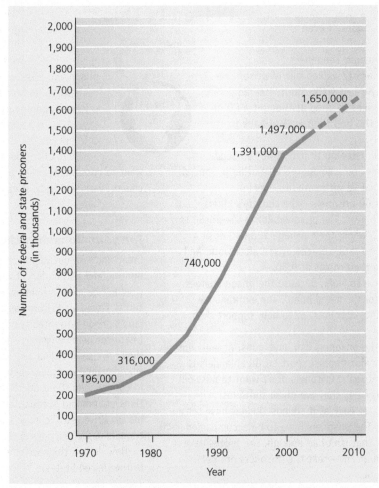

Sources: By the author. Based on *Statistical Abstract of the United States* 1995:Table 349; 2007:Table 334. The broken line is the author's estimate.

DEVIANCE AND SOCIAL CONTROL

	Table 3 **Inmates in U.S. State Prisons**	
Characteristics	**Percentage of Prisoners with These Characteristics**	**Percentage of U.S. Population with These Characteristics**
Age		
18–24	26.4%	9.9%
25–34	35.4%	13.5%
35–44	25.2%	14.8%
45–54	10.4%	14.3%
55 and older	1.0%	22.7%
Race-Ethnicity		
African American	47.3%	12.8%
White	36.9%	66.9%
Latino	14.2%	14.4%
Asian Americans	0.6%	4.3%
Native Americans	0.9%	1.0%
Sex		
Male	93.4%	49.3%
Female	6.3%	50.7%
Marital Status		
Never Married	59.8%	28.2%
Divorced	15.5%	10.2%
Married	17.3%	58.6%
Widowed	1.1%	6.4%
Education		
Less than high school	39.7%	14.8%
High school graduate	49.0%	32.2%
Some college	9.0%	25.4%
College graduate (BA or higher)	2.4%	27.6%

Source: By the author. Based on *Sourcebook of Criminal Justice Statisitcs* 2003:Tables 6.000b, 6.28; 2006:Tables 6.34, 6.45; *Statistical Abstract of the United States* 2007:Tables 12, 14, 23, 55, 216.

one out of eight African American men ages 20 to 34 is in jail or prison (Butterfield 2003). Finally, note how marriage and education—two of the major techniques society has of "anchoring" us—provide protection from prison.

As I mentioned earlier, social class funnels some people into the criminal justice system and diverts others away from it. This table illuminates the power of education, a major component of social class. You can see how people who drop out of high school have a high chance of ending up in prison—and how unlikely it is for a college graduate to have this unwelcome destination in life.

For about the past 20 years or so, the United States has followed a "get tough" policy. "Three strikes and you're out" laws upon conviction for a third felony have become common. When someone is convicted of a third felony, judges are required to give a mandatory sentence, sometimes life imprisonment. While few of us would feel sympathy if a man convicted of a third brutal rape or a third murder were sent to prison for life, these laws have had unanticipated consequences, as you will see in the following Thinking Critically section.

Thinking Critically

"Three Strikes and You're Out!" Unintended Consequences of Well-Intended Laws

In the 1980s, the violent crime rate soared. Americans grew fearful, and they demanded that their lawmakers do something. Politicians heard the message, and they responded by passing the "three strikes" law. Anyone who is convicted of a third felony receives an automatic mandatory sentence. Judges are not allowed to consider the circumstances. Some mandatory sentences carry life imprisonment.

In their haste to appease the public, the politicians did not limit the three-strike laws to *violent* crimes. And they did not consider that some minor crimes are considered felonies. As the functionalists would say, this has led to unanticipated consequences.

Here are some actual cases:

- In Los Angeles, a 27-year-old man was sentenced to 25 years for stealing a pizza (Cloud 1998).
- In New York City, a man who was about to be sentenced for selling crack said to the judge, "I'm only 19. This is terrible." He then hurled himself out of a courtroom window, plunging to his death sixteen stories below (Cloud 1998).
- In Sacramento, a man who passed himself off as Tiger Woods to go on a $17,000 shopping spree was sentenced to 200 years in prison (Reuters 2001).
- In California, a man who stole 9 videotapes from Kmart was sentenced to 50 years in prison without parole. He appealed to the U.S. Supreme Court, which upheld his sentence (Greenhouse 2003).
- In Utah, a 25-year-old was sentenced to 55 years in prison for selling small bags of marijuana to a police informant. The judge who sentenced the man said the sentence was unjust (Madigan 2004).

for your Consideration

Apply the symbolic interactionist, functionalist, and conflict perspectives to mandatory sentencing. For *symbolic interactionism*, what do these laws represent to the public? How does your answer differ depending on what part of "the public" you are referring to? For *functionalism*, who benefits from these laws? What are some of their dysfunctions? For the *conflict perspective*, what groups are in conflict? Who has the power to enforce their will on others?

The Decline in Violent Crime

As you saw in Figure 2, judges have put more and more people in prison. In addition, legislators passed the three-strikes laws and reduced early releases of prisoners. As these changes occurred, the crime rate dropped sharply, which has led to a controversy in sociology. Some sociologists conclude that getting tough on criminals was the main reason for the drop in violent crime (Conklin 2003). Others point to higher employment, a drop in drug use, and even abortion (Rosenfeld 2002; Reiman 2004; Blumstein and Wallman 2006). This matter is not yet settled, but both tough sentencing and the economy seem to be important factors.

Recidivism

A major problem with prisons is that they fail to teach their clients to stay away from crime. Our **recidivism rate**—the percentage of former prisoners who are rearrested—is high. For those who are sentenced to prison for crimes of violence, within just three

Beneath the humor of this cartoon lies a serious point about the high recidivism of U.S. prisoners.

Figure 3   **Recidivism of U.S. Prisoners**

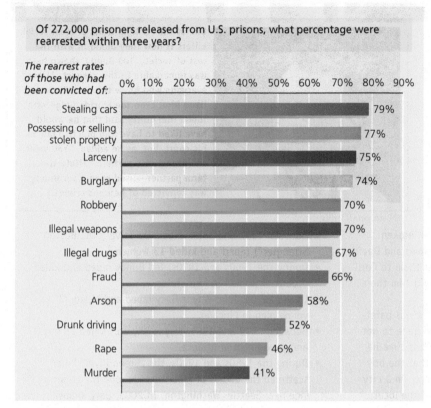

Of 272,000 prisoners released from U.S. prisons, what percentage were rearrested within three years?

The rearrest rates of those who had been convicted of:

Stealing cars	79%
Possessing or selling stolen property	77%
Larceny	75%
Burglary	74%
Robbery	70%
Illegal weapons	70%
Illegal drugs	67%
Fraud	66%
Arson	58%
Drunk driving	52%
Rape	46%
Murder	41%

Note: The individuals were not necessarily rearrested for the same crime for which they had originally been imprisoned.

Source: By the author. Based on *Sourcebook of Criminal Justice Statistics* 2003:Table 6.50.

years of their release, two out of three (62 percent) are rearrested, and half (52 percent) are back in prison (*Sourcebook of Criminal Justice Statistics* 2003:Table 6.52). Figure 3 shows recidivism by type of crime. It is safe to conclude that if—and this is a big if—the purpose of prisons is to teach people that crime doesn't pay, they are colossal failures.

The Death Penalty and Bias

Capital punishment, the death penalty, is the most extreme measure the state takes. The death penalty is mired in controversy, arousing impassioned opposition and support on both moral and philosophical grounds. Advances in DNA testing have given opponents of the death penalty a strong argument: Innocent people have been sent to death row, and some have been executed. Others are passionate about retaining the death penalty, pointing to such crimes as those of the serial killers discussed in the Down-to-Earth Sociology box on the next page.

Apart from anyone's personal position on the death penalty, it certainly is clear that the death penalty is not administered evenly. Consider geography: The Social Map shows that where people commit murder greatly affects their chances of being put to death.

The death penalty also shows social class bias. As you know from news reports on murder and sentencing, it is rare for a rich person to be sentenced to death. Although the government does not collect statistics on social class and the death penalty, this common observation is borne out by the average education of the prisoners on death row. *Most* prisoners on death row (51 percent) have not finished high school (*Sourcebook of Criminal Justice Statistics* 2006:Table 6.81).

Figure 5 shows gender bias in the death penalty. It is almost unheard of for a woman to be sentenced to death. Although women commit 9.6 percent of the murders, they

capital punishment the death penalty

The Killer Next Door: Serial Murderers in Our Midst

I WAS STUNNED BY THE IMAGES. Television cameras showed the Houston police digging up dozens of bodies from under a boat storage shed. Fascinated, I waited impatiently for spring break. A few days later, I drove from Illinois to Houston, where 33-year-old Dean Corll had befriended Elmer Wayne Henley and David Brooks, two teenagers from broken homes. Together, they had killed 27 boys. Elmer and David would pick up young hitchhikers and deliver them to Corll to rape and kill. Sometimes they even brought him their high school classmates.

©Bettmann/Corbis

One of the striking traits of most serial killers is how they blend in with the rest of society. Ted Bundy, shown here, was remarkable in this respect. Almost everyone who knew this law student liked him. Even the Florida judge who found him guilty said that he would have liked to have him practice law in his court, but, as he added, "You went the wrong way, partner." (Note the term partner—used even after Bundy was convicted of heinous crimes.)

I talked to one of Elmer's neighbors, as he was painting his front porch. His 15-year-old son had gone to get a haircut one Saturday morning; it was the last time he had seen his son alive. The police insisted that the boy had run away, and they refused to investigate. On a city map, I plotted the locations of the homes of the local murder victims. Many clustered around the homes of the teenage killers.

I was going to spend my coming sabbatical writing a novel on this case, but, to be frank, I became frightened and didn't write the book. I didn't know if I could recover psychologically if I were to immerse myself in grisly details day after day for months on end. One of these details was a piece of plywood, with a hole in each of its four corners. Corll and the boys would spreadeagle their victims handcuffed to the plywood. There, they would torture the boys (no girl victims) for hours. Sometimes, they would even pause to order pizza.

My interviews confirmed what has since become common knowledge about serial killers: They lead double lives so successfully that their friends and family are unaware of their criminal activities. Henley's mother swore to me that her son was a good boy and couldn't possibly be guilty. Some of his high school friends told me the same thing. They stressed that Elmer couldn't be involved in homosexual rape and murder because he was interested only in girls. I conducted my interviews in Henley's bedroom, and for proof of what they told me, his friends pointed to a pair of girls' panties that were draped across a lamp shade.

Serial murder is the killing of several victims in three or more separate events. The murders may occur over several days, weeks, or years. The elapsed time between murders distinguishes serial killers from *mass murderers*, who do their killing all at once. Here are some infamous examples:

- Between 1962 and 1964, Albert De Salvo ("the Boston Strangler") raped and killed 13 women.
- During the 1960s and 1970s, Ted Bundy raped and killed dozens of women in four states.
- In the 1970s, John Wayne Gacy raped and killed 33 young men in Chicago.
- Between 1979 and 1981, Wayne Williams killed 28 boys and young men in Atlanta.
- During the 1980s and 1990s, the "Green River" killer scattered the bodies of prostitutes around the countryside near Seattle, Washington. In 2003, Gary Ridgway was convicted of the crimes and given 48 consecutive life sentences for killing 48 women.
- In 2005, in Wichita, Kansas, Dennis Rader pleaded guilty as the BTK (Bind, Torture, and Kill) strangler, a name he had proudly given himself. His 10 killings spanned 1974 to 1991.
- The serial killer with the most victims appears to be Harold Shipman of Manchester, England. From 1977 to 2000, this quiet, unassuming physician killed 230 to 275 of his elderly women patients. While making housecalls, he gave the women lethal injections.
- One of the most bizarre serial killers was Jeffrey Dahmer of Milwaukee. Dahmer fried and ate parts of his victims. When he did, he felt a "unity" with the victim.

Almost all serial killers are men, but an occasional woman joins this list of infamy:

- In North Carolina, Blanche Taylor Moore used arsenic to kill her father, her first husband, and a boyfriend. She was tripped up in 1986 when she tried to poison her current husband.
- In 1987 and 1988, Dorothea Montalvo Puente, who operated a boarding house in Sacramento, killed 7 of her boarders. Her motive was to collect their Social Security checks.
- In Missouri, from 1986 to 1989, Faye Copeland and her husband killed 5 transient men.
- In the late 1980s and early 1990s, Aileen Wuornos, hitchhiking along Florida's freeways, killed 7 men after having sex with them.

Many serial killers are motivated by lust and are sexually aroused by killing, so the FBI sometimes uses the term "lust murder." As with Ted Bundy and Jeffrey Dahmer, some have sex with their dead victims. Bundy returned day after day to the countryside to copulate with the corpses of his victims. Other serial killers, however, are more "garden variety," motivated by greed, like Dorothea Puente, who killed for money.

Is serial murder more common now than it used to be? Not likely. In the past, police departments had little communication with one another. When killings occurred in different jurisdictions, seldom did anyone connect them.

Today's more efficient communications, investigative techniques, and DNA matching make it easier for the police to conclude that a serial killer is operating in an area. Part of the perception that there are more serial killers today is also due to ignorance of our history: In our frontier past, serial killers went from ranch to ranch. Some would say that mass murderers wiped out entire villages of Native Americans.

for your Consideration

Do you think that serial killers should be given the death penalty? Why or why not? How do your social locations influence your opinion?

---

make up only 1.6 percent of death row inmates (*Sourcebook of Criminal Justice Statistics* 2006:Table 3.129). It is possible that this statistic reflects not only gender bias but also the relative brutality of the women's murders. We need research to determine this.

Bias used to be so flagrant that it once put a stop to the death penalty. Donald Partington (1965), a lawyer in Virginia, was shocked by the bias he saw in the courtroom, and he decided to document it. He found that 2,798 men had been convicted for rape and attempted rape in Virginia between 1908 and 1963—56 percent whites and 44 percent blacks. For attempted rape, 13 had been executed. For rape, 41 men had been executed. *All those executed were black.* Not one of the whites was executed.

After listening to evidence like this, in 1972 the Supreme Court ruled in *Furman* v. *Georgia* that the death penalty, was applied, was unconstitutional. The execution of prisoners stopped—but not for long. The states wrote new laws, and in 1977 they again began to execute prisoners. Since then, 67 percent of those put to death have been white and 33 percent African American (*Statistical Abstract* 2007:Table 340). (Latinos are evidently counted as whites in this statistic.) Table 4 on the next page shows the race-ethnicity of the prisoners who are on death row.

serial murder the killing of several victims in three or more separate events

---

Figure 4   **Executions in the United States**

Executions since 1977, when the death penalty was reinstated.

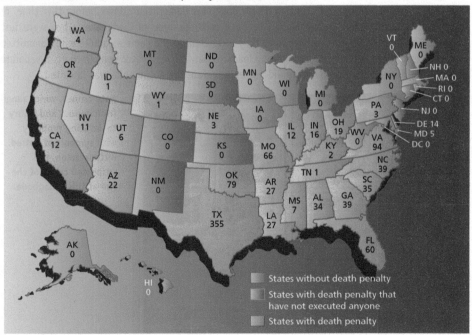

Source: By the author. Based on *Statistical Abstract of the United States* 2007:Table 341.

Figure 5 Women and Men on Death Row

98.4%

1.6%

Men   Women

Source: By the author. Based on *Sourcebook of Criminal Justice Statistics* 2006:Table 6.81.

Table 4 The Racial-Ethnicity of the 3,486 Prisoners on Death Row

	Percentage	
	on Death Row	in U.S. Population
Whites	45%	68%
African Americans	42%	12%
Latinos	11%	14%
Asian Americans	1%	4%
Native Americans	1%	1%

Source: By the author. Based on *Sourcebook of Criminal Justice Statistics* 2007:Table 6.80 and Figure 12.5 of this text.

Legal Change

Did you know that it is a crime in Saudi Arabia for a woman to drive a car (Fattah 2007)? A crime in Florida to sell alcohol before 1 p.m. on Sundays? Or illegal in Wells, Maine, to advertise on tombstones? As has been stressed in this chapter, deviance, including the form called *crime,* is relative. It varies from one society to another, and from group to group within a society. Crime also varies from one time period to another, as opinions change or as different groups gain access to power.

Hate crimes are an example of legal change, the topic of the next Thinking Critically Section.

Thinking Critically

Changing Views: Making Hate a Crime

Because crime consists of whatever acts authorities decide to assign that label, new crimes emerge from time to time. A prime example is juvenile delinquency, which Illinois lawmakers designated a separate type of crime in 1899. Juveniles committed crimes before this time, of course, but youths were not considered to be a separate type of lawbreaker. They were just young people who committed crimes, and they were treated the same as adults who committed the same crime. Sometimes new technology leads to new crimes. Motor vehicle theft, a separate crime in the United States, obviously did not exist before the automobile was invented.

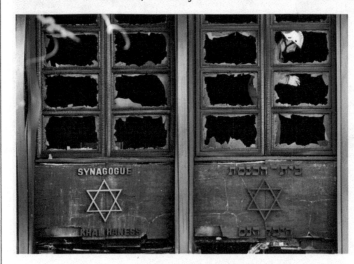

Hate crimes, which range from murder and injury to defacing property with symbols of hatred, include arson, the suspected cause of the fire at this synagogue.

FABRICE COFFRINI/AFP/Getty Images

In the 1980s, another new crime was born when state governments developed the classification **hate crime.** This is a crime that is motivated by *bias* (dislike, hatred) against someone's race-ethnicity, religion, sexual orientation, disability, or national origin. Before this, of course, people attacked others or destroyed their property out of these same motivations, but in those cases the motivation was not the issue. If someone injured or killed another person because of that person's race-ethnicity, religion, sexual orientation, national origin, or disability, he or she was charged with assault or murder. Today, motivation has become a central issue, and hate crimes carry more severe sentences than do the same acts that do not have hatred as their motive. Table 5 summarizes the victims of hate crimes.

We can be certain that the "evolution" of crime is not yet complete. As society changes and as different groups gain access to power, we can expect the definitions of crime to change accordingly.

Table 5 Hate Crimes	
Directed Against	**Number of Victims**
Race-Ethnicity	
African Americans	3,494
Whites	1,027
Latinos	646
Asian Americans	272
Native Americans	102
Religion	
Jews	1,086
Muslims	202
Catholics	68
Protestants	48
Sexual Orientation	
Male Homosexual	902
Homosexual (general)	314
Female Homosexual	213
Heterosexual	32
Bisexual	18
Disabilities	
Mental	49
Physical	24

Source: Statistical Abstract of the United States 2007:Table 308.

for your Consideration

Why should we have a separate classification called hate crime? Why aren't the crimes of assault, robbery, and murder adequate? As one analyst (Sullivan 1999) said: "Was the brutal murder of gay college student Matthew Shepard [a hate crime] in Laramie, Wyoming, in 1998 worse than the abduction, rape, and murder of an eight-year-old Laramie girl [not a hate crime] by a pedophile that same year?"

How do you think your social location (race-ethnicity, gender, social class, sexual orientation, or physical ability) affects your opinion?

The Trouble with Official Statistics

Both the findings of symbolic interactionists (that stereotypes operate when authorities deal with groups such as the Saints and the Roughnecks) and the conclusion of conflict theorists (that the criminal justice system exists to serve the ruling elite) demonstrate the need for caution in interpreting official statistics. Crime statistics do not have an objective, independent existence. They are not like oranges that you pick out in a grocery store. Rather, crime statistics are a human creation. One major element in producing them is the particular laws that exist. Another is how those laws are enforced. Still another is how officials report their statistics. Change these factors, and the statistics also change.

Consider this: According to official statistics, working-class boys are clearly more delinquent than middle-class boys. Yet, as we have seen, who actually gets arrested for what is influenced by social class, a point that has far-reaching implications. As symbolic interactionists point out, the police follow a symbolic system as they enforce the law. Their ideas of "typical criminals" and "typical good citizens," for example, permeate their work. The more a suspect matches their stereotypes (which they call "criminal profiles"), the more likely that person is to be arrested. **Police discretion,** the decision of whether to arrest someone or even to ignore a matter, is a routine part of police work. Consequently, official crime statistics always reflect these and many other biases.

hate crime crimes to which more severe penalties are attached because they are motivated by hatred (dislike, animosity) of someone's race-ethnicity, religion, sexual orientation, disability, or national origin

police discretion the practice of the police, in the normal course of their duties, to either arrest or ticket someone for an offense or to overlook the matter

Reactions to deviants vary from such mild sanctions as frowns and stares to such severe responses as imprisonment and death. Some sanctions are formal—court hearings, for example—but most are informal, as when friends refuse to talk to each other. One sanction is to label someone a deviant, which can have powerful consequences for the person's life, especially if the label closes off conforming activities and opens deviant ones. The degradation ceremony, in which someone is publicly labeled "not one of us," is a powerful sanction. So is imprisonment. Official statistics must be viewed with caution, for they reflect biases.

The Medicalization of Deviance: Mental Illness

Another way in which society deals with deviance is to "medicalize" it. Let's look at what this entails.

Neither Mental Nor Illness?   To *medicalize* something is to make it a medical matter, to classify it as a form of illness that properly belongs in the care of physicians. For the past hundred years or so, especially since the time of Sigmund Freud (1856–1939), the Viennese physician who founded psychoanalysis, there has been a growing tendency toward the **medicalization of deviance.** In this view, deviance, including crime, is a sign of mental sickness. Rape, murder, stealing, cheating, and so on are external symptoms of internal disorders, consequences of a confused or tortured mind.

> **medicalization of deviance** to make deviance a medical matter, a symptom of some underlying illness that needs to be treated by physicians

Thomas Szasz (1986, 1996, 1998), a renegade in his profession of psychiatry, argues that *mental illnesses are neither mental nor illnesses. They are simply problem behaviors.* Some forms of so-called mental illnesses have organic causes; that is, they are *physical* illnesses that result in unusual perceptions or behavior. Some depression, for example, is caused by a chemical imbalance in the brain, which can be treated by drugs. The depression, however, may appear in the forms of crying, long-term sadness, and lack of interest in family, work, school, or one's appearance. When someone becomes deviant in ways that disturb others, *and* when these others cannot find a satisfying explanation for why the person is "like that," a "sickness in the head" is often taken as the cause of the unacceptable behavior.

Attention deficit disorder (ADD) is an excellent example. As Szasz says, "No one explains where this disease came from, why it didn't exist 50 years ago. No one is able to diagnose it with objective tests." It is diagnosed by a teacher or a parent complaining about a child misbehaving. Misbehaving children have been a problem throughout history, but now their problem behavior has become a sign of mental illness.

All of us have troubles. Some of us face a constant barrage of problems as we go through life. Most of us continue the struggle, perhaps encouraged by relatives and friends and motivated by job, family responsibilities, religious faith, and life goals. Even when the odds seem hopeless, we carry on, not perfectly, but as best we can.

Some people, however, fail to cope well with life's challenges. Overwhelmed, they become depressed, uncooperative, or hostile. Some strike out at others, while some, in Merton's terms, become retreatists and withdraw into their apartments or homes, not wanting to come out. These are *behaviors, not mental illnesses*, stresses Szasz. They may be inappropriate coping devices, but they are coping devices nevertheless, not mental illnesses. Thus, Szasz concludes that "mental illness" is a myth foisted on a naive public by a medical profession that uses pseudoscientific jargon in order to expand its area of control and force nonconforming people to accept society's definitions of "normal."

Szasz's extreme claim forces us to look anew at the forms of deviance that we usually refer to as mental illness. To explain behavior that people find bizarre, he directs our attention not to causes hidden deep within the "subconscious," but, instead, to how people learn such behaviors. To ask, "What is the origin of someone's inappropriate or bizarre behavior?" then becomes similar to asking "Why do some women steal?" "Why do some men rape?" "Why do some teenagers cuss their parents and stalk out of

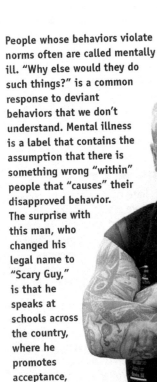

People whose behaviors violate norms often are called mentally ill. "Why else would they do such things?" is a common response to deviant behaviors that we don't understand. Mental illness is a label that contains the assumption that there is something wrong "within" people that "causes" their disapproved behavior. The surprise with this man, who changed his legal name to "Scary Guy," is that he speaks at schools across the country, where he promotes acceptance, awareness, love, and understanding.

AP Images

the room, slamming the door?" *The answers depend on those people's particular experiences in life, not on an illness in their mind.* In short, some sociologists find Szasz's renegade analysis refreshing because it indicates that *social experiences,* not some illness of the mind, underlie bizarre behaviors—as well as deviance in general.

The Homeless Mentally Ill

Jamie was sitting on a low wall surrounding the landscaped courtyard of an exclusive restaurant. She appeared unaware of the stares that were elicited by her layers of mismatched clothing, her matted hair and dirty face, and the shopping cart that overflowed with her meager possessions.

When I saw Jamie point to the street and concentrate, slowly moving her finger horizontally. I asked her what she was doing.

"I'm directing traffic," she replied. "I control where the cars go. Look, that one turned right there," she said, now withdrawing her finger.

"Really?" I said.

After a while she confided that her cart talked to her.

"Really?" I said again.

"Yes," she replied. "You can hear it, too." At that, she pushed the shopping cart a bit. "Did you hear that?" she asked.

When I shook my head, she demonstrated again. Then it hit me. She was referring to the squeaking wheels!

I nodded.

When I left, Jamie was pointing to the sky, for, as she told me, she also controlled the flight of airplanes.

To most of us, Jamie's behavior and thinking are bizarre. They simply do not match any reality we know. Could you or I become like Jamie?

Suppose for a bitter moment that you are homeless and have to live on the streets. You have no money, no place to sleep, no bathroom. You do not know *if* you are going to eat, much less where. You have no friends or anyone you can trust, and you live in constant fear of rape and other violence. Do you think this might be enough to drive you over the edge?

Consider just the problems involved in not having a place to bathe. (Shelters are often so dangerous that many homeless people prefer to sleep in public settings.) At first, you try to wash in the rest rooms of gas stations, bars, the bus station, or a shopping center. But you are dirty, and people stare when you enter and call the management when they see you wash your feet in the sink. You are thrown out and told in no uncertain terms never to come back. So you get dirtier and dirtier. Eventually, you come to think of being dirty as a fact of life. Soon, maybe, you don't even care. The stares no longer bother you—at least not as much.

Mental illness is common among the homeless. This man, who hangs out near Boston Commons in Boston, Massachusetts, has been homeless for 44 years. This gives you an idea of the depth of the problem of rehabilitation.

No one will talk to you, and you withdraw more and more into yourself. You begin to build a fantasy life. You talk openly to yourself. People stare, but so what? They stare anyway. Besides, they are no longer important to you.

Jamie might be mentally ill. Some organic problem, such as a chemical imbalance in her brain, might underlie her behavior. But perhaps not. How long would it take you to exhibit bizarre behaviors if you were homeless—and hopeless? The point is that *just being on the streets can cause mental illness*—or whatever we want to label socially inappropriate behaviors that we find difficult to classify. *Homelessness and mental illness are reciprocal:* Just as "mental illness" can cause homelessness, so the trials of being homeless, of living on cold, hostile streets, can lead to unusual thinking and behaviors.

Joe Raedle/Getty Images

The Need for a More Humane Approach

As Durkheim (1895/1964:68) pointed out, deviance is inevitable—even in a group of saints.

> Imagine a society of saints, a perfect cloister of exemplary individuals. Crimes, properly so called, will there be unknown; but faults which appear [invisible] to the layman will create there the same scandal that the ordinary offense does in ordinary [society].

With deviance inevitable, one measure of a society is how it treats its deviants. Our prisons certainly don't say much good about U.S. society. Filled with the poor, they are warehouses of the unwanted. They reflect patterns of broad discrimination in our larger society. White-collar criminals continue to get by with a slap on the wrist while street criminals are punished severely. Some deviants, who fail to meet current standards of admission to either prison or mental hospital, take refuge in shelters, as well as in cardboard boxes tucked away in urban recesses. Although no one has *the* answer, it does not take much reflection to see that there are more humane approaches than these.

Because deviance is inevitable, the larger issues are to find ways to protect people from deviant behaviors that are harmful to themselves or others, to tolerate those behaviors that are not harmful, and to develop systems of fairer treatment for deviants. In the absence of fundamental changes that would bring about a truly equitable social system, most efforts are, unfortunately, like putting a Band Aid on a gunshot wound. What we need is a more humane social system, one that would prevent the social inequalities.

Summary *and* Review

What Is Deviance?

From a sociological perspective, **deviance** (the violation of norms) is relative. What people consider deviant varies from one culture to another and from group to group within the same society. As symbolic interactionists stress, it is not the act, but the reactions to the act, that make something deviant. All groups develop systems of **social control** to punish **deviants**—those who violate their norms.

How do sociological and individualistic explanations of deviance differ?

To explain why people deviate, sociobiologists and psychologists look for reasons *within* the individual, such as **genetic predispositions** or **personality disorders.** Sociologists, in contrast, look for explanations *outside* the individual, in social experiences.

The Symbolic Interactionist Perspective

How do symbolic interactionists explain deviance?

Symbolic interactionists have developed several theories to explain deviance such as **crime** (the violation of

norms that are written into law). According to **differential association theory,** people learn to deviate by associating with others. According to **control theory,** each of us is propelled toward deviance, but most of us conform because of an effecti ve system of inner and outer controls. People who have less effective controls deviate.

Labeling theory focuses on how labels (names, reputations) help to funnel people into or divert them away from deviance. People who commit deviant acts often use techniques of neutralization to continue to think of themselves as conformists.

The Functionalist Perspective

How do functionalists explain deviance?

Functionalists point out that deviance, including criminal acts, is functional for society. Functions include affirming norms and promoting social unity and social change. According to **strain theory,** societies socialize their members into desiring **cultural goals.** Many people are unable to achieve these goals in socially acceptable ways—that is, by **institutionalized means.** *Deviants,* then, are people who either give up on the goals or use deviant means to attain them. Merton identified five types of responses to cultural goals and institutionalized means: conformity, innovation, ritualism, retreatism, and rebellion. **Illegitimate opportunity theory** stresses that some people have easier access to illegal means of achieving goals.

The Conflict Perspective

How do conflict theorists explain deviance?

Conflict theorists take the position that the group in power (the **capitalist class**) imposes its definitions of deviance on other groups (the **working class** and the **marginal working class**). From the conflict perspective, the law is an instrument of oppression used to maintain the power and privilege of the few over the many. The marginal working class has little income, is desperate, and commits highly visible property crimes. The ruling class directs the **criminal justice system,** using it to punish the crimes of the poor while diverting its own criminal activities away from this punitive system.

Reactions to Deviance

What are common reactions to deviance in the United States?

In following a "get-tough" policy, the United States has imprisoned millions of people. African Americans and Latinos make up a disproportionate percentage of U.S. prisoners. The death penalty shows biases by geography, social class, race–ethnicity, and gender. In line with conflict theory, as groups gain political power, their views are reflected in the criminal code. **Hate crime** legislation was considered in this context.

Are official statistics on crime reliable?

The conclusions of both symbolic interactionists (that the police operate with a large measure of discretion) and conflict theorists (that the capitalist class controls the legal system) indicate that we must be cautious when using crime statistics.

What is the medicalization of deviance?

The medical profession has attempted to **medicalize** many forms of **deviance,** claiming that they represent mental illnesses. Thomas Szasz disagrees, asserting that they are problem behaviors, not mental illnesses. Research on homeless people illustrates how problems in living can lead to bizarre behavior and thinking.

What is a more humane approach?

Deviance is inevitable, so the larger issues are to find ways to protect people from deviance that harms themselves and others, to tolerate deviance that is not harmful, and to develop systems of fairer treatment for deviants.

Thinking Critically

1. Select some deviance with which you are personally familiar. (It does not have to be your own—it can be something that someone you know did.) Choose one of the three theoretical perspectives to explain what happened.

2. As is explained in the text, deviance can be mild. Recall some instance in which you broke a social rule in dress, etiquette, or speech. What was the reaction? Why do you think people reacted like that? What was your response to their reactions?

3. What do you think should be done about the U.S. crime problem? What sociological theories support your view?

Additional Resources

What can you use MySocLab for? 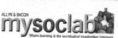 www.mysoclab.com

- **Study and Review:** Pre- and Post-Tests, Practice Tests, Flash Cards, Individualized Study Plans.
- **Current Events:** *Sociology in the News,* the daily *New York Times,* and more.

- **Research and Writing:** *Research Navigator, Writing About Sociology,* and more.

Where Can I Read More on This Topic?

Conklin, John E. *Why Crime Rates Fell.* Boston: Allyn and Bacon, 2003. The author analyzes the reasons that experts have suggested for why crime rates have fallen: changes in policing, imprisonment, drugs and gun usage, age, and social institutions.

Fox, James Alan, and Jack Levin. *Extreme Killing: Understanding Serial and Mass Murder.* Thousand Oaks, Calif.: Sage, 2005. As the authors analyze the various types of serial and mass murders, they examine the characteristics of both killers and their victims.

Goffman, Erving. *Stigma: Notes on the Management of Spoiled Identity.* New York: Simon & Schuster, 1986. First published in 1968. The author outlines the social and personal reactions to "spoiled identity," appearances that—due to disability, weight, ethnicity, birth marks, and so on—do not match dominant expectations.

Heiner, Robert, ed. *Deviance Across Cultures.* Oxford: Oxford University Press, 2007. Cross-cultural norms and behavior are the focus of this collection of classic and contemporary articles on deviance.

Lintner, Bert. *Blood Brothers: The Criminal Underworld of Asia.* New York: Palgrave MacMillan, 2004. Maps out the topography of organized crime in East Asia.

Lombroso, Cesare, Guglielmo Ferrero, Nicole Hahn Rafter, and Mary Gibson. *Criminal Woman, the Prostitute, and the Normal Woman.* Durham, N.C.: Duke University Press, 2005. This translation of a classic work from the 1800s on women and crime is put in current social context by two researchers on female criminals.

Paul, Pamela. *Pornified: How Pornography Is Transforming Our Lives, Our Relationships, and Our Families.* New York: Henry Holt, 2005. Based on interviews, the author's thesis is that for many people pornography is replacing intimacy and creating emotional isolation.

Rathbone, Cristina. *A World Apart: Women, Prison, and Life Behind Bars.* New York: Random House, 2006. A journalist's account of the four years she spent investigating MCI Framingham, the oldest women's prison in the United States.

Reiman, Jeffrey. *The Rich Get Richer and the Poor Get Prison: Ideology, Class, and Criminal Justice,* 8th ed. Boston: Allyn and Bacon, 2007. An analysis of how social class works to produce different types of criminals and different types of justice.

Rodriguez, Luis J. *The Republic of East L. A.: Stories.* Los Angeles: Rayo, 2003. These hard-hitting vignettes let the reader know what life is like in this poverty-plagued section of Los Angeles.

Silberman, Matthew, ed. *Violence and Society: A Reader.* Upper Saddle River, N.J.: Prentice Hall, 2003. As the authors of these articles analyze the social factors that underlie violence, they focus on social inequality, culture, and family, sexual, and criminal violence.

Journals

Criminal Justice Review: Issues in Criminal, Social, and Restorative Justice and *Journal of Law and Society* examine the social forces that shape law and justice.

INDEX

Role confusion, 70
Roman Catholic Church
  and Internet, 133
  as ecclesia, 124
  member characteristics, 125
Romance, 72–74
Roughnecks," the, 148–149
Rural poor, 53
Russia capitalism in
  and religious persecution, 109–110
  in NATO, 13

S
Sacred, defined, 106
"Saints," the, 148–149
Same–sex marriage, 66–67, 84
Sanctions, 142
"Sandwich generation," 92, 89
Saneros, 122
Schools.
  and social class, 148–149
  preschools, 47
Science.
  and morality, 132, 144, 150
  and religion, 132
Sears, 152–153
"Second shift," the, 70–72
Sects, 121, 123
Secularization
  of culture, 111
  of religion, 129–131
Self control, 146–147
Self, the.
  and labels, 147–149
Self–fulfilling prophecy
  and corporate inner circle, 17
  in marriage, 98
September 11th, 111
Septuplets, 83
Serial fatherhood, 94
Serial murder, 162–163
Sexism.
  and diversity training, 18–19
  and violence, 95–97
Sexual attraction, 72–74
Sexual behavior, 141
Shaming, 142–143
Shoshone, the, 81
Shunning, 113
Single mothers
  and child rearing, 76–77
  and poverty, 52, 54–55, 82
  births to, 55, 82, 87–88

Slavery
  and religion, 114
  in earlier societies, 117
  in the United States, 51, 114
Social change
  and deviance, 150
  and religion, 109, 115–116
  and technology, 9
  and voluntary associations, 15
  in India, 72–73
Social class, 31–61
  among African Americans, 51, 78–79
  and advertising, 31
  and child rearing, 46–47, 76–77
  and college attendance, 41–42
  and crime, 47–48, 144–145, 152–157,
    159, 161, 165
  and crime statistics, 165
  and death, 45
  and death penalty, 161
  and delinquency, 148–149, 165
  and deviance, 144–145, 148–149, 165
  and divorce, 46
  and education, 41–42, 47, 49–50, 152
  and health and health care, 44–45, 59
  and marriage, 46, 73, 76–77
  and mental illness, 45–46
  and politics, 38, 47
  and religion, 47
  and socialization, 76–77
  and technology, 48
  and the family, 46–47, 76–79
  and voting, 35
  automobile industry as example of, 44
  components of, 32–38
  consequences of, 44–48
  contradictory locations in, 40
  defined, 32
  in criminal justice system, 47–48,
    148–149, 155–157, 161
  models of, 38–44
  of religious groups, 125–126
  of the homeless, 31, 43–44
Social control.
  and norms, 141–143
  as a function of religion, 106
  functionalist perspective on, 149–155
  of workers, 21–22
  reactions to deviance, 157–168
  symbolic interactionist perspective
    on, 145–149
Social inequality
  and income, 32–35, 41
  in criminal justice system, 47–48,
    155–157, 161–164
  in marriage, 68

Social inventions
  bureaucracy, 7–14
  capitalism, 6
  corporations, 17–25
Social isolation, 70
Social mobility, 48–50
  and gender, 49–50
  and religion, 125, 130
  and the family, 50
  and women, 49–50
  myth of, 58–59
  of African Americans, 51
  pain of, 50–51
Social movements
  civil rights, 109
Social order, 141
Social Register, 41–42
Social solidarity, 107
Social stratification, 30–61
  and social mobility, 51
  caste system, 73, 123
  conflict perspective on, 32
  in India, 72–73
Socialization
  and social class, 76–77
  of children, 76–77
  prisoners of, 146
Societies
  dependent on norms, 140–141
  types of, 5–6
Sociobiology, 144
Sociology
  and biology, 144
  and feminists, 49
  and study of religion, 106, 125
  and value judgments, 150
Solidarity, 107
Sony, 24–25
Southern Baptist Convention, 124
Spouse abuse, 95–97
State religions, 109
Statistics, interpreting
  and chances of marital success/
    failure, 89–91, 98
  misuse of, 98
  on crime, 165
  on social mobility, 49–50
Status inconsistency, 38–39
Status symbols, 37–38
Stereotypes
  and corporate culture, 17–19
  and gangs, 153
  held by the police, 165
  of the poor, 52, 54, 56
Stigma, 140